ARIADNE'S
BOOK OF
DREAMS

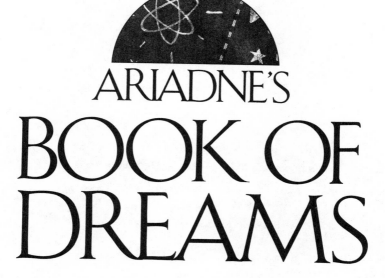

ARIADNE'S
BOOK OF
DREAMS

A DICTIONARY
OF ANCIENT AND
CONTEMPORARY
SYMBOLS

ARIADNE GREEN

A SKYLIGHT PRESS BOOK

WARNER BOOKS

An AOL Time Warner Company

Copyright © 2001 by Ariadne Green and Skylight Press
All rights reserved.

Warner Books, Inc., 1271 Avenue of the Americas, New York, NY 10020

Visit our Web site at www.twbookmark.com.

For information on Time Warner Trade Publishing's online publishing program, visit www.ipublish.com.

 An AOL Time Warner Company

Printed in the United States of America
First Printing: September 2001
10 9 8 7 6 5 4 3 2 1

Library of Congress Cataloging-in-Publication Data

Green, Ariadne.
    Ariadne's book of dreams : a dictionary of ancient and contemporary symbols / Ariadne Green.
        p. cm.
        Includes index.
        ISBN 0-446-67752-3 (trade pbk.)
        1. Dream interpretation. 2. Dreams. 3. Symbolism (Psychology) I. Title.

BF1091 .G73 2001
154.6'3'03—dc21   2001026069

Book design by H.Roberts Design
Cover design by Diane Luger

This book is a tribute to my mother, Valentene, who was inspired to name me Ariadne after the goddess of the labyrinth and who taught me to pay attention to every detail of life. And to my daughters, Nitsa and Vianna, who sacrificed so much for the sake of my spiritual quest and whom I acknowledge as having inspired a truer purpose. And finally it is a tribute to all my students and friends whose dreams have offered me wisdom and creative inspiration.

Contents

The Myth of Grace

ARIADNE AND DIONYSUS

A long time ago, King Minos ruled Crete. He had dominion over everything except for one thing: Poseidon's prized white bull, which was ravaging the countryside killing the king's men. Before King Minos ordered the bull to be killed, Minos' wife, Pasiphae—under the spell of Zeus—had one wild night of love-making with this fabulous bull. As a result she gave birth to the Minotaur, half-bull and half-man.

Although Minos was humiliated, he was obligated to appease Poseidon in his treatment of the Minotaur. He commissioned Daedalus to construct a labyrinth, in the center of which he placed the Minotaur. Every three years young maidens, children, and effeminate youths would be sent into the labyrinth to be sacrificed to the beast. This practice continued until one day a brilliant young hero named Theseus sailed onto Crete from Athens.

Theseus courageously volunteered to enter the labyrinth in order to slay the beast and spare the maidens, a task of heroic proportion. Minos' beautiful daughter, Ariadne, fell deeply in love with Theseus. She offered him her help in entering the labyrinth in exchange for a promise of marriage. Theseus agreed, so Ariadne gave him a ball of thread, which they tossed into the labyrinth to roll to its center. Following the thread, Theseus traveled into the center of the labyrinth and slayed the Minotaur. He returned to Ariadne's arms victorious. As promised, they married and sailed back in the direction of Athens, stopping on an island called Naxos to rest.

Once Ariadne fell asleep on the beach, Theseus seized the opportunity to abandon her there. Unfortunately for Theseus, however, he forgot to change his sails from black to white as he had agreed to signal his safe return to Athens. Instead the sail was black, which announced to Theseus's father that Theseus had been killed by the Minotaur. His father was so distraught that he committed suicide. In his grief over his father's needless death, Theseus committed suicide himself.

When Ariadne realized she had been abandoned on Naxos, she mourned and lamented the loss of her beloved as the greatest tragedy of her life. However, the god Dionysus had loved Ariadne from afar and rescued her from the island. They united in a sacred marriage. He gave Ariadne a crown of flowers, which he later threw up into the heavens. The crown became the aurora borealis.

Ariadne is an archetype of feminine wisdom who guides us with a magical thread through the labyrinth of the soul, the subconscious. The characteristics she represents were abandoned for six thousand years with the advent of patriarchy; only now are they awakening within us. She symbolizes the thread of insight and intuition into our dreams and their mystery. She is the guide who directs us to slay the negative aspect of the Minotaur that is chained and demonized and to embrace the creative power of its Taurean nature that Poseidon's bull really represents. By discovering the

Minotaur's true innocence and brilliance we discover a deeper aspect of ourselves that is innocent and seeking recognition.

Without Ariadne, Theseus was separated from his soul and from the nurturing and wise qualities of the labyrinth goddess. He couldn't survive without her. Ariadne, on the other hand, had been waiting a long time on that island to be embraced for all of her wisdom and divinity—in the end, Dionysus took on that privilege. As the god of ecstasy and intoxicated love he brought the enchantment and celebration back to Ariadne's life. Through him, she ascended to her royal throne as a queen of the heavens, and Dionysus is her king. He appreciates Ariadne for embracing her divine wisdom and depth and helping to bring them the recognition they deserve, for it is love that we are all looking for at the center of that labyrinth. That love for the self, which we define as home.

Through the union of the ideals of Ariadne and Dionysus, all of humanity can embrace mystical knowledge and life's wisdom.

Introduction

I take no dream lightly. From the two thousand dreams a year that I have had the honor of reading or hearing—whether they're from my clients, submitted to me at DreamThread: Online Dream Interpretation Service, or heard while standing in line at the supermarket, at the coffee shop, or from the teller at my bank—I have learned that each dream holds value not only to the dreamer, but also to anyone who is willing to hear it.

Each dream has put me on a path of discovery about the dreamer's inner story, about the mysterious nature and language of the soul, and has led me to some truth about myself. Dreams have given me a wealth of wisdom.

In 1985 I was completing my master's degree in educational psychology. I took a special interest in the study of dreams, children's stories, fairy tales, and myths. I was particularly inspired by the writings of Joseph Campbell, whose vast explorations of mythology as a public dream led me to recognize the mythological significance of such popular stories as *The Wizard of Oz*, *The Jungle*

Book, and *The Little Mermaid*. Although I had been a counselor in community mental health for thirteen years, I had never before explored a mythological perspective of human consciousness.

During this juncture of my professional career, I had also embarked on an inner journey, not so much voluntarily as out of a profound call to heal myself. I had a series of important dreams and visionary experiences that precipitated a transformation deep within my soul and rocked my reality. The first was a dream in which I pulled a snake up through the center of my body, from the base of my spine all the way up through the crown of my head. The dream was accompanied by a burning fever and sensations of electricity shooting through my body. I slipped in and out of a delusional state, semiconscious for three days. When I awakened fully I possessed extraordinary psychic ability and a profound sense of oneness with everything around me. I have come to recognize this dream event as my call to be a shaman.

For me, as well as for other mystics and shamans who have expanded their consciousness beyond the perception of an ordinary world into a mystical experience, life is a meaningful dream.

Our whole universe is born out of creative source and process. All of us are imaginative beings deeply connected to this creativity we call life. We hold a creative intelligence not only in our minds, but in every cell of our bodies. This is a dreaming intelligence. The world around us—where images, signs, and symbols appear on every corner—is a beautiful reflection of this creativity. If we took a moment to note and then to contemplate the meaning of this world and its symbols, all of life would be meaningful.

I, like most shamans, have come to know that both day and night hold mystery and meaning. Shamans are the interpreters of the metaphors in life. We are the translators of the mythic elements that exist beneath the surface of all things. From the shaman's perspective, every symbol that exists in our waking reality can hold as deep a meaning as those that emerge from within our night dreams.

Any object in the world can become a symbol if a group of people ascribes meaning to it. Some symbols have cultural significance, and others possess a universal meaning. For instance, an NFL football helmet is an American cultural symbol that might represent masculine power and protection. A heart, on the other hand, is a universal symbol of love.

Cultural and universal symbols are all around us, and all these symbols hold meaning. They may also hold personal significance if we open our minds to the possibility that they are messages from our creative intelligence.

This dictionary presents the most wonderful and yet the most common meanings of the symbols we encounter in our daily life, as well as those that appear in our night dreams. The aim of this book is to offer you a thread of meaning and wisdom through which you may begin to interpret your life as if it were a dream and your night dreams as significant to your life.

From what has been a fifteen-year integration of a personal journey to wholeness, a professional journey from psychotherapist to shaman, counselor to healer, and spiritual seeker to spiritual teacher, I can now share some of the wisdom gained along the way.

NIGHT DREAMS

Most of us are baffled by our night dreams. Their language appears either too complex or too silly for our rational mind to comprehend. However, our dreams are full of images and symbolic information that can bring meaning to our existence. Without interpretation they remain simply elusive images.

We can embark on a personal journey of healing and transformation through the conscious exploration of our night dreams.

Making the conscious effort to remember and journal our dreams allows us to bring to light important facts about the conflicts we carry around inside. It can open up levels of creativity that can heal our minds and our bodies. Most important, the exploration of our dreams can bring spiritual meaning to our daily life.

THE SOUL AND ITS CREATIVE NATURE

The soul reveals its creative intelligence through the story lines of our waking life as well as through our night dreams.

The force and direction of the stream of creativity we call dreaming is set into motion by the soul's creative imagination. And as the soul knows no boundary, there are no limits to what the soul can create. In our dreams we can excel with superhuman strength. Our soul demonstrates through its creativity the potential to re-create our lives at any given moment by changing our thoughts and actions.

The soul is eternal. It lives on and on through many incarnations. With each incarnation, it evolves psychologically and grows spiritually. The soul may bring the lessons from previous incarnations into this life in order to master further some spiritual principle. For example, it might take many lifetimes to understand and express the power of unconditional love. The soul may create numerous scenarios through which we consciously choose to be more unconditionally loving. Repetitive themes in night dreams also may point out these important life lessons so that we can master them in this life.

THE CONSCIOUS DREAMER

Our daytime experiences can also be viewed as dreams. Most of us have had the experience of hearing a song on the radio at just the moment when we needed to hear the lyrics most. Perhaps the lyrics offered inspiration that changed our mood, opened our heart, or validated some idea that we were holding in our minds at that very moment. Or perhaps the song answered a question that we had posed just an instant before. Most of us dismiss an event like this as coincidence.

But the conscious dreamer is one who sees meaning in every moment and event. Through the open eye of the conscious dreamer, all of life is full of miracles and revelations that bring us closer to wholeness and to our essential self. With this open eye, everyone who makes an appearance on life's stage can provide keys to achieving self-knowledge and self-love.

I remember going to a Starbucks on Sunset Boulevard in Hollywood and being greeted outside by a homeless man. I refer to him as the Black Sage of Morning Coffee. He asked me if I had any change. "You know change: a nickel, a dime, a quarter, a dollar, a hundred dollars, a thousand, a million. It's all the same. It is change. It's all about change." When I walked out of Starbucks, the Black Sage of Morning Coffee was singing the song "I Believe I Can Fly" and I stood next to him and began to sing with him. This man appeared in what is called dream reality to teach me something about the way to think about money. "Free yourself up, ask for what you want, and fly" was the sum of his message. Asking for a nickel is the same as asking for a million. There is no difference. What if I acted on what I had been taught early in childhood, that one should not talk or listen to strangers? I might have missed the wisdom of this sage and seen him as a threat to my safety rather than as someone with an important message. This is also true of our night dreams. Those fearsome characters may really be angelic messengers who have come here to teach us an important lesson.

In dream reality, essential truths are delivered symbolically through synchronistic experiences. Synchronicity is defined as a "meaningful coincidence." Just like the song on the radio, it sends a lightning bolt to the conscious mind, shocking us to wake up to the magic of life. Each day may be filled with synchronicities and meaningful information that can guide us in the right direction—if we expect and welcome them. Every sign and symbol can be savored and digested as a reflection of a meaningful dream in which we are both the creator and the participant. Therefore, we can interpret the signs and symbols within our environment the same way we interpret them in the morning after a night of dreaming.

What is dream reality? What we normally view as the real world is what mystics and spiritual teachers call the third dimension, or fixed concrete reality. Dream reality is the fourth dimension. This is where our creative and intuitive intelligence views, and in many ways re-creates, our world. Our powers to do so are what help us perceive synchronistic moments, embrace messages that come from our own unconscious, and experience little miracles. Dream reality is our deepest wisdom becoming apparent to us.

Life becomes full of synchronistic moments in which the symbolic world attacks the rational and logical mind. The Mickey Mouse T-shirt worn by someone walking in front of us on a crowded city street, for example, can remind us to visit the "Magic Kingdom" of our imagination rather than indicating someone's visit to Disneyland.

If we stop to pay attention to the signs and cues, we may discover a life that is meaningful and more spiritually fulfilling.

THE SHAMAN'S VIEW

Shamans exist in every culture, including Western culture. Shamans are mystical and priestly figures whose origins can be traced as far back as the Paleolithic period. In indigenous cultures their sacred and social activities are still central to tribal life and serve many functions. Shamans heal the sick, communicate spiritual knowledge, foretell the future, intervene politically, offer spiritual advice, and in general restore the community to harmony and balance with the gods and with nature. Shamans exist in a contemporary world, too. They perform their sacred activities through many roles. They are healers, mystics, mediums, artists, spiritual writers, and psychologists. Their activities in Western culture are less central because their spiritual power is often denied.

Shamans have always been the interpreters of the myths and dreams of their culture. They bring the interpretations of their visions and their dreams to their community to inspire faith in the spiritual dimension that exists and interfaces with life.

In viewing the world from the perspective of a shaman, one who mediates the spiritual dimensions with the dimension of this world, all of life is infused with spirit. Shamans tell us that spirit exists within the natural world. This connection to the natural world is what I call a "heart connection," which reveals normally unseen dimensions. From a heightened state of awareness, or "heart vision," one may interact with nature intimately. The rocks speak, the trees speak, and the oceans roar out messages. Shamans tell us to listen to nature's secrets and to see through the illusions of our preconceived notions of the world. For the shaman, nature is the envelope that, when opened, reveals the messages from the Great Spirit of the universe. The shaman has a sacred relationship to nature in which she is connected deeply to its wisdom.

Shamans teach that we need not venture beyond our own backyard to connect with the spiritual dimension. All the answers are within each experiential moment if we choose to see with our hearts and our mystical eye.

I believe I am a shaman. We all hold the potential within us to be shamans. We may slowly awaken to this potential through the conscious exploration of our dreams.

THREE-WORLD MODEL

From the shaman's view, there are three interconnected dreaming worlds: the Lower World, the Middle World, and the Upper World. The sacred tree of life symbolically connects these worlds with an image that shows its roots penetrating the depths of the Lower World, its trunk established in the Middle World, and its branches extending into the Upper World. The sap, which runs through the tree, is the spiritual power or life force.

For the shaman, the Upper World contains many spiritual dimensions through which he can travel, receive the revelation of spiritual truths, and touch the light. The Middle World is the place where we consciously interact with nature. It is where a spiritual life is lived. The Lower World is where nature's primordial power, or spirit power, may be tapped and used to heal others. It is also where our ancestors were laid, whose mythical history may be tapped into. These worlds are all connected: In the Lower World, we recognize the importance of our history and embrace it; in the Middle World, we live compassionately as expressed by our emotions, thoughts, ideas, and actions that influence our world; in the Upper World, we live enlightened through our spiritual connection to the God Source.

DREAM PRECEPTS

The following basic principles will help you understand the dreaming process. I am struck by how many individuals believe their dreams are meaningless processes of their minds. Dream wisdom tells us that in honoring our dreams we are given valuable psychological tools for personal and spiritual growth.

Precept 1

Every single dream is of service to the dreamer. No dream is meaningless or the result of a too-heavy meal eaten the night before. Every fragment, image, symbol, and sign in a dream has meaning. Therefore, every element deserves further exploration so that the dream's intended message can be understood by the dreamer. It is not enough to witness the emotional quality of the dream, nor is it accurate to generalize dream information as merely a recapitulation of daily events. It is important to look at every symbol and element as if one were savoring the separate flavors in a meal.

Precept 2

Every dream has an intended message and meaning for the dreamer. Every dream does not *have multiple meanings.* There are a number of associations, both objective and subjective, that can be made about each dream's symbols that may eventually lead the dreamer to an accurate conclusion about a dream's meaning. The dream's meaning is not coded information in an unintelligible language meant to trick the mind or ego. It is not designed to fool us or to prevent us from bringing to consciousness the secrets of the subconscious. The subconscious does hold memories and emotions that are stored deep within. One of a dream's functions is to reveal these subconscious memories and the repressed emotions associated with them in order to relieve us of tension and bring insight into the origin of these conflicts. Sometimes it is the conscious mind of the dreamer that fights against receiving the dream's message.

Precept 3

Dream language is beautiful, meaningful, poetic, and pure. In most cases, each symbol in a dream acts as a metaphor for a larger idea or is an understated truth about what one feels or believes. A symbol may also arrive as a metaphor of greater truth from a higher intelligence. Thus, a pink rose may symbolize the qualities of love and feminine beauty, and serve to remind us that we possess them. A fishhook may appear in a dream to indicate an emotional response to a situation where one feels "hooked" by someone's intention to reel one in. Or it may offer a solution to a financial problem—as a means to fish for the wealth that is around us. The key to understanding dreams is understanding and listening to the basic language—not with the intellect pulling it apart, but by using intuition about what each element is saying, as if it had a recognizable voice of its own.

Precept 4

All characters of a dream are equally important. Characters may play more than one role. The characters in dreams do not necessarily represent various parts of our personality. They can, however, mirror parts of our soul brought as messengers in the dream. For instance, the appearance of a clown may act as a reminder of our forgotten sense of fun and playfulness and may be there to coax out our laughter.

Some of the characters in a dream may, of course, be aspects of our personality. For instance, we may have incorporated our mother into our personality and a dream may reveal how she is still controlling the direction of our life by placing Mom in the driver's seat of our car. Yet, the mother-symbol is deeply connected to our soul because as the primary messenger and embodiment of the feminine principle, our mothers are responsible for the nurturing of our souls and personalities. No matter how she succeeded or failed, she served as a messenger of a lesson about maternal love.

Precept 5

Dreams are good. Therefore, there is nothing to fear in a dream. Even our worst nightmares may come as a warning of conflict that demands resolution within the psyche. Nightmares may be a signal that we are ready to start working to clear away the conflict. Villains and terrorists who threaten us in a dream may point to our own fears about showing our personal power and authority in the world. By confronting the demons in our dreams, we vanquish the fears that paralyze us.

Precept 6

Dreams are valuable gifts to be opened and cherished. Dreams are treasures from the depths of the soul, jewels of meaning unearthed from the subconscious. Each is full of symbolic information that needs to be investigated and appreciated. These gifts are too precious to disregard or to cast away as trivial or not worthy of attention. As stated in the Talmud of Judaism, a dream not understood is like a letter unopened. Would we discard a letter from a friend before reading it? Even the most common dream can bring an uncommonly important message. Therefore, making an effort to remember dreams through mental suggestion before retiring, or placing a dream journal on the nightstand, welcomes the gift of a dream.

Precept 7

Dream wisdom tells us that we need not seek to control our dreams and we need not be controlled by them. Dreams come from a wise and intelligent source. The soul is united with a higher creative intelligence ready to work out any conflict that disturbs the natural balance of the internal world. For any mental virus or unwanted stimulus bent on destroying this balance, the psyche concocts an antivirus to disarm its power. For example, the psyche may quickly compensate for the obstacles that we face in our life by offering us a picture of fulfillment. Or it may respond with some implicit advice to change course when we are moving away from our authentic nature.

Lucid dreamers who attempt to master their dreaming life by redirecting the dream's course toward their desired outcome may be defeating their dream's purpose. This precept argues against forcing any action in a dream based on an ego-desired outcome. The outcome we want may not serve the balance of dreaming life.

Just as we need not control our dreams, we need not be controlled by the negative emotional qualities within dreams that reflect the forces in our lives. All that is secretly held within the subconscious seeks to be recognized and brought to the conscious mind to be transformed. In so doing, one is freed from the prison of infantile emotions and shadow-forces that seek to annihilate the authentic self. These shadow-forces are often repressed fears, anger, guilt, and other dangerous beliefs that live in our subconscious and torment us daily.

Precept 8

Dreams offer the keys to wisdom about the self. Dream dictionaries are a tool. Our dreams unlock the secrets within the subconscious whose meaning may be veiled from the conscious mind. No dream dictionary can interpret our personal history for us. Nor can it give us a definitive answer as to the meaning of a symbol from a dream, which is personal. It can, however, offer us valuable insights into what a symbol may mean in a general sense. It can help us unravel what is often confusing metaphorical language by suggesting some possible interpretations.

Each symbol in a dream may also have subjective meaning, to be discovered through our personal associations. This meaning may be different from the objective meaning presented in a dream dictionary. For instance, we may have a negative personal association with eating ice cream because our mother fed us ice cream when she felt guilty for punishing us. Thus, ice cream in our dream may really point to hidden emotions related to early childhood abuse rather than to suggest that we are enjoying a luscious treat. On the other hand, the same symbol may present both a subjective and an objective meaning. For example, ice cream could be objectively translated into "I scream," pointing to the need to express the emotional response to abuse. In this case there were two meaningful interpretations of the same symbol, one subjective and one objective. Each interpretation adds meaning to the other.

Any dream dictionary is limited to the writer's general understanding of the language of the soul. Unfortunately, many dream dictionaries on the market offer outdated interpretations based on superstition and conjecture, such as a cat in a dream being a bad omen, or the appearance of an owl meaning that someone in your family will die. They reflect the fear-based popular beliefs of their time and purport an unenlightened view of dream language.

This dictionary presents over twelve hundred common symbols, most of which list several interpretive meanings. They have been compiled from the thousands of dreams I have had the opportunity to listen to and to read from dreamers all over the world. They have also been gathered from my personal experience as a conscious dreamer viewing my life as a dream reality.

It offers an array of modern symbols and brand names—everything from Coca-Cola to Zest soap—as well as traditional symbols whose history may be traced back to antiquity. Some are commonly delivered through our night dreams. Others are more likely to arrive in the synchronistic moments in our walk about the Middle World as conscious dreamers. Some may come as signs pointing to some future event; others will offer a thread of wisdom into the soul's legacy. However, most of the symbols and their interpretations will explain some of the everyday concerns, ideas, attitudes, beliefs, and feelings that emerge from within our dreams and that most of us can relate to.

Some of the symbolic interpretations in this dictionary offer esoteric meanings that relate to the mystical traditions from which the symbol originated. In this case, I have not inferred what the meaning might represent to you. These symbols emerge from the Lower World, or the mythic level of the subconscious, and carry with them archetypal significance. You may discover their relevance and significance through your own inquiry and this will allow you to bring their wisdom into your life and into your personal spiritual journey.

A letter next to the entries indicates the world (Lower, Middle, or Upper) from which the symbol has likely emerged. As mentioned, these worlds are intertwined, so some symbols may reflect elements from one or more worlds. In this way you can better distinguish those wonderful dreams that arrive as spiritual messages from those that reflect daily concerns.

How to Use the Dream Dictionary

You may use this dictionary to interpret the outstanding symbols emerging from your night dreams whose meaning may perplex you. First, allow yourself to contemplate the meaning of the symbol through your own intuition, jotting down a list of both objective and subjective associations. Then refer to the symbol entry in this dictionary to validate or add to your meaning.

Let us say, for example, that a vase emerges from within a dream as an outstanding symbol from the Middle World. In the dream, you are holding and examining this vase. When you awake, write down in your dream journal every detail that you remember about the vase—its shape, the material it is made of, whether there are any designs etched or painted on the surface, and its condition. Ask yourself what the object is normally used for. Since a vase is usually defined as a receptacle for holding flowers, you may also want to consider the meaning of flowers, a Lower World symbol.

Let us say that the vase is made of clear crystal glass. You may also consider the meaning of glass or crystal. What does glass represent to you? Perhaps it means something clear, transparent, and fragile. Jot down a few objective meanings.

Then ask yourself if a vase like this sparks any personal associations or memories. Perhaps you broke your grandmother's favorite vase as a child or your mother always had fresh flowers on the dining table in a similar-looking vase. Write down any of these personal associations. Next, look up the meaning in this dictionary for vase, flowers, glass, and crystal and enter them in your journal. Look over all the objective meanings and your personal associations and decide which ring true for you after weaving the meanings together. You may, for instance, conclude that the meaning of the glass vase refers to the delicate and transparent nature of your own feminine body, which may hold the fragrance and expression of your authentic beauty. It may also suggest that you perhaps view yourself as fragile or easily broken. Consider that you may feel too fragile or transparent to others or how you may desire that others see your inner beauty.

As a last step, close your eyes and revisualize the glass vase. Notice if any other images appear that may deliver additional information or clarify the meaning. Remember that using your intuition is the most accurate method for discovering the symbol's true meaning. When you feel you have deciphered the intended meaning of the symbol, write it down and highlight it in some way. You may also create an affirmation that puts to use the meaningful information derived from this process. One example could be: "I affirm that others will see the true expression of my inner beauty."

This dictionary may also be used to interpret the symbols and signs that arrive as synchronistic events in your waking life. A general rule of thumb I use as a conscious dreamer is that if I notice a particular image or symbol three times in a single day, then it is meaningful. You can begin the process of collecting these symbols that arrive repetitively or those that your intuition deems meaningful by jotting them down in your daily dream journal. You may see a definite correlation between the elements in your night dreams and those in your waking dream reality as they blend together.

Use this dream dictionary wisely. Its content is not gospel. The interpretations of dream symbols offer meaningful and insightful suggestions. Remember that the real answers lie within you. That is the wisdom of dreams.

"All of life is a dream within a greater dream."
—*Shakespeare*

CHAPTER 1

The Lower World

The Lower World is the deepest dimension of our soul. It contains nature's secrets, the primordial power that is instinctual to our nature. The Lower World contains the imprints of every thought and idea planted and cultivated by humans throughout our history. These thoughts have germinated into public dreams, or what we call mythology. Within each cell of our bodies this mythic legacy exists, ready to be tapped by the dreaming process. Mining the gold of our dreams brings the wealth and wisdom of the ages and nature's mysteries to the light of the conscious mind.

The Lower World is rooted in the natural world. It is the terrain of a primordial reality in which the power of the earth, its elements, and its kingdoms may be encountered so that their wisdom and power can be brought forward into life.

For the shaman who travels deep into the Lower World, it is a sacred journey of initiation. Traditionally, shamans make their descent into the Lower World to retrieve their power through a potent dream or through an altered state of consciousness. They may enter the earth's body through an opening such as a cave, a hollow tree, or a deep pool to descend and die a mythic death so that they may be reborn in some way. The visions from their subterranean journeys are brought back to the tribal culture to be reenacted through sacred rites and seasonal ceremonies.

Some Native American cultures such as the Pueblo and Hopi, ancestors of the Anasazi of the southwestern United States, still use structures called kivas that replicate the portal into the Lower World. Kivas are circular chambers made of earth and limestone that are entered by descending a ladder. Once there, the initiate is prepared through prayer and ceremony to obtain the mythic knowledge of his culture. Through secret teachings by tribal elders and through his own visions, the initiate ascends, transformed and empowered to inspire and renew the faith of his community.

Modern psychology uses the term *collective unconscious* to describe the Lower World, where powerful archetypes dance with the elements of nature and still influence our personalities today.

According to Carl Jung, the father of analytical psychology, archetypes, or patterns of energy that influence the human personality and emerge spontaneously in dream material, are carried within the vast collective unconscious. These archetypes, what Jung calls mythological motifs, point to a mythic life we live, perhaps without knowing it. The qualities and dynamic tensions expressed by these archetypes are set in bold letters, demanding attention within the text of the subconscious. They summon us to transform ourselves by acknowledging their power, embracing their positive qualities, and resolving the conflicts they act out. We accomplish this through a process called creative dreaming.

ARCHETYPAL DREAMS

The kings, queens, tricksters, fools, gods, goddesses, and mythical and natural creatures, as well as demons, may bear gifts for dreamers in the form of a spiritual message. These characters are often forces of dark and light waging war with each other. The queen, for instance, may come to signify the honor bestowed on the mature feminine persona, and at the same time may present the lessons of the evil, jealous queen who wants to destroy the emerging individual who is rival to her throne. She also demonstrates the maternal aspect of the personality, which may rule the subconscious and may not want to give way to a more liberated feminine aspect.

In archetypes dreams, which are also referred to as "big" or "grand" dreams, the gods and goddesses play out their dramas within the psyche. They ignite passion, celebrate beauty, bring reason, demonstrate the courage of a hero, or offer a theme for further exploration into the soul. These archetypes are a blueprint for spiritual knowledge that is the basis of the values we recognize as intrinsic and necessary to our wholeness. They express clearly what it is to be a truly multifaceted human being. For instance, a dream of Mercury wearing his winged helmet and racing through a field may speak to a dreamer's desire to run forth with quicksilver speed and deliver an important message to someone—or to the world.

The gods and goddesses in our dreams may emerge clothed in modern dress as celebrities. In the drama of our dreams, they express the same qualities and values as the gods and goddesses. Our fascination with celebrity seems to represent a fascination with qualities we cannot achieve within ourselves.

The appearance of Madonna in a dream, for example, may come as none other than the Greek goddess Aphrodite, who won the prize of Paris as the most beautiful goddess in competition with Athena and Hera on Mount Olympus. Madonna is sexy and expressive, bringing power and recognition to feminine sexuality. She emerges as a seductress, summoning a woman to embrace her own unique beauty, and as the temptress of a man's unexpressed desires. In this way, she may fulfill an unconscious desire to express sexuality more freely.

I once had a dream that I was at the breakfast table with Mel Gibson and was straddling his lap asking for a commitment. I associated Mel with the qualities that his character portrayed in the film *Braveheart*. In this role he was a courageous hero who was willing to fight for a mission that was heart-inspired. At the time of the dream, I was hunting for my own masculine qualities, which could bring me the focus and bravery necessary to fulfill a longtime vision.

THE SHADOW

A powerful archetype, the shadow, perhaps the most disowned and denied power within the subconscious, may appear out of nowhere to threaten the goodwill of the dreamer. It may appear as a villain, an assassin, a tyrant, or even as the Devil himself to torment and threaten our sense of worth or fulfillment. Like the Grinch (who stole Christmas) or the Wicked Witch of the West, the shadow may indicate the power of evil, which must be confronted and challenged in order to win back our innocence and embrace fulfillment. The nightmarish quality of a shadow dream may bring about fear and terror. Most of us have had a confrontation with the shadow in a dream, in which we are being chased, threatened, or robbed of actualization. We may run or hide when he pursues us and awaken with a jolt. The shadow rests in our subconscious, the place where we may deny the evil within ourselves in order to live moral lives. Our shadow nightmares reveal this conflict within ourselves.

One of my students dreamed that her boyfriend doodled an inscription on the skin of her leg through a hole in her jeans that read *JC/Satan*. This dream expressed perfectly the conflict between good and evil, between Jesus Christ, the resurrected son of God, and Satan, the fallen angel. It was clear that this deeply embedded conflict was imprinted in her "genes."

Our shadows cannot be denied, bargained with, or destroyed. They must be faced, or their evil will continue to haunt our dreams and rob us of our opportunities for fulfillment and pleasure in life.

There is a natural attraction to what we repress or deny within the subconscious. An example might be a woman who is attracted to a "bad boy," a lover who seduces or tricks her and perhaps even abuses her. She may really be yearning to embrace her own disowned antisocial desires. The danger is in the trap of believing that she does not deserve better because of the shame of such dark yearnings.

Those within the culture who are attracted to negative symbolism, who wear tattoos of devils and images of death, may act out the disowned shadow for the culture as a whole. Positive or negative overidentification with archetypes may be dangerous because this assigning of black or white devalues other pieces of the self that, when integrated, offer a more complete picture of the individual.

Modern positive archetypes such as Mickey Mouse, Big Bird, or Winnie-the-Pooh hold significant power and archetypal meaning. When we were children, they taught us important values through their stories and characterizations. In adulthood, their messages still urge us to adopt their principles. Mickey is a jovial character who teaches us to appreciate the Kingdom of the Magical Child. Winnie-the-Pooh shows us ways to uncondition-al love. Big Bird demonstrates the value of having a special friend. Each reminds us of important spiritual and human values.

INDIVIDUATION: TIMES OF CHANGE

Dreams of mythic proportions usually come at times when the personality is ready to individuate from the imposed struc-tures and patterns of society, family, and the beliefs of a culture. During the peak of a transformational cycle or a ripe opportunity in life when change is forced or welcome, whether it is a period of maturation such as adolescence or a transition such as divorce, a dream may come as a call to venture deep into the Lower World. Like Alice in *Through the Looking Glass* or Dorothy in *The Wizard of Oz*, a mythic dream may take one into a dark forest as a hero or heroine to slay the demons that block the path. We might have to slay our father, our mother, a witch, or a monster shadow figure who may seek to devour us or rob us of our power. Once that figure has been slain, the ego can move past its old identity and claim one that reflects growth. The personality no longer seeks refuge in the safety of the known world, and it is compelled to accept a deeper connection to nature and a truer, more authentic expres-sion in life.

Adolescents who are between the ages of twelve and sev-enteen commonly have dreams that mark the passage into adulthood. This period in one's life is seldom recognized in Western culture. In more primitive societies, the transition is celebrated through specific rite-of-passage rituals. Adolescents frequently have difficulty making the transition from childhood to adolescence, and their dreams may reveal the conflicts they face. Their quest to individuate and for self-exploration is often interrupted by parents and educators who exert an opposing force, pulling them into different levels of conformity. While the soul struggles to resolve these conflicts creatively, the adolescent's creativity may turn inward, resulting in emotional tension and depression. It may also turn outward, resulting in antisocial behavior.

When my daughter was twelve, she had a very important dream in which she was confronted by two men with strange-looking futuristic guns. These men were also wearing spider rings on their fingers. She wrestled away a gun and shot the strangers. Rather than bullets, the guns emitted rays of light that dissolved the men. She then descended into the basement of the house, where she discovered a treasure chest full of jewels and spider rings. A guide in the dream told her that she could take as many of the jewels as she wanted. No matter how many jewels and spider rings she took out, the treasure chest remained full. In the dream, she was talking to her father on the telephone, telling him about the dream experience. He in turn told her that he had the same dream when he was her age.

My daughter's dream marked her transition into puberty and pointed to the discovery of her creative power drawn from the Lower World. In the dream, she had conquered her fears through the power of the light and made a descent to find the treasures within her subconscious, symbolized by the basement. The spider ring is a symbol of fertility and creativity, an amulet of power that would protect her and offer her a symbolic connection to her own creative potential. The jewels within the treasure chest represented the radiant qualities and regenerative potential of her sexuality. They also represented the wealth and abundance that may be claimed when she touches the depth of her own creative potential.

Dreams like these are milestones in a psychological as well as a biological process. Recognition and celebration of such a dream may ease the crisis of adolescence and bring to light the psychological tasks necessary to embrace growth.

THE CALL TO SHAMANIZE

Dreams from the Lower World may also be calls to shamanize, to retrieve the power within nature in order to use it for healing. Intense energy or heat—even fever—may accompany such dreams. They may be seen as the milestones of deep psychological work that push forward the soul's evolution. Shamans often are called to their profession through a dream in which they are met by an animal power who will later become the shaman's ally, guiding him into the many dimensions of the soul.

A dream in which a wild animal appears and threatens to devour or dismember us may represent a confrontation with a natural or supernatural power. Animal power dreams are common but are seldom recognized as a call to shamanize. Often the dreamer will avoid the call by running from the animal and thus avoid the deepest connection to nature and its power.

I recall a dream where I was being chased through the forest by a bear. I ran straight to my mother's house, where the bear waited patiently for me outside. The dream remarked on my avoidance of my role as a shaman and healer through my adherence to the belief that to be successful I needed to pursue doctoral studies. My mother's house represented the safety of accepting her conventional beliefs that higher education was the formula for success.

Animal powers, from the perspective of the shaman, are not symbols. They are strong allies or spirits who lend their energies as power to the shaman through a special kinship. The Lakota Indians, for instance, subscribe the name "relations" to the animal power that they encounter in the spiritual realms. For the Lakota as with other tribal cultures, the power of the animal is familial and sacred. For instance, Brother Eagle is a guide to the spiritual realms. He brings the power of Great Spirit into life and offers a "bird's-eye" view of life from a spiritual perspective.

When animal powers emerge from within a dream we can commune with an extraordinary power and potential. If not fought off or chased away, the animal may offer its wisdom as medicine for the soul, supernatural power for healing, and instinctive power to strengthen the personality. Whether it is the healing energy of a snake or the pride and confidence of a lion, each possesses an extraordinary power that connects us to an instinctual side of ourselves.

The ancient Egyptians believed that animals were closer to God because they were in touch with the mysteries within nature. They assigned godlike qualities to animals and worshiped their power. Many dream analysts interpret animals in dreams symbolically and ascribe negative characteristics to them. They consider animals as reflecting lower drives, which humans should rise above by virtue of the intellect. This view separates man from the mysteries of nature and thus denies the power and potential of the Lower World.

SACRED UNION

More than twenty years ago, I had an important dream. In the dream I was giving birth to an androgynous god with both male and female genitalia. I believed it to reveal the true nature of the soul—that it is androgynous. The male side expresses the forces of reason, logic, and action. The female offers the qualities of intuition, receptivity, creativity, and emotionality. If encountered dancing together in a dream, these archetypes express the union of opposites merged in a sacred expression. A wedding in a dream may suggest the celebration of this sacred union.

Dreams often express this struggle to balance the male and female aspects in order to actualize them creatively.

For both men and women, the unconscious female is wounded by the patriarchal male, who imposes structure and obedience to negate feminine power. A modern myth, "The Little Mermaid," first written as a children's fairy tale by Hans Christian Andersen, has been transformed in recent years by the myth-makers at Disney Studios. This animated movie points to the reemergence of the feminine voice at a time when our culture needs to regain the balance and sensitivity of the feminine principle. Growing legs out of fins, which were only useful when hidden in the sea of the subconscious, Ariel, in her archetypal female adolescence, must reclaim her voice from the demonized sea witch named Ursula. The struggle to reclaim the voice of intuition and wisdom is difficult to resolve. Through the defeat of the sea witch, Ariel is embraced by her masculine aspect. This myth illustrates the individuation process as Ariel leaves her father's side and her familiar ocean world, as well as speaking to the sacred union of the male and female.

NATURE'S ELEMENTS AND RESOURCES

From within the Lower World, the natural elements may erupt in dreams as weather patterns that offer insight into the mood of the dreamer. These elements have corresponding meanings as they relate to man: fire (passion), water (emotions), air (mind), and earth (the body). As weather, these elements combine to create storms, floods, and winds of all sorts to express our own feelings or moods. Earth activity, such as earthquakes and aftershocks, in dreams may reveal deep emotions or responses to situations that rock our lives.

Dreams of tidal waves and hurricanes may offer a magnified picture of our emotions. A stream may represent the flow of life force; a river may indicate vital sexual energy. A cave may be the womb, a mountain peak the crown. Dreams reflect the deep connection between man and the elements of nature.

MINING THE JEWELS AND ORE OF THE EARTH

Minerals, the jewels and treasures of the earth, are excavated from deep within the Lower World to offer up their radiant qualities and to help us glimpse the spiritual light within. Dreamers have reported being presented with a special crystal, such as an amethyst, in a dream by some wise woman or sage. Such a gift of power may awaken intuition and spiritual vision. More commonly, dreamers may find themselves wearing a special piece of jewelry containing a gem that may signify a special quality: Diamonds reflect radiant clarity, and pearls represent wisdom and enlightenment. Each brings a definition to an aspect of the soul. As a synchronistic gift, a dreamer may later acquire such a crystal or piece of jewelry in his or her waking life in order to work with its power more consciously.

The ore of the earth, when refined into precious metals, has meaning as different aspects of the soul. Silver as feminine and gold as masculine, together, bring balance. Raw metals such as iron may denote strength of character.

The process of alchemy, which turns base metals into gold, represents the refinement of the soul into its purified and untarnished state of wholeness. Ancient alchemy symbols may also appear in dreams to further our understanding of ourselves.

NATURE AND HER CYCLES

If a garden serves as the dream environment, the varieties of plants, trees, and flowers offer messages to the dreamer. Each flower or plant offers a unique quality that reflects natural characters within the individual. Therefore, a rose may represent qualities of feminine beauty and a daisy may reflect a ray of sunshine into one's heart.

A beautiful dream told to me by a seventeen-year-old revealed the protective quality that nature bestows. In the dream, she sat beneath a sacred tree whose branches were expansive. For a time her family was there with her, but then they turned away, leaving her beneath the tree. When she journeyed away from the tree and down a path, the tree's branches reached out and continued to shelter her for quite a distance. In this dream, the tree is the tree of life, and its branches of wisdom offer protection while she embarks on an important rite of passage. It signifies her innate connection to nature's wisdom. The path leads her to mystical knowledge.

Seasonal changes may be announced to the dreamer attuned to the cycles of nature. A dream of a fox in a snow-blanketed forest may forecast more accurately the arrival of winter than the day marked on a calendar. Seasons in dreams may also represent the seasons of life. With each season of life, we are asked to embrace the milestones and the wisdom that come with each age. Spring calls us to embrace innocence, summer the magical, fall the mystical, and winter our wisdom.

In cultures where the seasons were celebrated by festivals and ceremonies marking the solar cycles such as the solstices and equinoxes, connections were made directly to the cycles of feminine fertility. In modern culture, we seem to celebrate the seasons with sports activities: soccer in spring, baseball in summer, football in fall, and hockey in winter. The male consciousness, with its preoccupation with competitive sports, may reflect a spiritual need as well. These games offer empowerment, much like the contests of any other warrior society that tested the strength of the masculine will.

ANCIENT SYMBOLS

Mined from the depths of the Lower World, ancient symbols bring forth a rich history of associated meanings. Whether historical or religious, ancient symbols may be traced to mythological origins. The ancient symbol of the ankh, for instance, is associated with the healing power of Isis, the Egyptian goddess. In her mythology, she restored the life of her dismembered husband, Osiris, pointing to the healing power of the great goddess as a life-giving and life-renewing force.

Ancient symbols may offer esoteric meanings that are related to mystical traditions. Sometimes these symbols occur randomly within our dreams, even when we may not have any personal relationship to the tradition from which the symbol originated. They appear as part of a rich legacy of the collective unconscious. These symbols may be researched in ancient religious texts or in more modern encyclopedias of ancient symbols.

From basic shapes and elementary symbols to the complex geometric forms, a vast array of symbols that rest within soul memory may appear in dreams. The most common first scribbles of children are circles and crosses, basic symbols of wholeness and spirit. Concentric circles, or circles within circles, for instance, have a long historical association that depicts the cosmos and its spheres as a microcosm within a macrocosm. These early shapes are imprinted deeply in the soul, emerging through expressive art forms and within dreams quite spontaneously.

More complex symbols such as mandalas, Hebrew letters, labyrinths, and the yin and yang offer examples of a legacy of spiritual history that connects man to the journey of the soul and its spiritual origins. Mandalas, with their intricate patterns, display rays that conjoin at the center of a wheel that has no beginning and no end. They express an order and symmetry to man in his quest for spiritual attainment. The Hebrew letters were offered as the word of God; the labyrinth is the pathway of the inner journey. The symbols of yin and yang represent the balance of male and female opposites.

The primordial power symbols and archetypes of the Lower World have accumulated their meaning over thousands and thousands of years. The symbols of the Lower World differ from those of the Middle World in that their meanings are imprinted deep within us as part of a universal consciousness that is separate from our personal experience. We may form associations, however, with symbols from the Lower World that may be positive or negative. Sometimes these associations are born of biased opinions or because of a personal historical reference to them. Thus, we may miss the deeper spiritual meaning these symbols seek to convey. Other symbols can be seen as a doorway to sought-after wisdom that leads to deeper knowledge. Their psychological pull is strong—so strong that when one's own beliefs challenge the archetypal patterns, conflict arises and must be addressed and resolved through conscious effort. Through conscious contact with a symbol and the pattern of energy the symbol holds, we may discover some deeper truth. In this way, meditation on an ancient symbol, such as the cross or a five-pointed star, may induce a physical experience that brings a deeper, truer understanding of the symbolic message. This can be a profound awakening experience to the meaning of a symbol.

The deepest aspects of the soul exist within the Lower World. Thus, Lower World dreams transform the soul at the most fundamental level and leave a collective imprint for future generations.

CHAPTER 2

The Middle World

The playground on which we creatively play out life's comedies and tragedies is called the Middle World. Here is where we live, work, play, interact with others, fall in love, fall out of love, serve our families, serve others, find enjoyment, and commune with nature.

From a shaman's perspective, the Middle World is the manifest world where spirit, soul, and ego move into action. In the Middle World, we give birth to our ideas. We also tear them down or allow them to die when they have served their purpose. The Middle World is the ground on which we experience our successes and suffer our failures.

In the Middle World, there is an eternal compromise between our ego's desires and the desires of the soul. The world is meant to sustain and fulfill us, but, unfortunately, it sometimes falls short of its promise. This is partially due to our sometimes narrow view of the world and the way we interpret our circumstances. We often feel isolated, alone, forced to lead an unsatisfactory life. Few people live the life they want or the life they deserve. Few feel their days are filled with wisdom and meaning.

Whether our desires are satisfied in the world depends a lot on the attitudes and beliefs we hold about ourselves and the world in general. We improvise on the playground of life to achieve our goals each day and to fulfill our greater dreams. Sometimes we succeed and sometimes we fail. Sometimes life gives us what we expect, but more often it presents us with what we need in order to grow psychologically and morally. If we embrace all of life as a lesson where each challenge or obstacle becomes the perfect circumstance for personal growth, we honor life's tests. We understand that each obstacle has been set before us to strengthen our personality and evolve our soul. Whether we are to learn the value of forgiveness or the value of patience, each test in confronting our anger or impatience offers an opportunity for a new attitude or course of action, and a more fulfilling outcome.

The role of Middle World dreams and their symbolic language is to reflect our concerns, emotions, attitudes, and actions back to us so that we may gain meaning from our experiences. Therefore, the signs and symbols of the Middle World, whether presented through the synchronicities of life or through the replaying of our night dreams, offer us wisdom through which we may grow emotionally, psychologically, and spiritually. Simply put, dreams in the Middle World offer us concrete guidance for how we can move about our lives constructively, making new choices, taking new direction, making changes in our attitude, all of which promote the fulfillment of our personal goals.

THE SECRET PLAYGROUND

The Middle World is full of secrets. It is a veritable playground of psychic information that our conscious minds rarely notice, but our subconscious minds pick up and stores. The symbols of society are everywhere on product labels, on T-shirts, on the faces of buildings, on billboards, and on television. Every object we notice, manipulate, or experience centers the data bank of our subconscious mind. It is stored there as day residue and projected onto the screen of our night dreams. There it is translated into a symbolic language, which is usually metaphorical. Some of the symbols of dreams can be personally translated based on our personal associations. But most have another, objective meaning, one the subconscious understands and attempts to convey. The translation of that subconscious message is self-generated and thus may be viewed as the soul's translation. The soul's translation of symbolic language is woven together into a meaningful story and delivers insights into the dreamer's mind. In night dreams, the message will persist through many cycles of dreaming until it is understood by the dreamer.

In the waking dream, or dream reality, these messages often arrive as synchronicities. These synchronistic messages may appear as a sign pointing the way to live a more morally or spiritually authentic life. The appearance of Winnie-the-Pooh several times in a day on a T-shirt, for instance, may be offering the sound advice to begin loving unconditionally. The appearance of a rubber band on a curb while crossing the street to meet a friend may be seen as encouragement to "hold it together emotionally." The fact that we notice and process these seemingly benign details of symbolic information means that our higher or "creative intelligence" is seeking to bring meaning to our existence by offering them as food for thought. Our creative intelligence is making connections between what we notice and the concerns of our subconscious that are aching to be addressed.

A conscious dreamer who is awake in the dream of the

Middle World (i.e., alert to the larger story of symbols around him) holds a panoramic view, receiving guidance and information at every turn. Coincidences, then, are most often an expression of our own openness to personal enlightenment!

THE WISDOM ON THE PLAYGROUND

Dreams are ingenious theatrical productions that ask us to take a seat in the audience and view how we have been operating and behaving. The subconscious is giving us feedback. For instance, if I traded terse words with my husband while I watched Rosie O'Donnell on TV, she may show up in a night dream to reveal anger that was unexpressed in the real argument. My subconscious would be using Rosie as an outspoken, gutsy celebrity to express my withheld emotional response to the argument. The subconscious would not only be using what was on television during the argument to replay the feelings, but it would also be demonstrating that Rosie herself was a messenger. Rosie's name itself could also be significant. It could have served as an arrow pointing to a dysfunctional pattern of behavior. "Rosie" could translate into an "everything is rosy" attitude. In this way, she may have been mocking the smoothing over of unexpressed rage through a divine play on words.

In our normal waking state, we disregard the background and stay focused on the foreground and thus miss hidden messages of the Middle World. At night, the subconscious erupts with a dream expressing what has been concealed from view. We need to wake up within the dream of life and learn to interpret each situation as if it were a scene in a dream.

Night dreams that emerge from the Middle World are often direct responses to life's occurrences, and they demonstrate our psychological achievements in handling these events. They render into metaphorical images our deepest feelings, beliefs, and attitudes, which we may conceal from others or even from ourselves.

Whether we are plagued by guilt or rage, or uplifted by a positive experience, the subconscious may have something to say about it. It informs us of shifts in belief or attitude that we may need to make consciously. It may commend us on ones that we have already made. In this way, our dreams offer a little constructive criticism and a lot of encouragement.

Some dreams from the Middle World not only show us where we are in achieving our goals for fulfillment but also inform us about where we have been and where we are going. They highlight the major lessons of our life and show us the sequence of milestones we have passed and those that we will soon be approaching. They unravel the underlying self-limiting beliefs that we ascribe to that may thwart our progress on our evolutionary journey. These dreams are important reviews and previews of our quest for psychological wholeness. They note every time we fail to resolve the pattern and applaud us when we have had a major breakthrough. Those who do serious dream work may uncover such a dream in one of their journals years after they had the dream. Thus, dreams that tell us a little about our past, comment on the present, and project the future are navigational maps to our ultimate destination.

REFLECTIONS OF THE MIRROR

The night dreams of the Middle World present many characters. Some are reflections of ourselves; some are reflections of those who are close to us. Parts of our personality may emerge— the child, the adult, the wise self, the coward, the hero, the third-party caller, members of our family of origin, an invisible self, and a cast of other characters who all have some piece in working out the creative process of dreaming. They demonstrate that there are different parts of our personality seeking expression and working on our life problems. A dream may indicate when a destructive part of our personality is taking over. An example might be the inner teenager who overindulges in junk food when the adult is confronted with true sexual intimacy. Or the child who is allowed to drive the car in a dream and runs it off the road, signifying perhaps that one is being driven by one's childish behavior or emotions a little too often. Wise aspects may also be operating to offer solutions and more mature ways of approaching the problem. They may come to present a symbolic gift or a tool, which might be a metaphorical remedy. For example, a strange woman may show up in a man's dream, handing him a pacifier as a solution to living with his nagging wife.

Our friends in life often make up for qualities we lack. They may possess attributes we need to take on. They may also enter our lives to present us with reflections of earlier relationships with sister, brother, mother, or father. They may show up to help us develop our wholeness as well as to offer us companionship. They, like everyone else in our lives, can be viewed as teachers whose lessons may be overt or covert.

Our friends may make appearances in our night dreams as representatives of different aspects of our personality. For instance, if we have a best friend who is usually curt and opinionated, he or she may reflect that part of our own personality. Or if the "too nice" part of ourselves needs a more assertive voice, a friend with those tendencies might arrive as a primary character in our dream. Making a mental list of the traits we associate with a friend who appears in a dream could bring to light an aspect of our own personality and show us where we need to focus.

In some dreams, friends and acquaintances reveal who they

really are inside. The psyche witnesses hidden information that our conscious mind ignores, so it may pick up an individual's good or bad intentions. A dream may reveal what our friends are thinking inside or doing behind our back. These psychic cues may be delivered in a dream as a full-length feature story about individuals and what they have hidden in their closets. The closer the connection to a friend, the more likely we are to dream about him or her. For instance, it is not unusual for a woman to dream about her husband's infidelity or another secret he's holding. A word of caution: It is often difficult to determine whether such a dream is expressing an underlying fear rather than an actual betrayal, as dreams may reveal our own fears and anxieties as well.

Often, we will have a sense of someone in the dream but do not get the full view of who they are. The figure may be riding next to us in the passenger seat of our vehicle or be in the room with us as we interact with other characters in the dream. Invisible partners in dreams signify underdeveloped aspects of our personality with which we are not well acquainted. They can represent a part of us that picks up the psychic cues of life. In this way they come to represent the intuitive function.

FAMILY

Members of our family of origin offer deep emotional and soul ties. At a soul level they brought to us a legacy of genealogical information containing patterns of behavior and attitudes and beliefs that we lived with throughout our childhood. Children live the unconscious lives of their parents up to the age of seven, which means that the conflicts carried in the soul of the parent are transferred psychically to the children. Some of these patterns override our conscious choices in adulthood, and, no matter how hard we try to make a mental shift in attitude, the influence of a particular family member may still overpower our quest to be our own person. Dreams reveal these unconscious strongholds over our will as family members collaborate in the dreamscape. For example, if you are living with your father in a dream, or are lying in bed with him, or are letting him drive your car, your dream is expressing the powerful influence of his psyche on your life choices. The father often represents the patriarchal values and defines a way of moving outward in the world in the area of personal achievement and success. The mother represents our view of nurturing and our emotions. Loyalty to good old Dad or to Mom's attitudes, therefore, may hold us back from actualizing our dreams in the Middle World. Our night dreams will reveal to us how their imprinted patterns are interfering.

Sisters and brothers, who have usually shared our childhood experiences, are often with us to express the bond with our personal history. However, each sibling may perceive identical situations in the home quite differently. Some may be weakened by them and others strengthened. The appearance of a sibling in a dream, then, may signify that you are addressing a wound of childhood. Siblings may also show up in a dream to fulfill a role that they played in our childhood. Perhaps a brother was the family scapegoat, and so he arrives to point to our own feelings about being victimized in one way or another. A cousin may arrive as a character who expresses a more distant relationship to the family values and attitudes, sharing some of the family history but not all.

We may live in our parents' house in our dreams until we have fully individuated from their value structures and have discovered our own. Dreams in which we are in the house with our parents or in the various houses we grew up in may signify a time of working through family-of-origin issues. This is usually a good time to seek the help of a counselor experienced in working with dreams to complete the inner work.

MINOR CHARACTERS

Minor characters, despite their cameo appearances in a dream, may bring a big message whether they arrive through the back door or the front door. As stated in Precept 4, all characters are equally important. From a shamanistic perspective, all the characters of our dreams are messenger spirits who may have a significant gift of wisdom for the dreamer. Their message may be conveyed through some action or enactment in the dream. The brevity of their appearance brings attention to them that may be different from other, seemingly more relevant, characters. The view that not all characters in our dreams are parts of ourselves is an important aspect of dream work, as it clears confusion when dreams have come from another dimension, from the Lower or Upper Worlds.

Each detail and action of the characters in our dream is important. Their attitudes and their identities may be expressed through the clothing they are wearing, an object they hold, or through the behavior they enact in the dream. For instance, a character's Victorian dress might suggest that he or she is expressing outdated values that suppress sexual expression. Or if a messenger in a dream appears in army fatigues, he may have arrived to recruit the dreamer to some social action, such as promoting peace. Thus, clothing can express one's identity or profession as well as one's values.

THE SCENES

The environments of the Middle and Lower Worlds are intertwined in our waking dream and are the arenas and landscapes where we explore life. The dreamer can experience the power and spiritual dimension within nature. These environments are the ground upon which we play out our life's potentials. Whether they are a natural environment, such as a desert, oasis, mountain, beach, or forest, or a man-made area, such as a city, town, or country farm, each offers us resources and experiences that are unique and meaningful to our existence.

Natural metaphors exist within nature that bring extraordinary experiences to the conscious dreamer. For instance, geomorphs, rocks that take on the characteristics of an animal or the shape of a human, may so shockingly resemble them that we must take a second look in our amazement. Another example of nature's communication may be the stray cat meowing at your front door, possibly to announce that you have been lost but are now ready to embrace your potential. A diseased tree might signify living a diseased life. And hornets at the front door may indicate that the dreamer is about to enter a house of jealousy and anger. Such natural-world metaphors of the Middle World bring meaning to every aspect of life and are a reflection of our deep connection and interaction with nature.

Cities and towns where we live and work deliver society's direct messages and metaphors for us to witness and digest. The symbols of society may bombard the senses with subliminal messages filled with deep personal meaning, which may be more complex than a serene natural environment. Walking down a city street for the conscious dreamer may bring about a pocketful of miracles. Synchronistic messages from the signposts along the way, such as messages on license plates, the make of a car, the message on a billboard, or the brand name of clothing worn by a passerby, may all deliver an important message to the conscious dreamer about the direction and course of his or her life. For the awakened eye of the conscious dreamer, everything in life has a message, sometimes literal, sometimes metaphorical. Noticing someone walking by wearing Converse sneakers may indicate that something is being "conversed about" in the current dialogue that he or she is failing to hear. A helicopter flying overhead may come as a message to "hover" over a present complex problem in order to get a clearer perspective.

The symbolic sign or literal sign may also come to announce an opportunity that may be presented shortly. For instance, encountering several school buses on the road to an important business meeting may announce that one will learn something unexpected at the appointment. The environment where we live, work, and play, therefore, is full of messages if we are open to receiving them.

THE ENVIRONMENTS IN NIGHT DREAMS

In night dreams, there is a more mystical or magical quality to the primordial gardens of the Lower World versus the ordinary appearance of these environments in dreams from the Middle World. Consider the example from Chapter 1 where the tree followed the young girl on her path toward spiritual knowledge.

The environments in our night dreams that are inspired by the Middle World point to the area of life upon which the dreamer needs to focus. Being outdoors in a dream suggests being involved in activities of outward expression, such as achievement and play. Being indoors can reflect interior concerns and preoccupations, such as domestic issues, family dynamics, and self-exploration.

Enrolling in a new school may signify new lessons in life that one may need to learn in order to bring the soul and personality into balance. Eating at a restaurant might reflect how one experiences receiving social nurturing. Sitting by a lake can represent one's spiritual concerns.

A house with many rooms to explore often signifies the interior layout of the soul itself. We may enter a room and notice every detail of the furniture, the paintings on the wall, the floors, and the carpeting. Each element represents an idea or belief we might possess in our subconscious. Antique furniture may suggest that one is living with the legacy of the past, which may or may not fulfill desires in the present. During times of psychological repair, remodeling may represent the deep soul work that has become necessary to transcend the past and transform the future.

CHANGING SCENES

Scene changes in dreams reflect a shift from one concern or thought to another. Progressive scene changes may direct us to look through the layers to the emotional patterns that surround a particular concern. Moving from the inside to the outside expresses movement from idea into action.

A sudden or abrupt scene change may move the dreamer closer to a more detailed explanation of the dream. It may reflect creative problem-solving undertaken to remedy a situation. Some dreams offer resolution; others do not. But each dream is an attempt to resolve the conflicts creatively and meaningfully in service to the dreamer's well-being.

EMOTIONS AND MOODS

Life in the Middle World is full of emotional ups and downs. We may respond to criticism in our life by putting up defenses. We may avoid our feelings by holding up a mask of happiness when we are miserable. Or we may collapse into a heap or even throw a tantrum at a perceived loss or betrayal.

Emotions are healthy responses to life. If we store them away because we feel unsafe or because we feel we don't have permission to express them, our dreams may bring them in a tidal wave, sometimes quite literally as a symbol to make the point.

Since the moment of conception, our experiences in our mother's womb are stored as imprints deep within the cells of our bodies. We bring the psychic information from our past and spill it into the present. Some of the repressed material from childhood may be long held in cold storage as frozen feelings until they have thawed out into fluid movements within our dreams, helping us to heal those core wounds.

Dreams render our feelings into metaphorical images. A centipede may crawl on us if we are afraid to embrace the vicious sting of our own anger. Or a box of Kleenex on the bed may point to grief around having lost a lover. Water flooding our home may appear as a response to our worry and concern about family relationships. It may demonstrate the guilt we have felt around an emotional outburst that requires some conscious cleanup.

The emotions in our dreams may be discovered in a secret hiding place. We may find ourselves in a warehouse or a closet, opening boxes that we have hidden in an effort to stow away traumas and hurts from as far back as our childhood. Our night dreams give us an opportunity to witness from the point of view of the observer the feelings and their associated wounds that were tucked away out of sight for long periods of time. We may then sort through them objectively in order to resolve the conflicts they have created.

We may wake up with a strong emotional response to our dream, fearful about confronting the dream's secret. Negative emotional responses to dream material may impede our progress and hinder us from looking more deeply at what the dream is really trying to tell us. If you have a terror of spiders, for instance, and one appears on the floorboard of your car in a dream, it might cause a "freak-out." But the spider may have been a messenger pointing to the creative power with which you are moving forward in life. It may have come with the message to cultivate, appreciate, and embrace your creative nature.

Each individual deals with the stress in the Middle World differently. Some roll with the punches and others run and hide. Fearfulness may be an obstacle to psychological health. Our dreams often reflect our stress by offering a confused jumble of images at night. Anxiety dreams in which we have lost our books for class or misplaced an important document for work are examples most everyone has had at one time or another. They reveal our nervousness, anxiety, and feelings of unpreparedness.

By identifying the emotion that is revealed in the dream, we can begin the process of inner work to heal previously unidentified wounds and to gain objectivity regarding more recent emotional issues.

PROBLEM-SOLVING IN THE MIDDLE WORLD

Our walk about the Middle World presents us with many problems to solve. Family relationships, work, finances, health, love, and self-expression may all be of concern. We may need the assistance of a higher intelligence to find a creative solution to the challenges of life. Dreams demonstrate the creative problem-solving ability within the subconscious. Conflicts resolve ingeniously within the repository of memories from which the conflict arose in the first place. The creative juices of our dreams rewrite our internal scripts, sometimes without any conscious effort. In this way, they compensate for the disappointments we have confronted and help fulfill our wishes. Therefore, a dream in which we are reunited with our ex-spouse through love, for example, resolves the internal feelings of abandonment or disharmony we were left with in the dissolution of the relationship. The dream fulfills an internal wish.

Dreams may replace a bad attitude with a good one. If we are in conflict about attending a workshop or a family reunion, a dream may demonstrate the possible benefits of going by offering a preview. In other words, what we may have dismissed as not important enough to pursue may be presented as an opportunity for fulfillment and growth by our subconscious adviser.

DREAMS AND HEALTH

Dreams can reveal hidden health issues before the symptoms appear in the physical body. Often, dreams of floods or tidal waves may warn of the brewing of an illness caused by unexpressed emotions. Not only may our dreams reveal the illness, but they may also explain its origins and scene-by-scene causality, as well as offer a prescription for healing. Miraculously, a dream may even bring forth the creative energy to heal the illness. Remarkable recoveries have been known to be precipitated by the healing potential within dreams.

One such example was a woman whom I saw in my private practice. In her dream, a young boy about ten years of age appeared and grabbed the cane of a crippled old man and beat him to death with it. The woman, who suffered from a crippling form of arthritis, discovered that her symptoms were miraculously disappearing after the dream. The child in her dream represented a renewal of her masculine will and a more youthful energy that she needed in order to conquer the crippled aspect of her personality. The dream reflected the attitudinal change that she no longer would accept being crippled. Although it is difficult to explain this type of remarkable recovery from a medical perspective, it demonstrates the creative power within the subconscious to heal the physical body. Using dream information to initiate behavioral and attitudinal changes may be life-saving. The practice of journaling dreams during a health crisis or any other crisis in one's life may offer important clues that are necessary to recovery.

LOVE, RELATIONSHIP, AND INTIMACY

Life in the Middle World is all about love. Whether we admit it or not, we seek to be loved and to express love. Dreams reveal the beauty of love relationships as well as the challenges we confront with those we love. The arrival of a mysterious stranger on our balcony may announce readiness for a romantic lover. A box of chocolates delivered in a dream may relate the sweetness and enjoyment of some love relationship. The gift of a wedding ring may come to solidify through commitment the bonds of a relationship. Each of these examples indicates a readiness to accept the power of love in our life.

Dreams sometimes replay the early relationships that molded our beliefs about love. A dream in which our present wife or husband transforms into our old flame from high school may reveal that they are one and the same character. The dream reveals how we are still haunted by the memories of an old, unresolved relationship. If our old flame was unfaithful, we may be tormented by the fear of infidelity in our present relationship. Our dreams will reveal these fears with scenes where our lover is seduced by another. Dreams unravel the patterns we most fear, allowing us to grow from them so that our true love stories may eventually have happy endings.

Intimacy and sexuality are common themes in dreams as we attempt to heal the shame and fear around sexuality. Dreams taking place in the bedroom bring concerns we have about our sexual nature and our sexual desires into the foreground. An unmade bed may be a remark on the lack of attention and care that one takes around one's sexual behavior. Having numerous people in bed with us may indicate that many differing attitudes about sexuality are vying for space. Garbage in the bed may remark on trashy thoughts about sex. The metaphors express the disharmony we may feel as we confront intimate relationships. As we confront the limiting beliefs about our sexuality and intimacy through dreams, we heal the most sacred part of what it is to be human.

HORROR STORIES OR COMEDIES

Whether they involve falling, being chased by a shadow figure, having your car stolen, or being violently assaulted in some way, nightmares are disturbing occurrences that can produce a great deal of anxiety and interrupt normal sleep patterns. Nightmares, or "bad dreams," often relate to anxiety, fear, or apprehension about life. They may come as responses to events or circumstances that threaten our well-being or thwart our progress toward our goals. Sometimes nightmares are caused by repressed experiences or feelings that have been buried in childhood and surface as conflicts in adulthood. These nightmares are often like a loud knock on the door, demanding to be brought out of the darkness and into the light of examination.

Dream researchers identify two types of nightmares. The first type, night terrors, usually occur within the first two hours of sleep and are characterized by fitful or restless sleep from which the dreamer may awaken screaming out loud. The content of the dream most often is not recalled. Young children are more frequently plagued by night terrors because of their sensitivity and openness. Whatever the cause of these night terrors, their occurrence tends to diminish as the child grows.

The second type of bad dreams, nightmares, are anxiety dreams that occur in the later part of the sleep cycle and are usually recalled in great detail. The content of these dreams can be quite disturbing and often violent. Individuals who are characterized as having thin boundaries or are labeled as "sensitives" are most likely to suffer from nightmares. Creative, artistic individuals usually fall into this category of nightmare sufferers because of their openness and ability to tap into other dimensions of consciousness more easily

Developing insight into the meaning of stress-related nightmares can bring freedom from the fears and anxieties that are their source. Confronting the demon in a dream may strip it of its power.

Sometimes what we may think is a nightmare may really be a comical exposé of our behavior in life. The dreamer can tell the difference by the emotional response the details elicit. I recall a dream where a stockroom boy was filling the shelves in the aisle of a supermarket with junk food. A gang suddenly burst through the door with machine guns and shot him dead. But I was not horrified. The dream was a response to a radical diet that I had initiated during that time. It was a comment on the extreme approach I had taken in order to lose weight.

Dreams such as flushing decapitated heads down a toilet or slaughtering a cow may simply and poignantly remark on getting rid of negative thinking. They are not growling nightmares bent on terrorizing our well-being. Instead, they imaginatively and graphically point to something about our behavior or thinking that has changed. In such a dream, the dreamer is usually an observer of the violent act rather than the victim, and seems aware of a certain benign atmosphere that permeates the scene.

True nightmares will usually be accompanied by fear, anxiety, and even panic, and are more likely to recur.

SELF-CONCEPT AND BEAUTY

We wear many masks in the world in an effort to fit in and gain recognition. Being authentic may be farthest from our minds as we attempt to validate ourselves through cultural norms of success and beauty. Dreams reveal insecurities and fears about our appearance, identity, and performance in the world. A woman who tries on new clothes in a department store in her dreams may be looking for a fresh attitude to put on or to change her image. Discovering that one is standing naked in front of an audience may be a response to feeling overexposed and embarrassed after revealing too much about oneself. Participating in a beauty pageant may speak to a competitive attitude about one's physical appearance. Dreams attempt to bring into full view our self-concept, which may not reflect our true individual inner and outer beauty. A dream in which one dreamer found herself in a coffin next to Princess Diana with a newspaper headline reading I CAN AUTHENTICATE WHAT IS BEAUTIFUL AND WHAT IS NOT brought wisdom and resolution to a long history of self-defeating thoughts about her physical beauty.

FULFILLMENT

Life in the Middle World propels us to put our ideas into action in order to fulfill our goals and desires. The projects we create through our work in the world can be represented as construction sites in our dreams. And dreams reveal how close we are to fulfilling the goals we set for ourselves. If we find ourselves on a building site whose foundation has just been laid, this may reveal that a creative idea is in the making. Putting icing on a cake or putting the last piece in a puzzle are metaphors for completion. Serving and eating a cake may represent enjoying the product of one's creativity and may indicate that one has reached fulfillment.

The roads and thoroughfares in our dreams represent the path we have chosen to our destination. A bumpy, unpaved road may suggest that one has chosen a difficult passage, and a freeway may be a comment that one has chosen the road to independence. Ultimately, the roads in our dreams bring us closer to our destination, closer to fulfilling our dreams, and closer even to fulfilling our destiny.

Every twist and turn we take on our journey through life is meant to be a learning experience, whether we ever fulfill our desires or reach our destination. The lessons we choose may torment us or may liberate us. We make the choice through our interpretation of the event. The ultimate experience of fulfillment is the celebration of ourselves and the celebration of life in the Middle World as a dream we have created. Living an enlightened life means appreciating the total picture as well as the single moments. Appreciating our dreams requires the same. Our dreams offer us the opportunity to have lives filled with meaning, wisdom, and respect for our soul's journey.

CHAPTER 3

The Upper World

Dreams from the Upper World offer a wealth of wisdom and inspiration for the dreamer. Whether they are a profound message from a celestial guide, being touched by the light, a spirit visitation from a dead relative, or a paranormal encounter of the third kind, Upper World dreams connect us to the potential that is beyond this ordinary world. These dreams are heaven sent.

When the spiritual dimensions of the Upper World collide with the consciousness of the dreamer who has inexplicably broken through the barrier of the Middle World, the bounty of inspirational gifts and spiritual revelations reaches the dreaming mind like a lightning bolt. A message from some visible or invisible messenger may offer a directive or an assertion of a transcendent truth. If a dreamer hears voices of angels summoning him or her to experience angelic light or to see the apparition of some saint who brings moral advice, the dream is delivering a divine power. In such dreams the individual has the rare opportunity of communing and communicating with a spirit source. Guides may deliver spiritual encouragement through a difficult time such as a death or another transition in life. They may summon one to renew a spiritual path or offer a message as simple as "All you need is love."

Most of the messages in dreams from the Upper World are easily interpreted. They arrive as literal messages rather than as metaphoric material that requires deciphering. A message can arrive as a headline on a newspaper, a number or name on a license plate, or an image on a billboard in front of one's face in a lucid moment just before waking. The message is signed, sealed, and delivered in such a way that the dreamer may have little question as to its validity.

I was recently told a dream by a friend to whom a male angel appeared in white robes and a "mod" haircut. The dreamer was descending a rapid waterway with raging force. The angel told her to remember to keep the soles of her feet up in the air. After discussing the dream, the dreamer commented that she believed the angel was suggesting that she surrender to her emotions and let the life force carry her. The soles of her feet represented her own soul, and thus the message was an encouragement to feel uplifted.

Dreams such as this one are referred to as "big" or "grand" Upper World dreams. They are not easily forgotten because they are often vivid and their message is profound. When taken to heart, such a dream might drastically alter one's life course. It can shift one's attitude or thinking in such a way as to offer a new momentum to fulfill long-sought desires.

Big dreams guide the dreamer to transcend in some way the darkness of the manifest world. Much like Dorothy's travels from Kansas to Oz, the experiences of Upper World dreams awaken the senses to the metaphysical world. The dreamer's eyes become open to the spiritual power that can interface with life. Such dreams are truly peak experiences or spiritual openings.

The spiritual dimensions of the Upper World are octaves above what we experience in our daily existence. In the Upper World, light and sound are the pulse of the universe and heavenly bodies. Here, angelic beings may converge on the consciousness of the dreamer. Christianity identifies the Upper World as heaven, and as one climbs the spiritual ladder through spiritual acts of goodness or in death, he or she may receive the grace of God. Symbols such as ladders, spiral stairways, treetops, or a mountain peak may appear in a dream as a portal for entering the dimensions of the Upper World. The dreamer may ascend to revel in a magical realm, similar to the way a shaman travels to an otherworldly dimension to receive a special power or to consult with the spirits.

I recall a dream where I found myself scaling a high mountain. When I reached the top, the entrance to the Upper World, a bright orange sun rose from behind the mountain. I heard a voice reverberate a message that penetrated every part of my consciousness. "What God cannot accomplish, man can accomplish" jolted me out of a deep sleep and continues now, months later, to echo in my mind. The dream came at a time when I was questioning whether I could ever fulfill what was being presented as my destiny. I felt that what was expected exceeded my knowledge and abilities. The dream demonstrated that I was a vehicle for bringing God's plan forward. It motivated me and bolstered my confidence enough so that I could take steps toward fulfilling my purpose. Not only did this dream inspire, but it announced the entrance of a man who possessed the abilities I lacked and who could join me in this spiritual mission. Such a dream conveys to the dreamer the certainty that a higher power exists.

DREAM PROPHESY

Since antiquity, prophets have gifted to humanity their visions and revelations obtained from dreams. As the intermediaries between God and humanity, their role and profession were often that of divine service. The Egyptians believed the gods communicated directly with the pharaohs through their dreams. The Greeks, too, celebrated dreams as the avenue of connection to the gods and goddesses of Mount Olympus who might grant a good dream as a gift for service. Oracular temples were erected throughout Greece, and initiates traveled long distances to receive a dream of healing or divination from the gods. The birth of Christ was announced to Joseph through a dream, and a dream later warned him that he should flee Egypt with Mary and the child to avoid Herod's soldiers. Queen Maya, Buddha's mother, was foretold of the birth of her son through a dream in which she was pierced by six ivory elephant tusks and carried to a high Himalayan peak. Shamans and Native American medicine men have always empowered their people through the sharing of dream visions that offered solutions to extreme hardship.

Present-day prophets come clothed in modern dress and live among us. Dreams reveal that anyone can tap into the spiritual dimensions and receive what might be termed a prophetic dream. Dreams that predict a change coming on the horizon are frequently among the pool of dreams collected on my Web site, DreamThread: Online Dream Interpretation Service (www.dreamthread.com). DreamThread collects dreams of a prophetic nature from individuals around the world. These dreams often shed light on the meaning of events in the news, such as political unrest, economic shifts, and social changes. Often characterized by the dreamer viewing an event with a crowd of people across the ocean or in the sky, these dreams sometimes point to an evolutionary change that may be necessary to bring balance back into the world.

FLYING DREAMS

More common experiences of the Upper World dimension are dreams of flying. The phenomenon of flying dreams, in which the dreamer finds himself soaring above treetops, over houses, and through the air, is a common experience of travel into the Upper World. Just about everyone has had such a dream. The dreamer is granted the supernatural power of flight, bringing him or her freedom from the gravity of life. Such dreams usually signify freedom from the limitations that life imposes. They usually come at a time when the dreamer has broken through a form of limited thinking or has overcome a major psychological obstacle. As a response to times of great success or when one has taken an extraordinary risk, a flying dream may signify one's personal liberation and a new ability to touch previously untapped potentials.

Some dreamers report that they always remember flying in their dreams. Others recall that sometimes they join others in flight and find themselves teaching others how to fly. The dreamer who has difficulty taking off or landing gracefully may master these skills in subsequent dreams. Flying is a particularly common experience in childhood, before the young mind conforms to the earthbound restrictions placed on it by the world. For most of us, sadly, flying dreams are infrequent occurrences because we adhere to limiting beliefs that restrict us from freely expressing our unique talents and desires. We become lead-footed, stuck to the ground in the concrete aspects of our world.

PSYCHIC DREAMS

Dreams demonstrate that there is no limitation on what we can perceive through the psychic powers and dimensions of the subconscious. Through our dreams we can predict the future, communicate with someone on another continent, and experience events that may affect our world.

Every night, our dreaming body (or astral body) escapes the confines of the Middle World and enters a dimension of the Upper World where existence is timeless. We realize that we are connected soul-to-soul and to everything that "is," that exists. In this dimension, we are all psychic.

There are three types of psychic dreams, and they are quite common. They are precognitive, telepathic, and clairvoyant dreams. Once we are awake, these dreams baffle us: We define ourselves as separate from others and see events through constructs of space and time.

A dream that seems to have predicted a future event is identified as a precognitive dream. For example, dreaming about a friend one has not seen in years and then running into the person in a supermarket the next day would be deemed a precognitive dream experience. These dreams can predict good news as well as bad news, and even death. They may be quite accurate in revealing even the tiniest details of an event that will take place sometime in the future.

A dream where we may have touched the consciousness of another person and have accurately revealed his or her thoughts or actions is referred to as a telepathic dream. For instance, dreaming that a relative is sick and discovering that he or she is in the hospital the next day demonstrates our ability to communicate with each other in the dream state through telepathic channels. A dream may receive information about a loved one as far away as another continent or as close as the next room.

Dreams where we have psychically connected with an object or situation in the world are referred to as clairvoyant dreams. These remarkable dreams include dreams of natural disasters and noteworthy social events. Having a dream of an earthquake and waking to a special TV report of an earthquake halfway around the world can give us goose bumps. The dreamer's clairvoyance in such instances is magnified. He or she has received information that may be very detailed and that is seldom elicited. Individuals who receive such information may experience a great deal of anxiety as a result. Some may turn off their intuitive powers or even shut down the conscious connection to their dreaming life out of defense.

Clairvoyant dreams offer evidence that we are not separate from the body of the earth and that changes or disturbances in the earth can readily be perceived by the dreaming mind. Such psychic abilities are natural to those who have awakened to a hidden potential of the mind that is closed off or hidden during the normal waking state. I remember a dream in which I opened a box and hundreds of Portuguese man-of-wars jumped out onto my skin. I woke up with a burning sensation all over my body. I turned on the news the next evening and listened as the anchorperson announced the Kuwait crisis and Operation Desert Storm. I immediately realized the meaning of my dream and that I had been psychically affected by this conflict.

There are some unique individuals who report having precognitive, clairvoyant, and telepathic dream experiences with great frequency. An individual with such ability is called a psychic sensitive. In a shamanic culture, an individual with such powers might take the role of a shaman, using his or her abilities in service to other members of the community.

In interpreting dreams, it is important to differentiate a dream that comes as telepathic, clairvoyant, or as a precognitive event from dreams that are more personal and relate to the constructs of one's own psyche. It is often difficult for the novice to verify a paranormal dream, since the event it predicts can arrive far after the vision. The dream experience may not manifest in life until years later. For instance, it is common for a woman to have her "dream man" and future husband show up in a dream as much as ten years before his actual arrival.

An analytical approach to dream interpretation proves useless in determining whether a dream is precognitive. It is only the intuitive mind that can perceive the difference. By developing an open-door policy toward dream work, one may more easily recognize the truth about a dream. Following up on the hunches from a dream that is thought to be a telepathic message from a friend is one way of beginning.

Another paranormal dream experience, which has received a great deal of attention through the recent work of Linda Lane Magellan, is the phenomenon of mutual dreams. These dreams demonstrate that two or more individuals may participate in the same dream on a given night. Quite common for husbands and wives or close friends, these dreams merge two dreaming minds into a psychic partnership to collaborate in the dreamscape. Dreamers may collaborate, sharing similar themes, elements, and experiences of the dream. They may or may not be aware of each other's presence within the dream. If they are aware of the other's presence, the mutual dream is referred to as a shared dream. If the dreamers have no recollection of the other person's presence in the dream but do experience similar themes, settings, or symbols, the dream is referred to as a meshed mutual dream. Most dreamers do not realize they have been mutual dreaming until they share their dreams in the morning.

What these dreams demonstrate is that the dream is its own world that can be entered communally. I shared one such experience with a roommate. My roommate woke up in the morning and began to share her dream of a blue horse that she had brought down off a mountain. As she descended with the horse, it transformed, shrinking into a small pony. I also had a dream of a blue horse that same night. As I sat on top of the same mountain, I heard words come from a source outside myself, a source I could not identify: "To choose the power of the blue horse is to choose life." Excitedly, we spent half the morning interpreting the dream, and finally agreed that each image offered significant information of a spiritual nature. The mountain represented the spiritual center and portal of the Upper World. In ascending the mountain, we were both greeted by the blue horse, an otherworldly spiritual power and archetype that unified a Lower World animal with an Upper World transcendent aspect, signified by the color blue. The color blue we also associated with the power to communicate spiritual truth. Our dreams revealed that when one brings spiritual power down from the Upper World and attempts to express it in life, the power is often diminished by our lack of faith and confidence. We minimize our spiritual power perhaps out of a need to conform to the expectations of the world and, therefore, accept a diminished view of ourselves. I believe my personal message was that it was important for me to choose a spiritually purposeful life. Mutual dreams like this one bring credence to the statement "What worlds these dreams are made of" and to the view that many dimensions exist as realities for the dreaming mind.

DREAMS AND CREATIVE EXPRESSION

Symbols that meaningfully convey transcendental truths are all around us. Artists whose dreams and visions have brought these revelations into art have met the responsibility of keeping alive the Upper World and its cosmology. They remind us that we need not feel divided. It is through these artists' creative connections that we can again find ours, and with their eyes we can see again the representations of spirituality. From the iconography in churches and their religious representations to the label on a Budweiser can, one can find elements of redemption through pictorial representation of spiritual power. A picture of Simba from *The Lion King* may have as much spiritual significance as a portrait of Jesus. Both convey a similar mythological journey of a redeemer who makes a heroic journey to bring salvation to the world.

The world is full of reminders that spiritual dimensions interface with the physical world. A fascination with the symbolic representations of angels has re-emerged more recently. We find angel pins, angels on mugs, angels on T-shirts, angels on TV. We are thus reminded that angels have always been in service to humanity and can lend a helping hand—if only one believes.

The music we listen to may also be inspired by dreams. Musicians often rely on the dream state to work out lyrics and musical scores. These inspirational melodies are often described as the work of a higher intelligence that could not have emerged during the normal creative process. Writers also contribute through visionary experiences and dream states. A visionary novel *The Kin of Ata Is Waiting for You* written by Dorothy Bryant is an excellent example. Our cultural lives, then, may be enhanced by the spiritual dimensions to which the dreaming minds of the artists, musicians, and mythmakers connect.

ASTROLOGY AND LUNAR CYCLES

Dreams can be influenced by celestial bodies, the constellations of the stars, and the rotations of the planets within our galaxy. First plotted by astronomers through mathematical calculations, stars were linked together to form patterns of radiant energies. Each of these patterns was seen further to resemble personifications of gods and animals, which were later transcribed into the mythologies of the world.

Astrology, which assigns to these patterns certain personality traits and characteristics, plots the course of the stars and planets onto the coordinates of an individual's birth time and place. Although there is some rebuttal to the scientific validity of astrology, it has remained a science of metaphysics that is used by the masses to divine one's destiny.

In archetypal astrology, we see mythology and its archetypes as connected to the stars and planets. We also see that dreams may reveal these archetypal patterns and underline their influence on our personalities. When archetypes such as the sun and moon emerge in a dream, they may come to symbolize powerful energies at work. The sun emerging from behind a mountain may indicate that it's time for our masculine side to take center stage. The moon partially covered by a cloud may indicate a shadow of fear veiling one's intuition. Saturn appearing in a dream may signal a time for material lessons, and Venus may signify that one has fallen in love.

Each sign in the Zodiac brings with it associated elemental energies that stimulate our dreaming. When a planetary alignment coincides with the natal chart of an individual, transformational waves are set in motion that may offer opportunities for psychological work and growth through conscious dream work. These opportunities are like windows of time that allow one to use the power of the Upper World to advantage. It can be helpful for a conscious dreamer periodically to have a progressive chart cast by a reputable astrologer in order to pinpoint these opportunities. In this way, one may become conscious of the influence of celestial bodies on the psyche.

The lunar cycles affect the tides of our dreams. Many dreamers report that their dreams tend to be more vivid during a full moon than in other phases. When the moon is in a particular astrological phase, dreams may emerge that relate to the characteristics of that particular sign. For instance, dreams during a Scorpio full moon may contain material related to one's sexuality and offer opportunities to work through sexual conflicts. Dreams during a Cancer full moon may include water, reflecting the state of our emotions. And dreams when the moon is in Pisces may be more mystical or prophetic.

By keeping detailed dated dream records, noting the phases of moon and astrological sign placement of the sun and moon, you can learn more about how your dreams are influenced by the cosmos. This will point you to times when transformational energies may offer you more opportunity for personal growth.

SPIRITS AND VISITORS OF THE THIRD KIND

The spirit world, often referred to as the astral plane, may flood dreams with welcome and unwelcome spirit visitations. Through collecting dreams from dreamers all over the world, a large and interesting sample of dreams has been gathered that appears to contain such remarkable visitations. It is not unusual for a dreamer to have a parent or grandparent who has transitioned from life return for a surprise visit. Usually, such visits will help reconcile in some way the dreamer's feelings of loss at the passing of the loved one. They let the dreamer know that the loved one is in a good place and is still available. The direct communications by the spirit visitor may contain evidence of the visitor's authenticity, revealing some piece of information only the dreamer or someone very close to the deceased could know. Through a hidden doorway or veil, the dreamer may be led into a room filled with light to meet his or her loved one and to receive some gift or message. A recent dream shared by a student of mine offers an example of such a visitation. The visitation was from his grandmother, who in the dream handed him a cup of peas. In deciphering the symbol of the cup of peas, we agreed that his grandmother had come to soothe him with a cup of "peace."

Just as some visitations may be welcome, others may be from visitors of a ghostly character unknown to the dreamer. They may haunt or torment the dreamer during the night. Reports come from dreamers everywhere who have had a frightening presence appear in the dream state. When they awakened, they were still aware of the presence around them. Such spooky experiences may become repetitive and quite disturbing for some. The dreamer may even feel attacked in some way or may have the feeling that he or she is being taken over by the presence—literally pulled away from his or her own body. I have discovered that these dreams are usually frequent in individuals whose psychic space has been corrupted or compromised in some traumatic way, as through sexual abuse. Without adequate boundaries, they attract unwanted intruders. The individual may need to learn psychic self-defense methods in order to overcome these unwanted visitors.

VIRTUAL WORLDS

Lucid dreams are other phenomena that are often viewed as a transcendent experience by dreamers who have mastered conscious control over the dreaming process. The experience of lucid dreaming is most commonly defined as when the ego of the individual wakes up in the dream, realizes that he or she is dreaming, and takes control of the dream. Often precipitated by flying, the dreamer lands in some scene, observes for a while, makes decisions, and takes conscious action to change the dream in some way. Lucid dreams offer insight into the hidden potentials of the mind and demonstrate that our dreaming mind creates a virtual-reality playground, which we may visit consciously.

The dreamer often experiences vivid colors, bright light, and a great sense of personal freedom in these moments of lucidity. The heightened emotional quality and vivid impression of the imagery of lucid dreams differentiates them from the ordinary dream experience. Dreamers relay feelings of joyfulness and even ecstasy as they play with the element of the dream consciously.

Many individuals consciously seek to train the conscious mind through particular techniques to awaken within the dream and begin the lucid process. Although these practices will improve the frequency of lucid-dreaming events and demonstrate that with training, manipulation of the dreaming process is possible, it is questionable as to whether induced lucidity is in the dreamer's best interest. It is my opinion that the psyche's creative intelligence moves naturally toward wholeness and creatively resolves the conflicts present in dreams. Induced lucid dreaming may actually be detrimental, as it disrupts this more natural process. The conscious ego is not always the best adviser in matters of the heart or the best guide to the integrity of the soul. Ego decisions in lucid dreams, like those in real life, are often in direct opposition to one's homeostasis and balance of the soul.

Another type of lucid dream is one where the supra-conscience or the higher self of the individual intervenes in the dream. As in other lucid dreams, the conscious mind is aware that it is dreaming. However, rather than manipulating the direction of the dream, it appears to surrender to a higher power, which may sweep the dreamer in another direction or resolve a conflict in a dream in a magical way. This remedy may produce less of a sense of ego mastery in the dream, yet it can impart a greater sense of spiritual intervention.

In supra-lucid dreams, a direct experience of "true light" often accompanies the dream. These dreams are also characterized by vivid colors and clear light penetrating the dreamscape. Enlightening experiences such as embracing one's beauty, innocence, or spiritual nature may come as a peak experience in a supra-lucid dream. A dream of my own in which I was drowning in water and suddenly became lucid while transforming into a shark's body was an exhilarating example. As the shark, I propelled with supernatural power to the deepest part of my subconscious to find an Almond Joy wrapper on the ocean floor. The interpreted message was "Find the joy from deep within." When I awoke, I couldn't believe that I wasn't soaking wet, because the dream felt like such a real experience.

Tibetan Yoga dream practices attempt to elicit such supra-lucid dream experiences. They offer complex spiritual practices composed of meditation techniques that, when practiced before going to sleep, prepare the individual spiritually and mentally for a lucid dream. These meditative methods enhance dream recall and open the power centers of the body to channel "true light" into the dream state.

WHEN WORLDS UNITE

By bringing meaning to the signs, symbols, archetypes, and elements of the Upper World, whether through night dreams or collected through the synchronistic events of the waking dream, we discover that the otherworldly intersects the worldly. Symbols of a divine origin, such as angels, halos, rainbows, suns, moons, and stars, bring the qualities of the Upper World of dreams into life. By engaging in meaningful play with these symbolic representations from our dreams, we may thus realize that our world can be traced to divine origins.

Upper World dreams deliver us into the certainty that spirit is all around us, assembled in the moment. And at any given moment our lives may take new, more positive direction if we choose to become lucid in our waking life and accept the grace around us. Enlightenment is the realization that heaven's dream is here on earth and we need not seek to leave our bodies to ascend. Dreaming itself is a process of ascension.

Dreams in general are of transcendent value to the spiritually centered mind. The related psychological work may even be viewed as spirit-driven. Each growth step we take through conscious dream work affects the collective unconscious, which includes every soul and every living thing. The reverberation of our progress transforms the organism of the universe. We may ourselves become like shamans and mediate the Upper World with the Middle World through recognizing dreams of a transcendent quality and bringing the visions and information they communicate to those around us. By doing so, we bring inspiration and wisdom to our community of friends.

Spirituality and psychology have come together within the field of transpersonal psychology, which investigates transcendent states as an integral part of the whole of an individual. For the conscious dreamer, the exploration of dreams is a quest for personal truth and spiritual certainty. By honoring the dreams from the Upper World as containing sacred information, one may be guided and supported toward life's fulfillment.

The Symbols

Signs and Symbols A to Z

Abercrombie & Fitch (M) Shopping for this brand-name street wear suggests that you may be ready to try on a more youthful presentation and authentic way of expressing yourself in the world.

Ace Hardware (M) An Ace Hardware store as the setting of a dream may symbolize your search for self-realization and a quest for wholeness. Ace equates with looking out for number one. Roaming the aisles of an Ace Hardware store may offer you the tools of your trade.

Adding machine (M) An adding machine, whether the old-fashioned kind or an electronic calculator, computes business expenditures and may point to your frustration about finances. It may also indicate that you should look at how and where you are spending your money. A machine meant to add up numbers properly may also be a sign that something does not "add up," indicating that your suspicions may be warranted.

African American (M) An African American may lead you to discover the value of your roots or heritage. As a character, he or she may exhibit grounded or soulful qualities that you may need to discover within yourself. As a representative of a group that has been the object of discrimination, he or she may appear as a symbol of pride, whatever your ethnicity.

Air (L) As the breath of God, air represents that which carries the wish of the Creator. Air may also represent the activity of the mind. Symbolizing the wind, air may indicate a change of thought or ideas, as well as changes in the direction of one's life.

Aircraft carrier (M) An aircraft carrier may appear in a dream to suggest that you may need to prepare for a battle that may be in the air, such as a battle of wits, or a debate with a business partner, an argument with a customer, or an issue with a family member.

Airplane (M) A fast way of moving around the world, an airplane indicates global ideas or business. Usually associated with freedom, it may be a comment on the level of freedom you have attained. A plane crash may represent the failure of a business venture. Not being able to get your plane off the ground may represent difficulties in acquiring the capital for a project. Piloting your own plane may represent the ultimate success-driven venture and may mention your need to be your own boss.

Aladdin (L) As an archetype, Aladdin is the pauper and thief who becomes a prince. Through the power of grace and magic, he comes out of poverty into nobility. In this way, he may symbolize a man who has risen out of the ashes into glory. The appearance of the Disney character Aladdin may mean that you are about to get your wish.

Muhammad Ali (M) This colorful and controversial heavyweight boxer was known not only for his boxing skills and prowess but also for his independent and arrogant behavior. He was also known for long-winded speeches that nonetheless usually accurately predicted his wins in the ring. His appearance in a dream may indicate an egocentric personality trait you need to tame. On the other hand, it may indicate that the time has come in your life to fight with a positive, forward-looking attitude for something in which you believe.

Aliens (U, M) Aliens appear perhaps to remind us that we are not alone in the universe. Dreams of aliens arriving may present literal experiences and contact with beings from other galaxies. Such dream encounters may result in profound experiences of light and sound in which the dreamer feels altered in some way. Aliens crowding around you in your dream may also reflect your own feelings of living in an alien nation, indicating your sense of isolation and alienation from others.

Almond Joy (M) Discovering an Almond Joy candy bar wrapper in a dream may signify having found the ingredients for living a "joyful" life.

Altar (U) An altar, a sacred place for worship and prayer, may express concerns about your spiritual life. It may also indicate the need to sacrifice your desires in favor of a personal quest for spiritual enlightenment.

Aluminum (L) An alloy that combines both strength and lightness, aluminum may be a symbol of the coexisting qualities of lightheartedness and strength of will.

America (M) Taking a trip across America may represent entering a place where personal freedom and liberty are respected.

Amethyst (L) Radiating a violet ray within a quartz structure, the amethyst unearthed in a dream may awaken your third eye or spiritual vision.

Amsterdam (M) A dream set in Amsterdam may suggest that you are visiting a counterculture or tasting the wild side of life.

Amulet (U) Amulets are symbols of spiritual power. They may be granted to the dreamer who is ready to display and demonstrate his or her spiritual power. An amulet may also offer protection.

Amusement park (M) A dream that takes place in an amusement park may reflect a desire to experience more enjoyment. It may be a reminder of an experience in your waking life that was very amusing.

Anaconda (L) The largest of the snake family, the anaconda brings the message of huge creative potential that is on the way. This snake may also be calling on you to cultivate your sexuality through tantric practices in order to strengthen sexual vitality.

Angels (U) Angels descending into your dreams come as guides who assist humanity from above. They may appear to uplift you into the light or to deliver a profound spiritual message. However they may be clothed, they may take you into a flight to freedom or descend to give their gift of service. Angels in a dream may bring comfort when you have fallen from grace or suffered a profound loss. They may also open your heart.

Animals (L) Animals emerge from the Lower World as powerful archetypes and energies. They may lend their wisdom, attributes, and supernatural powers to the dreamer. The appearance of any animal in a dream may point out that man and nature are not separate but are intricately connected.

Ankh (L) The ankh is a symbol that dates back to ancient Egypt and is associated with the healing powers of the goddess Isis, the divine physician who was said to be able to breathe life back into the dead. If an ankh appears in a dream, the symbol may signify divine power, the power of healing, and even immortality. An ankh may also represent an initiation into the mystery of ancient healing arts.

Answering machine (M) Problems in retrieving messages from your answering machine may point to frustration in understanding a communication from someone you care about. It may be an indication that you are not listening.

Ant (L) Ants demonstrate a strong work ethic. Because they build large colonies, they may represent the strength of community effort. Carrying large loads many times their own weight, ants can appear in a dream to represent someone small with superior strength, a great deal of patience, and perseverance. Ants may elicit the dreamer to work hard and to cultivate patience in performing a task.

Anteater (L) Unlike the diligent ant, the anteater is an animal that may come to destroy what you have built. It is not necessarily an adversary, because it may be taking away what you were working on so that you can pursue your true or greater purpose. The anteater may be saying that you need not work so hard on fruitless projects.

Antelope (L) An antelope galloping in a dream may bring the message that it is time to spring into action in order to achieve your goals. An antelope signifies the energy necessary to move from stagnation and indifference into action. The antelope may also be urging you to flee from a situation that might threaten your well-being.

Apple (L) The apple is a symbol of wisdom. Associated with the Garden of Eden, the apple can represent carnal knowledge. When an apple is cut to reveal a cross section, a five-pointed star can be seen. This star is the symbol of feminine creativity and of the mysteries within nature. Reminding that "an apple a day keeps the doctor away," it may signify good health. Finally, the golden apple was associated with the goddess Aphrodite as the prize for her beauty.

Apple computer (M) Apple computers are known for being user-friendly and are preferred by most artists. One may appear in a dream to spark your creative side. As the apple represents wisdom, this symbol may indicate that it is time to go ahead and use your wisdom to create something beautiful.

Aquarium (M) Gazing into an aquarium in a dream may represent contained emotions. It may represent the microcosm, as it contains an entire ecosystem of life, and may invoke contemplation and relaxation.

Aquarius (U) The sign of the humanitarian, the appearance of Aquarius may signal that it is time to become concerned with your community and to offer serious solutions to global and social problems.

Architect (M) An architect may appear as a character in a dream to help remodel the house of the soul. An architect may point to the need for psychological help, appearing as a counselor or another expert who can help you work out psychological issues.

Archway (M) An archway inside a house may represent the entrance into an open and creative space of the imagination.

Aries (U) The power of the Ram, the fire sign, is that of a warrior or initiator. Appearing in a dream, Aries may be suggesting that you need to take initiative to get things done. It may denote playfulness.

Arguing (M) Emotions expressing themselves in a dream, which then result in an argument, may be a reference to a conflict between two aspects of your personality. Thus, arguing with your father may mean that you are in conflict with the rigid values you have internalized from your father. Arguing in a dream may also compensate for your inability to express your honest emotions with friends or family when you are awake.

Armored truck (M) Running into an armored truck may be a very direct sign that you have met someone who is well guarded emotionally. An armored truck may also signify the need to protect your bank account from yourself or others, or it may be an indication that you have met someone who heavily guards their money and other resources. (See *Truck*.)

Arms (L) Arms extend or reach out. Thus, a broken arm may indicate an inability to reach out to someone or extend yourself to others. It may also represent the inability to get your work out into the world. Carrying something in your arms signifies presenting something to the world.

Army base (M) Whether you have ever lived or worked on a military base, visiting or revisiting a place with extreme regimentation may indicate that you are back in an authoritarian stronghold, whether by your own design or someone else's.

Arthritis (L) Having arthritis in a dream may indicate that you lack the desire or ability to move forward with your purpose or cannot act on your dreams for fulfillment. The inflamed joints associated with arthritis may suggest an aggravation that is crippling an individual's ability to act. Arthritis may also appear as a sign of a possible illness, which may need to be medically treated.

Artichoke (M) As a play on words, an artichoke may mention that you are choking back your creativity, as in "Art I choke." Artichokes open to reveal the heart and also reflect flowering potentials. In that we usually eat the heart of an artichoke, it may comment "eat your heart out."

Asia (M) Arriving on the continent of Asia may mean that you are having concerns about family and tradition. Taking a trip to Asia may reflect Eastern spiritual ideals, such as developing inner peace and living a meditative life. Politically, Asia may represent a socialist point of view where a person is seen less for his or her individuality and more for what he or she can contribute to the society as a whole.

Asian person (M) An Asian character in a dream may indicate a need to adopt a more Eastern philosophy and approach to life. The Asian family tends to keep strong family values and respect family rituals. This may suggest that you need to honor your elders and tradition.

Asters (L) Asters signify hope. Resembling a star in shape, they conjure the adage "to wish upon a star."

Attic (M) Rummaging through the attic may suggest that you explore your family legacy to discover what has been hidden away in the subconscious. The attic represents the area of intuition; the attic window represents the third eye. Gazing out the attic window signifies using your psychic gifts.

Australia (M) In a dream whose scenes take place in Australia, you may be called to examine a rugged country where outcasts and criminals were once exiled. Australia may also represent your feelings of being displaced or persecuted.

Avalanche (M) Being caught in an avalanche may signify feeling buried by your own fears. An avalanche may mark a traumatic event that left you buried in the cold, such as the loss of a relationship.

Avenue (M) Strolling or driving down the avenue in a city or town offers a great deal to see and take in. An avenue may represent the concerns you have as you move forward in life. Avenues may also reflect the direction in which you are moving en route to your destination. An avenue may suggest that you take a turn that is unusual for you.

Axle (M) Having a broken axle on your vehicle may be synonymous with having a broken leg. You may not be able to stand on your feet for very long or move forward again without a change in attitude. Since a broken axle may occur while traveling on a bumpy road, this may reflect that difficult life passages may have broken your spirit.

Baboon (L) This primate represents emotions and may be commenting on an immature or inappropriate expression of feelings in public. On the other hand, the appearance of a baboon may mean you need to express your feelings more dramatically in a given situation.

Back (L) The back of the physical body reflects support issues. A feeling of weakness in the lower back may indicate that you do not feel supported by others. Scars or wounds on the upper back may reflect too many burdens. A hunched back may mean that you have been a martyr, carrying the burdens of others for too long. In general, looking at someone's back means you are looking at his or her history.

Backhoe (M) A backhoe is a heavy piece of construction equipment that digs a deep hole. It may stand for needing to unearth something from within the subconscious, perhaps a deeply embedded memory or emotion.

Baking (M) The act of baking in a dream may indicate a creative project you are about to undertake. (See *Betty Crocker foods*.)

Bald (L) A bald man appearing in a dream may represent a man who has lost his power. Baldness may also be a positive sign of maturity for a man.

Banana (L) The phallic shape of a banana may suggest the sweetness and power of a man's sexuality. In Hawaiian history, bananas were a forbidden fruit. Women were not allowed to eat bananas, which were to be enjoyed only by male royalty. Thus, bananas are the fruit of abundance for a select few who are worthy of their power. A banana in a dream may also indicate a woman's sense of disenfranchisement. A bruised banana may mean that you feel bruised by a hurtful experience.

Banana Republic (M) Since a banana is a phallic symbol, characters wearing this brand of clothing may hold the belief that this is a man's world or an abundant world.

Bank (M) Being in a bank in your dreams relates to concerns about your finances. A bank is an institution where you learn about money and its value, a place where you may save money and withdraw money. A bank may indicate that it is time to start saving money for the future or that you may need to withdraw funds for an important purchase or make an important investment.

Banquet (M) Dreaming about enjoying a banquet may mean that you have many choices for fulfilling a deep wish. It may signify the abundance of life you can find through social interaction. In a dream, attending a banquet in your honor may compensate for feeling unnoticed or taken for granted in life.

Barbecue (M) Turning meat on a barbecue may represent creating a meaty or meaningful experience for friends. It may also indicate a transformational experience or may mean that you are now "cooking," metaphorically speaking. In other words, you are on the right track.

Barbed wire (M) Being caught in barbed wire can indicate a painful entrapment or feelings of having been hurt by someone else's boundaries. Barbed wire in a dream may indicate difficulty in getting through to someone.

Barber (M) Sitting in the barber's chair may mean you have concerns about your masculine appearance. Getting a haircut in your dreams may indicate that you may be about to lose power in some way or face unwanted criticism.

Barbie doll (M) Barbie, the famous, ageless doll, may represent the unattainable image of perfection and body type. Her appearance in a dream may indicate a poor self-image or an addiction to perfection.

Barn (M) Since a barn is usually a fairly large and open space that houses animals, it may signify your animal instincts. The idea of rolling in the hay may indicate that you had a distasteful sexual experience. Living in a barn may be an indication that you are feeling exposed or living with too many other people's problems.

Baseball (M) Baseball has often been connected metaphorically with playing the game of life. Sometimes you may be delivered a curveball or a fastball, either of which may throw you off balance. There are nine innings in a baseball game, and the number nine symbolizes completion. The object of the game is to score a run by crossing home plate. Getting home may represent your spiritual destiny.

Baseboard (M) A baseboard joins and also separates the floor and the wall of a room. Therefore, it can represent the foundational structure of your personality. It may also represent your baseline beliefs. The baseboard may indicate that you feel "bored." It may also indicate that you need to pay attention to your underlying beliefs about yourself. Dreaming of the baseboards in a kitchen may indicate that you need to review what you believe about nurturing your family, for instance.

Basement (M) The basement of a house represents a dark place where things are stored and may be hidden. Therefore, entering the basement may mean that you are ready to face your fears, acknowledge your basic insecurities, or confront other hidden feelings.

Basket (M) As a container made of natural fiber, a basket may refer to sharing your natural qualities with others. When holding fruit, a basket represents receiving or giving the bounty of nature or the fruits of your labor.

Basketball (M) Basketball is a team sport made up of unusually tall men or women. A basketball game may represent a situation that calls you to stand tall and demonstrate pride. It may signify sinking a basket or clinching a deal through some competitive action.

Bathing (M) Taking a bath in a dream may indicate a need to be soothed from stress and worry. It may also suggest cleansing the body of impurities. A bathtub filled with water may suggest preparation for a spiritual or emotional cleansing.

Bathroom (M) The bathroom in a dream is the place where you release emotions and information that have been processed over a period of time. Being in a public rest room where there are no stalls on the doors may signify frustration about getting enough privacy, or difficulties in letting go.

Bay (M) A bay offers the calm waters of understanding to a dreamer and may bring subconscious patterns closer to consciousness. It may also represent the warding off of unwanted experiences until the time is right, as in holding something or someone "at bay."

Bay window (M) A bay window may represent the extension of your vision outward toward neighborhood or community. This window could also represent someone with a strong vision for the future. Sitting at a bay window may represent that you are in store for a long wait. (See *Window.*)

Beach (M) Lying on the beach may represent reaching the shore and, thus, finally understanding and solving some major problem in life. It may also indicate concerns, or the need for relaxation. Since the beach borders the ocean, it represents being close to the subconscious or to the emotions.

Beach ball (M) Multicolored and inflated with air, a beach ball may suggest playful emotions or thoughts. It may represent a symbol for your wholeness as the multicolored segments of the personality brought together in a totality.

Bear (L) For Native Americans, the bear comes to initiate the power of healing medicine and can represent a call to walk the path of a healer or medicine person. For the urban shaman, the bear's call may be to a profession in the healing arts such as massage therapy or reflexology. As an archetype, the bear possesses strength and a grounded connection to the earth. The bear often represents the nurturing or mothering aspect that comforts and heals as the primary relationship early in life.

Thus, an angry bear can signify a response to the devouring nature of your own mother.

Beard (M) A man with a beard may represent a father or another figure of authority. As Santa Claus had a full white beard, a white beard in a dream may signify an authority who brings gifts or wisdom.

Beatles (M) The Beatles may reappear onstage in a dream to represent a reunion of some sort. Their singing together may point up the importance of harmony in your life through tight-knit relationships. They may also represent a counterculture that transformed the mainstream, or they may come to demonstrate the power and success that are possible in a group achievement.

Warren Beatty (L, M) A character obsessed with vanity and unable to be pinned down, Warren Beatty may make a short appearance as Hermes, the messenger god. His reflection to a man may be his inability to commit. He may also deliver the message that it is never too late to embrace the institution of marriage or a real commitment to a woman. In a woman's dream, Warren may appear as the charming bad-boy lover who seduces her into thinking that she is the one.

Beautician (M) Sitting in a beauty salon may indicate your concerns about how you look. It may also point out that you need to pay some special attention to your appearance in order to feel good, or it could represent a desire for a different look or attitude. Hair often represents power. Therefore, a beautician may represent someone who is playing with your personal power.

Beauty and the Beast (L) In the fairy tale, Belle falls in love with the Beast and by doing so transforms him. This may symbolize the power of unconditional love in transformation.

Bed (M) As the place where you rest, sleep, and make love, the bed may point to concerns and feelings about resting or sexual intimacy. Having numerous people in bed with you may signify that there are many personality aspects or patterns from others influencing how you feel about intimacy. A woman in bed with her father may signify that she views her intimate partner as a continuation of her own father-daughter relationship. This connection does not necessarily reflect sexual abuse.

Bedroom (M) Being in a bedroom may reveal a great deal about your attitudes about sexuality and other areas of your personal life that are more private. A starkly neat bedroom may reflect your rigid views about sexuality. A messy child's bedroom may signify unruly behavior.

Bedspread (M) A bedspread represents the outer expression of your sexuality and beauty. Whether floral or tailored, it may express a great deal about sexual taste and what you may be looking for sexually.

Bed stand (M) A night table or bed stand in a dream may represent the space for ideas that we incubate during the night. The bed stand may be where you place the concerns you need to dream about or release at night.

Bee (L) The activity of a bee can signify business and hard work. Because bees pollinate, they have come to signify fertility and magic. The honey they create is a sweet nectar, which suggests that they bring sweetness to life. As the insignia for the royal lineage of the Merovingians, the magician kings, bees are associated with true royalty. A bee may arrive in a dream simply to say, "Let it be," or "Just be, and stop doing."

Beetle (L) As a bug that can be destructive to plants, the beetle might signify something eating up all that you have worked hard to cultivate. In this way, it may represent your bills. In that the beetle burrows in the ground, it may represent something destructive in the subconscious. As the scarab, the beetle may signify immortality.

Belt (M) A belt brings attention and definition to the waist and navel areas as well as functioning to hold up your pants. It may represent a powerful will for a man or woman who wears a belt with a large decorative buckle. A belt may also indicate that you must tighten your belt, thus curtailing expenditures. For a woman, cinching a belt may indicate her desire to appear curvier. A belt may also be associated with physical abuse for a child who was frequently whipped.

Bench (M) Sitting on a bench may represent waiting for someone. It may comment that you have set aside your ideas for a time in order to wait for a better moment to put them forth again.

Betty Crocker foods (M) As baking products that are associated with the modern homemaker, Betty Crocker cakes and mixes may appear on the shelf of your cupboard to help you whip up an extraordinary idea and turn it into a million-dollar business. Since Betty Crocker reflects the attitudes of a woman who is a good homemaker, an empty box of cake mix may indicate that you have lost your maternal instincts.

Bicycle (M) Riding a bicycle may represent a way of moving forward toward your goals that may take some effort. It reflects a person with an independent personality, one who is propelled by his or her own ideas. A bicycle may represent a desire to enjoy the outdoors.

Big Bird (L, M) This big yellow bird from *Sesame Street* can announce the arrival of a new loving friend or neighbor in your life. He may bring a tender message suggesting that you need to learn the basics about what it takes to be a good friend.

Billboard (M) A billboard may appear as a huge sign on the road of life. Its advertising message may bring wisdom or important information for you to take special notice of.

Bills (M) Going through your bills in a dream may represent deep concerns or worry about the level of your debt.

Birdhouse (M, U) A birdhouse may offer a sacred spiritual place in which to nest. Since birds are seen as symbolically mediating heaven and earth, a birdhouse may indicate that your home is your spiritual haven. A birdhouse in a dream may also indicate a need to concentrate on sheltering your spiritual nature, or it may be a sign of spring.

Birds (U) Birds are messengers delivering sacred information to the dreamer from the spiritual dimensions. Soaring high, they may demonstrate an opportunity to free yourself from the constraints of the world and the limitations you impose on yourself. Each species and variety of bird possesses particular qualities and attributes that may be relevant to your life or in fulfilling your life's purpose. (See *Canary, Cardinal, Crane, Dove, Eagle, Egret, Falcon, Flamingo, Hawk, Mynah bird, Ostrich, Parrot, Raven, Sparrow, Stork, Toucan, Vulture.*)

Birth (M) Giving birth represents giving life, not just the new life of a baby, but the new life of an idea or creative project. Difficulties with the birth process, such as hemorrhaging, may mean that you are losing your life force in order to birth someone else's product or project, or it may announce a new beginning.

Birthmark (L, M) A birthmark may represent a core or deeply imprinted attitude about yourself that mars your inner beauty. It may represent repressed shame or feelings of imperfection.

Biting (M) Biting someone in a dream may be a warning to look at your rage toward someone close to you. Biting into something may reflect a need to get more involved in a project or in a situation.

Black (L) Black represents the power of the darkness, the unconscious, what is hidden, and the manifest power of the earth. It may represent grief or morbidity. Black is also considered the color of death. Wearing a black dress in your dreams may suggest mourning, while a black hat suggests having good manners.

Blackboard (M) Writing on a blackboard may suggest that you have some lessons to give to others, and it may represent putting out an idea that you may want others to take notice of.

Blanket (M) Cuddling up with a blanket may express your desire for emotional warmth and compassion. An Indian blanket represents authenticity. A baby blanket may suggest that you require some tender loving care right now.

Blender (M) An appliance for blending and frothing up drinks, a blender may comment on mixing up a number of different ideas or the ingredients of a creative project. It also represents harmonizing.

Blind man (M) A blind man as a character may mean that you are blind to some truth or blind to seeing the whole picture or the true meaning in life.

Blizzard (L, M) A snowstorm metaphorically represents an extremely cold or fearful situation. It may also represent harsh conditions in your life that have made you feel fearful or generally apprehensive about the future.

Blouse (M) A blouse for a woman brings attention to the chest and breasts. Thus, it reflects how much of her heart she wants to express to the world. A woman wearing a bright orange blouse might indicate a bold, solid, and authoritative outlook. Slipping on a pink blouse may express the desire for a more loving and innocent image.

Blue (M, U) Blue denotes peace and serenity. Darker blues may indicate the need to give voice to your knowledge. Indigo blue combines violet with dark blue and thus denotes the expression of your mystical vision. Royal blue signifies nobility.

Blueprint (M) Reviewing the details of a blueprint may point to the plans that you are developing for some project in your life. You may need to take a closer look at the details before getting under way with your plans. A blueprint of the soul may indicate a place with many rooms and dimensions to explore. This blueprint could reflect overall changes that are in process through some inner work that will expand your thinking in some way.

Blush (M) Applying blush accentuates the cheekbones and may express a desire to add more contour to your face. In a dream, blush may mention the desire for a more rosy or loving self-expression. (See *Makeup*.)

BMW (M) The "Yuppiemobile" and status symbol of the corporate world may identify an individual who is successful as an entrepreneur.

Board game (M) Playing a board game may represent a strategic decision that you have just made in a business deal. A board game in a dream may also indicate that you are facing competition or opposition at work. A board game may literally mean that someone is playing games with you or deceiving you. Finally, it may indicate you are "bored" with a situation or with your present life.

Boats (M) Boats in our dreams ride on the waves and the surface of the subconscious, so they are connected to the emotional and creative currents of life. An ocean liner, carrying a large cargo of people and often goods, may or may not make it to port in our dreams. If it does, it would suggest that you will reap the riches you deserve.

Bodi tree (U) Buddha contemplated and reached enlightenment sitting under the Bodi tree. Thus, the Bodi tree symbolizes enlightenment through self-realization. The Bodi tree represents the tree of life and wisdom. (See *Buddha*.)

Bombs (M) Bombs going off may represent a big shock that has destroyed what you have built. A bomb might appear in a dream after a serious loss, such as the loss of a relationship or a necessary declaration of bankruptcy. Waiting for the bomb to go off in a dream may mean that there will soon be repercussions of actions you have taken.

Bones (L) Bones in dreams represent the basic structure of core beliefs. They may symbolize the legacy of your ancestral roots. Bones represent death and decay and thus may point to a symbolic death or a dismembering of your personality. Bones may also be dug up in a dream in order to reveal feelings of grief around a significant loss or the death of a friend or relative.

Boogie board (M) A boogie board is used to ride the waves on your belly and may suggest riding an emotional or creative wave and enjoying it. The board might also suggest that it is "time to boogie," or to move on.

Book (M) Finding a book may represent some hidden knowledge that was just discovered. The title of the book would present relevant information for you to take notice of. An autobiography may offer a review of your life and the events that were psychologically important.

Bookshelves (M) Browsing through a bookshelf may quench the desire for more knowledge and ask that you bring order and understanding to the information you have obtained.

Boomerang (M) When a boomerang is thrown well, it comes back to you. The boomerang in a dream may announce that what you did will come back to you, whether it was something positive or something negative.

Bow (M) Wearing a bow in your hair may point to a childish attitude. It may also suggest that you are trying to look too cute. On a wrapped gift, a bow may indicate that what you have to deliver to the world is being presented in a neat package.

Bow and arrow (M) Taking aim with a bow and arrow may comment on making the mark professionally and hitting the "bull's-eye" of your goals. It may also represent the act of hunting down prospects. As Diana, the huntress, is depicted with the bow and arrow, this may indicate a woman's need for self-protection and protecting her spiritual nature.

Boxing (M) Finding yourself in a boxing ring may mean that you are feeling challenged by someone else's beliefs and that you may need to fight back in order to realize your strength.

Bra (M) A bra, a harness for the breasts, may signify holding back or constricting your maternal tendencies. Throwing away your bra in a dream may indicate adopting a feminist attitude. Losing your bra may suggest losing control as a woman.

Brakes (M) Brakes on your vehicle in a dream reflect the ability to stop before proceeding forward. Putting on the brakes may indicate your hesitation in moving forward in life. Brakes that don't function may reflect feelings that you are unable to control or reduce the speed at which you are moving toward your goals. Brakes often wear out from riding them too long, suggesting the need to proceed with your plans.

Bread (M) Having a loaf of bread delivered in your dreams may suggest the arrival of some real dough or money. Bread represents spiritual fulfillment and the embodiment of Christ light or Christ-like qualities.

Bread rack (M) A bread rack holds bread that is cooling, and thus may mean that money will be available in the future but there may be a period of waiting before your finances change.

Breasts (L, M) For a man, a big-breasted woman may express the desire for maternal nurturing. For a woman, having larger breasts in a dream may remark on her desire to give more. Breast disease may be a response to feeling that you have given too much to others. Sore nipples in a dream also suggests that others have been sucking your energy and that you feel depleted.

Brick road (M) A brick road often has some historical value and may reflect that you have chosen a historical route or one that was built on traditional values. (See *Yellow Brick Road.*)

Briefcase (M) Carrying a briefcase represents concerns about work and travel. Losing a briefcase may represent loss of freedom at work. A briefcase holds important documents and may reflect the level at which you feel prepared.

Broom (M) Used to sweep a floor clean, a broom may suggest the need to clean up some dirt or negativity in your life.

Associated with witches, a broom appearing in a dream may point out that someone is acting like a witch or seems to have supernatural powers over you.

Brown (L) Earthy and rich, the color brown expresses your grounded nature. Brown may represent earthiness and cultural richness.

Bubble bath (M) Running a bubble bath may suggest the need to relax and soothe the senses. It may also indicate the need to pamper oneself.

Bucket (M) A bucket or pail is a vessel for carrying water, thus in a dream it may represent fulfillment through your work. An empty bucket may suggest that you came up short in a business venture.

Buddha (U) Meeting Buddha on the road in a dream signifies that you are on the path of enlightenment. Through compassion and a clear mind you may attain the light of the Buddha. (See *Bodi tree*.)

Budweiser (M) The beer may appear as a play on words. The bud as a newly formed flower may be wiser than the full blossom. Thus it may mean there is a young person with more wisdom than you whom you may learn from. Drinking a can of Bud may also point to enjoying a man's brew.

Bugs Bunny (L, M) The tall, lanky animated rabbit of Loony Toons fame may appear as the fool archetype. As an independent wiseguy, he may announce the arrival of a bachelor in a woman's life who will not commit to her. He may lead you into humorous situations or into more spontaneity. He may also suggest that you not take life so seriously.

Building (M) Building a house may signify construction of a new project in your business or building a totally new life. Building with Legos or building blocks may comment on needing to play with your ideas before putting them into action.

Bulldozer (M) A bulldozer may signify that you are feeling pushed away from what you want by another's intentions or will. Someone may be becoming too bullish for you to deal with effectively. A bulldozer may also indicate that extraneous things in your life may need to be cleared away—and cleared away quickly.

Bungee jumping (M) The act of jumping off a cliff tied to a bungee cord may be an indication of your bravery in facing some challenge in life. Taking a jump supported by a bungee cord may point to taking a risk that will allow you to bounce back even if the effort is not a complete success.

Burning heart (L) Symbolizing the transformation of the heart, the burning heart brings about a spiritual awakening or an embracing of divine love. It may represent passion, point to what your heart desires, or suggest that you have resisted love too long.

Bus (M) Chasing down a bus in a dream may reflect chasing after mainstream values. Riding on a bus may ask you to examine how much of your individuality you're willing to give up in order to be one of the crowd. Taking the bus may indicate that you will not arrive at your true destination, as the bus may not take you to your door. (See *Airplane, Vehicle*.)

Bush (L) With full foliage, a bush may represent expanded growth and fullness. The burning bush signifies spiritual transformation or spiritual awakening. Hiding behind a bush may represent your hesitation about being seen by others or your tendency to beat around the bush. A hedge of manicured bushes may represent your need to look perfect or neat.

Business card (M) Handing out business cards in a dream may point to the need to expand your business interests. Receiving someone's business card may predict an important future business contact.

Butterfly (L) This beautiful winged insect offers a message that a major transformation in thinking, attitude, belief, or action is under way. A butterfly spreading its wings may symbolize a time of liberation of the soul from the karma of previous lifetimes.

Cactus (L) This spiny, succulent desert plant may appear to indicate endurance through difficult circumstances. The cactus may encourage self-protection or represent a person you have difficulty communicating with. It may also represent a sticky situation.

Cadillac (M) The arrival of a Cadillac in your dreams may mean the arrival of someone with a big ego or an outdated view of what brings status in the world. The Cadillac may signify the need to think big in order to be successful.

Nicolas Cage (L, M) Playing characters who are often taken over by the shadow of addiction, the appearance of Nicolas Cage may remark on depression, addictions, or defeatist attitudes. Despite his fumbling and failures, he maintains a sense of humor. He may point to the humorous events in your life that you interpret as tragic.

Cake (M) A cake represents the result of your creativity. A cake with many layers may represent enjoying the many layers of an intriguing story or sweet conversation. A wedding cake represents the product of a sacred marriage or something that was created through the balance of your male and female aspects. (See *Betty Crocker foods*.)

Calculator (M) A calculator may indicate that you need to pay attention to numbers or finances in business. It may also mean you may have made an error or miscalculated something.

Campbell's soup (M) Soup in a dream combines many ingredients and simmers them into a hearty meal. Campbell's soup, for the dreamer who is versed in mythology, may mean you need to open up to a little Joseph Campbell wisdom as a hearty meal for the soul. (See *Soup*.)

Canary (L) This delicate, sensitive bird may come to dreams to warn of environmental hazards such as toxic pollution that could threaten your health. As they usually sing only when in pairs, a single canary may appear in a dream to represent the need for a mate or a new relationship. Canaries together point to the expression of joy through singing. (See *Birds*.)

Cancer (L, M) Having cancer in a dream may comment on fears or concerns about your health. Cancer may also suggest that you are harboring some destructive anger, which you may have suppressed. A dream about having cancer may be a literal early warning sign that should be taken seriously and lead you to seek medical advice.

Cancer the Crab (U) The sign of the crab is an emotionally nurturing astrological sign. The crab's appearance may announce that a nurturing and caring individual has come your way or signify a need to make your home a more comfortable place. Finally, Cancer, the Crab, may be a warning sign that you are becoming a mother hen.

Candle (M) Candles in dreams bring illumination to what is hidden in the darkness or deep within the subconscious. Candles may represent spiritual fulfillment, illumination, and enlightenment or bring to light the obstacles as well as the potential in life. Candles may be present to ask you to pray or to give a blessing.

Canned food (M) Stacking cans of food in the cupboard may suggest that you are preparing for the future or storing something for future use. A can may also point to contained emotions. Finally, it may warn that you could be fired from your employment, as in "getting canned." (See *Can opener.*)

Canoe (M) A canoe may represent synchronized action, since it takes teamwork to move a canoe. It may signify the need to team up with others in order to fulfill a longtime wish. Losing your paddle may mean that the progress of a project you are developing with others has been upset. A canoe may also signify that you feel like you have failed your team.

Can opener (M) Finding a can opener may represent that you have discovered an important tool for opening up someone to your way of thinking. Difficulty in opening a can may comment on difficulties in discovering the right ingredients to living a fulfilled life, or that you feel frustrated, or that you are unable to open up to someone else. (See *Canned food.*)

Capricorn (U) Earth, structure, foundation, and stability are the traits of Capricorn. Its arrival in a dream, whether as the goat or as its symbolic scripture, may signify a need to create more structure in your life. It may announce the arrival of someone who will offer stabilizing support, such as a financial benefactor.

Car (M) A car in a dream represents the most popular means by which we move forward in life toward our goals, desires, and destiny. Cars are objects of ego identification. They reflect how the world may view you, or they may be an indication of how you view yourself in the world. An automobile may also represent the physical body. Thus, car problems in your dreams may reflect difficulties you face in moving forward or breakdowns in how your body functions. The different colors, makes, and models of cars may be seen as expressions of the qualities of your character. (See *Truck, Vehicle.*)

Car accident (M) Having a car accident in a dream may indicate that some event or person has had a severe impact on your ego or self-esteem. It may be an indication that you are feeling insulted in some way. A rear-end collision may symbolize that some event, memory, or pattern of behavior from the past is still impacting you. A head-on collision signifies that your pursuits are in opposition to another's and that the result may have affected someone else negatively.

Cardinal (L) The cardinal's bright red robe brings the fire of passion to liberate sexual expression. Since cardinals are monogamous, the appearance of the bird may summon you to take flight with the expression of sexual feelings within a committed relationship. It may also be a reminder that your sexuality is innocent, since the cardinal is the liberator of wounds and fears concerning sexual expression. (See *Birds.*)

Carnation (L) A carnation may represent reincarnation or bachelorhood.

Carnelian (L) With its red-orange, deep, rich color, carnelian activates passion and the sexual or second chakra. Worn in a dream, it might announce your awakened sexual and spiritual power.

Carnival (M) Being at a carnival may represent your concerns about fulfilling a desire for more amusement and fun. A carnival may direct you to look back at an event within the last few days that brought you fulfillment, or point to a colorful and magical experience that you enjoyed immensely.

Carpenter (M) The appearance of a carpenter in a dream may suggest that you are ready to build something new in your life or make an addition to your present plan for the future. He may come to help you make some changes in your thinking patterns in order to construct a new attitude about yourself or your life. A carpenter may appear to represent Jesus and his salvation.

Carpet (M) Soft and luxurious or shabby with spots, the carpet may say something about the quality of comfort in your daily life. It may also reflect the lining of the womb or creative sexual center. Thus, cleaning the carpet may remark on cleaning up your sexual attitudes and clearing them of shame. Stains on the carpet are stains that mar the beauty of what you have laid as your foundation.

Carrot (L) Eating carrots may represent the need to be grounded in the earth by offering the body good nutrients from the earth to sustain itself. The proverbial dangling carrot suggests temptation.

Cash register (M) A cash register may signify that it is time to cash in on a business deal and usually is a sign of money coming in. On the other hand, it may be related to your concerns about making a profit in business. A cash register whose drawer is stuck may remark on your inability to make money.

Cassette player (M) Cassette tapes are the voices from the past, which may have influenced you and contributed to your psychological makeup. A cassette player may reflect those old beliefs or "tapes" that you are holding on to from the past.

Cat (L) Classically, a cat possesses an independent and self-reliant attitude. Thus, it may cross your path to challenge you to become more independent. Cats are the most psychic of all animals, and their psychic abilities may represent your own psychic power. The birth of kittens in your dream may announce the opening of intuitive abilities. A black cat appearing in a dream can represent the malevolent quality of psychic power and can reflect your fears in using your psychic abilities. You may falsely believe these abilities to be evil or destructive.

Cat in the Hat (M) The tall, lanky Cat in the Hat, created by Dr. Seuss, brings the message that reading is fundamental. He may suggest that it is time to crack open the books, do one's homework, or read for enjoyment. The Cat in the Hat may come to trick and coax you into having fun even with seemingly unpleasant circumstances of life. He may also represent cleverness.

Ceiling (M) The ceiling of a room may present the subject of your thinking or simply what is on your mind. Living in a house with cathedral ceilings may reflect your spiritual concerns. A slanted ceiling may represent ideas that are skewed in one direction.

Celebrities (L, M) Celebrities appearing on the stage of your dream are often acting out archetypal dramas and comedies, which we call myths. They may appear as some of the archetypes from the mythologies of the world, such as the Greek myths, which still drive Western culture. They may offer their associated character traits and roles to represent aspects of your personality, or they may come to represent an idealized version of a person in your life.

Celery (L, M) Stalks of celery may signify your desire for a larger "salary" at work, or they may be asking you to look at who may be "stalking" you. Celery may also point to a need to cleanse the bowels.

Cell phone (M) A character in your dream carrying a cell phone may take his business seriously. A cell phone denotes mobility and may represent an urgent need to communicate. It may also symbolize the need to communicate new information to your cellular memory, such as more loving thoughts. (See *Telephone*.)

Cement truck (M) This truck may signify the delivery of concrete and steadfast elements or ideas. Pouring cement may represent solidifying your plans by working out the details and making the necessary arrangements. The truck may also mean that you are ready to lay the foundation for a new project.

Cereal (M) A quick and easy food for breakfast, cereal may suggest that which brings nourishment and sustenance quickly. Eating a sugary breakfast cereal may comment on your gullibility as well as your poor eating habits.

Certificate (M) Being given a certificate in a dream suggests recognition for some accomplishment, whether it is in business or an indication of personal or spiritual growth. A certificate is a symbol of authenticity.

Chain saw (M) A chain saw is usually used to cut down trees. Someone who is coming at you with a chain saw may point to a shadow character who is ready to cut down your life.

Chairs (M) Chairs may represent ideas that you hold in your mind or that you are sitting on. Moving chairs around in a dream may signify playing with ideas. A wing-back provincial chair, for example, may reflect traditional ideas, and chairs in the Danish modern style might point to simpler ideas that do not involve a lot of detail.

Chalice (L) The chalice may represent the Holy Grail, the vessel that unites the recipient with Christ. As the prize of a spiritual quest, the chalice represents enlightenment. Holding wine, the blood of Christ, it is associated with communion. A chalice may also signify the container of the feminine principle or the goddess's wealth bestowed to you.

Chalk (M) Used to write on a blackboard, a crumbled piece of chalk may indicate not being able to get your point across. If the chalk erases easily, it may point to something communicated that does not have a lasting impact. Chalk is also associated with receiving a lesson.

Cheese (M) A solid dairy product, cheese can point to solidifying a deal that has some substance to it. Eating sharp cheddar may mean that you perceive motherly advice as critical. Swiss cheese might signify something lacking substance.

Cheetah (L) The fastest animal in the world, the cheetah indicates the power of rapid movement in the achievement of one's goals. The message to you is to get moving.

Cher (L, M) Cher may come to say "share" your talents and gifts by turning your volume up. As the archetype of an Amazon queen, she demonstrates success through separating herself from the institution of marriage and by becoming a queen without a king.

Cherries (L, M) Being fed ripe red cherries may signify having a sensual and pleasurable experience. It may also mean that everything is "just cherry" or well and good. As cherries have hard pits, this may point to feelings that life is the pits. Associated with gambling on a slot machine, cherries may signify receiving some petty cash.

Chess (M) As a slow game of strategy, playing chess in your dreams may represent that you have met your match in a business negotiation. A chess match may comment that you are involved in a power play where there is a lot at stake.

Chevy (M) As the Heartbeat of America, a Chevy may represent someone who is driven by his or her heart.

Chicago (M) As the heart of the Midwest, the arrival of a dreamer on the streets of Chicago may represent entering the mainstream values of Middle America, such as strong personal ethics and moral principles. The name *Chicago* means "strong or great." In that Chicago is the convention center of the world, it may be associated with the sharing of ideas in business.

Chicken (M) Being served chicken may comment that you are acting like a chicken because you are held back by your fears. Eating chicken may represent your desire for a "down home," nourishing experience. A live chicken may mean that there is a pecking order of dominance within a group that you are involved in; it could be a response to your feeling hen-pecked.

Chimney (M) Looking at smoke coming out of a chimney may mean that you are letting off some steam to dissipate your anger. The chimney breathes air into the hearth and, therefore, may represent fueling your passion or inner fire. It may also represent the opening or portal into the Upper World.

Chinese (M) A Chinese figure in a dream stereotypically represents someone who is working for the whole or who has socialistic values. This may be a comment on your need to conform, or it may indicate a need to adopt some strong traditional values. In dreams relating to your work, the Chinese may point to an open market.

Chiron (U) The newest heavenly body, Chiron is the sign of the wounded healer. It may announce someone who has coped with a great deal of emotional pain and thus learned compassion toward others. Chiron's appearance may call you to a healing profession. It may also represent the influence of karma in your life brought up from previous incarnations or any other transgressions of your soul.

Chocolate (M) Being given chocolates by a friend or lover may signify being given comfort and love. Chocolate is also associated with sensual pleasure and emotional satisfaction. Chocolates may also be a sign of your addictive behaviors.

Choker (M) A tight choker worn around the neck may reveal that you feel choked up and unable to communicate what is in your heart. A choker brings the eye of the observer directly to the throat, which is the center for self-expression. The woman wearing a choker may have a lot to say.

Chop suey (M) Eating chop suey may appear as a response to feelings that perhaps you have been chopped up and made into a meal to satisfy someone else's needs.

Christmas (L) Christmas represents a time of receiving the gift of fulfillment. It may also represent good cheer. Spiritually, it may refer to the birth of Christ. In a dream, Christmas may represent the fulfillment of long-held desires or refer to lasting impressions from childhood.

Chrysanthemum (L) A chrysanthemum is associated with the mothering aspect of the personality or nurturing principle.

Cinderella (L, M) Cinderella, the main character in the fairy tale of a waif turned princess, symbolizes the common psychological pattern of a woman who is waiting for her prince to come. She may not be able to see her value outside of a relationship, since the fantasy posits that attracting a man validates a woman's worth. The Cinderella story may also comment on a rivalry with other women.

Citrine (L) A yellow-orange gemstone that strengthens the will indicates the qualities of strength and personal power. Its appearance may also assist in magnetizing abundance and money.

City (M) Being in a big city in a dream may represent feeling that you are among the masses. A city may represent a hub of concerns ranging from success in your career to your ability to get along with others, or it may reflect the concerns you have about choosing the right livelihood.

Clairol hair products (M) Hair dyes in general indicate the desire to express your personal power. The message of Clairol may be to use clarity and care in expressing your power out in the world. Dying your hair red suggests passion and sassiness. Dying it black suggests looking more intelligent or mysterious. Blond hair expresses angelic and pure qualities. (See *Bathing*.)

Clam (L) A closed clam may state that you are shut tight as a clam and are cold emotionally. Eating steamed clams may be a response to an opening in a recent conversation that steamed things up.

Cleaning (M) Cleaning and tidying up may suggest preparation for someone new coming into your life. It may also remark on the necessity to clean up some unfinished business or to clean up a mess you have made in some relationship or situation. Cleaning could also represent having to clean up someone else's mess.

Cleanser (M) Cleansers are used to clean and to scour stains. Thus, a cleanser appearing in a dream may represent the need to purify the mind, the heart, or the body. Applied to a sink, a cleanser may indicate your readiness to rid the heart of some old emotional pain. In that they whiten surfaces, cleansers may symbolize your desire to clean up an old mess that may have corrupted your reputation. (See *Mr. Clean.*)

Climbing (M) Climbing a ladder in a dream may reflect an upward movement in your career. Climbing a mountain may reflect your desire for spiritual truth and understanding. Climbing a rocky incline may represent overcoming some huge obstacle in your life.

Bill Clinton (L, M) Like Zeus on Mount Olympus, former president Bill Clinton was responsible for the fate of humanity while he was in office. And like Zeus, Bill is known for his infidelity. He may appear in a dream to express your own leadership qualities. However, he may also point to the embarrassment of a public blunder.

Hillary Clinton (L, M) As a powerful first lady, noble and loyal, she emerges as the goddess Hera who values the institution of marriage above any other attribute of feminine concern. Whether she admits it or not, Mrs. Clinton's motto is "Stand by your man." She might arrive to comment on your loyalty to a relationship despite infidelity, embarrassment, and betrayal.

Clock (M) A clock on the wall may be a sign that it is time for something to happen. The time on the clock face may provide numeric significance. For example, nine o'clock may mark a time of completion of a psychological process, such as the ending of a negative emotional pattern. Twelve midnight may signify the dawn of consciousness and liberation from negative karma.

Closet (M) Your attitudes, symbolized as clothing, are often hung in the closet. The clothing may also represent a new self-image you may want to embrace. The closet may indicate something that you have hidden from yourself or something that was hidden from you. A walk-in closet may invite seclusion or hiding.

Clothes hamper (M) As the place where dirty clothes are stored, the hamper may signify having to pick up any of the negative thoughts you have left scattered around the house.

Clothesline (M) Hanging out clothing, particularly underwear, suggests that you are revealing your underlying attitudes to the public and may indicate an issue of an embarrassing nature. It could also mean that someone is handing you "a line."

Clothing (M) Clothing in general reveals the image that you want to project to the world. Each article of clothing reveals different concerns, qualities, beliefs, attitudes, and expressions. Even the color and conditions of the clothing may reveal significant information. For example, clothing that is tattered or torn may signify that you feel emotionally shredded by an experience. You may also be expressing a "poor me" attitude.

Clouds (L, U) As the alchemy of air and water, cumulus, cirrus, or stratus, dark or white clouds come to represent the manifestation of our thinking and our moods. In a dream, a cloudy sky may mean there is no sunshine in your life, and it can be a direct response to or prediction of your mood. A dark cloud ahead may signify a dark mood of depression and might forebode a negative experience you had better prepare for. Cloudless skies may indicate a positive shift in mood and attitude. Stratus clouds may comment that you are "out in the stratosphere" or unrealistic about your expectations.

Coach (M) A sports coach appearing as a character in a dream may signify the need to learn something new or to get some advice from an expert. He or she may offer solutions in playing the game of life fairly or may boost your ego by letting you know that you can excel and reach your goals.

Coat (M) A coat covers you up and protects you from the elements. Wearing a heavy, full-length coat may comment on your need to feel protected. It may also suggest that you are concealing something about yourself from others. Wearing a raincoat on a sunny day may bring attention to your fears of facing the nasty elements of your emotions, thus commenting on a pessimistic attitude.

Coca-Cola (M) The Coca-Cola brand has become the most recognized trademark in the world. Since 1886, Coke has been refreshing people everywhere and, therefore, might represent that the dreamer is having a refreshing thought or participating in a refreshing experience. Drinking a Coke in one's dream may also signify consuming the elements of success and gaining recognition from adopting American values in one's own business venture. Coke could also be a sign of a successful business venture. The shadow side may suggest consuming something with little nutritional value that is detrimental to the soul and spirit of the dreamer. It may also signify "the real thing." (See *Soda.*)

Cock (L) A rooster or cock may mean that it is time to wake up, thus signifying the need to become conscious of some external situation. It may point to a cocky individual or suggest that someone is half-cocked or out of his mind. A cock may also represent pride.

Cockroach (L) This seemingly indestructible and crafty creature lives in the dark and may represent unconscious, dark belief patterns that steal, rob, and multiply easily, spreading diseased thoughts. They scatter when they come in contact with the light, and thus defy consciousness.

Coffeepot (M) A coffeepot may comment on a conversation with friends in which you are pouring out something that may be viewed as stimulating, or it may signify that you desire more social interaction.

Coffee table (M) Sitting around a coffee table may signify socializing and having an interesting conversation. The objects on the table may represent the subject of the conversation. A coffee table marred with nicks and scratches may indicate that a conversation has gone sour.

Coffin (M) A coffin in a dream may indicate that one may need to embrace death as a natural part of the cycle of life. A coffin in a dream may also predict a death in the family or in your circle of friends and colleagues, but it suggests this very rarely. Death in a dream is usually symbolic rather than literal. Thus, a coffin may symbolize the end of a relationship or another important transition in life. It may also indicate that you have lost your enthusiasm for life.

Collar (M) A collar is a direct symbol of ownership and fellowship. A collar may be a symbol of identification with an organization. A priest's collar may be an indication of a pompous individual.

Colors (L, M, and U) Colors express qualities and attributes that may indicate your mood in a dream. Colors may add more detail to the attitudes and beliefs that are expressed in a dream. Thus, a woman wearing an orange T-shirt may be expressing a bold attitude. Whether it is the color of the clothing someone is wearing or the color of an object, each hue may reveal more specific information about the subject. (See individual color entries.)

Comet (U) Comets have always come as signs of change or destruction looming on the horizon. The appearance of a comet in your dream may also be a sign of changing events in life, which may bring some chaos into your life until things settle down.

Comet cleanser (M) Since a comet comes as a sign of a change on the horizon, scouring a sink with Comet cleanser may signify cleansing psychological or emotional stains that deeply mar your image. It may reflect the change that comes through an emotional cleansing. (See *Cleanser*.)

Compact disc (M) playing a CD of favorite music in your dreams may represent the desire to enjoy a moment of inspiration. It may also signify compressing information into a tight package.

Compass (M) A compass is a navigational tool that establishes direction. In a dream, a compass may appear to tell you that you are lost and need to be pointed in the right direction. A broken compass may indicate that you lack direction in your life. Pointing north, a compass signifies moving toward your vision of fulfillment. Pointing south, it suggests change. Pointing east it suggests spiritual or new beginnings. And if pointing west, a compass suggests issues regarding your emotions. (See *Four directions* and *East, North, South, West*.)

Computer (M) A PC may reflect your concerns about work. It may metaphorically stand for the ability to process information or for brain function. Problems with your personal computer may point to difficulties in processing data internally or in thinking clearly. For example, losing text may represent forgetting important information. Accidentally deleting something may indicate your losing information or forgetting ideas that are critical.

Computer mouse (M) Difficulty in controlling the mouse on your personal computer may suggest that you are losing control of the direction of your thinking. It may signify confusion. It may also indicate that you are acting like a mouse rather than a lion, a little too timid for your own good.

Computer station (M) A desk with compartments that houses your computer, this station may represent the human skull. It may also remark on concerns about organization at work.

Concert hall (M) Attending a concert may express concerns about your public image and whether you feel as though others are hearing you. It may also point to a desire to listen to music or to be entertained. Finally, it may suggest that you need to sit down and listen.

Sean Connery (L, M) Noble, fair, sincere, and mature, Sean may appear in his role as King Arthur or as Indiana Jones' father to bring the wisdom of a sage or the sovereign power of a king. As the archetype of the king, he may call you to your own wisdom and the dignity that comes with age. For a woman, he may appear as a fair father or a mature lover.

Construction site (M) A construction site is the ground on which you as the dreamer build your hopes and dreams for fulfillment. Depending on how far along the construction is, it will reveal the progress you have made in developing your ideas and plans. For instance, if the frame is up, this suggests that you have already created the foundation and skeleton of your project. A construction site may also be an indication of the progress of the psychological work you are doing. A truck on the site may mean you have all the necessary tools to embark on the construction of a new area in your life.

Converse brand (L, M) This athletic wear, whose trademark is the five-pointed star, brings ancient wisdom into modern dress. It may appear as a sign to focus on the power of your own creativity. It may humorously ask you to "converse" with someone who is standing beside you. The five-pointed star as the insignia of the feminine principle may point out the need to honor women's wisdom. The five points of the star also signify the five elements in the cycle of creativity, and such a star is the insignia of magic.

Cookie Monster (M) *Sesame Street*'s blue, fuzzy monster who just loves chocolate-chip cookies may indicate your lack of constraint and your inability to curb overindulgent behavior.

Cookies (M) Eating chocolate-chip cookies may suggest enjoying something or someone who is irresistible and chock-full of bits of love. These cookies appearing in a dream may also point to a pleasant or unpleasant childhood memory.

Cooking (M) Cooking in a dream may signify putting together the ingredients of a creative project that will perhaps nourish others. It may express your concerns about taking care of your family or about mothering your children. Burning something on the stove may comment that you are angry about a domestic situation.

Copper (L) A good conductor of heat and energy, copper may represent stability under fire as a personality trait.

Corn (L) Corn is a symbol of fertility in Native American cultures. Having the same connotation as wheat and barley, it may represent the sustaining power of the feminine nurturing principle. Spitting corn may indicate that someone is acting corny or silly.

Corner (M) Discovering something in the corner of a house may represent the discovery of something crucial that may bring two ideas together. Being in the corner of a house may point to feelings of being cornered or stuck.

Corona beer (M) The crown of beers, Corona, may signify the crown of glory for the dreamer who pursues a high-spirited life—not from literal intoxication, but from spiritual intoxication. It may also comment that you have become intoxicated by your own self-aggrandizement. Corona may also point to a regal friend in your circle of buddies.

Kevin Costner (M) A cavalry soldier turned Indian in *Dances with Wolves,* Costner represents the patriarchal hero who becomes a spiritual warrior of peace. He may come to mention the need to explore a more authentic path in life and the need to learn to value nature as one's teacher. He expresses the qualities of manliness as well as sensitivity.

Cougar (L) The cougar as the master of the mountain comes like Moses to the Israelites to bring messages from the spiritual world. The cougar can come to the dreamer as a call to become a spiritual teacher. Its power delivers higher truth through various forms of communication such as writing, channeling, public speaking, and media.

Country (M) Being in the country may point to your desire to escape from the busy world for a time. It may remark on concerns about lifestyles or a desire that reflects a more relaxed approach to life, or it may comment on a backward or too-simple lifestyle.

Courtroom (M) Being in a courtroom in a dream may reflect concerns about justice in a perceived unfair situation. It may point to the need to defend yourself or the tendency to judge others. The courtroom may also represent the act of courting another's wishes or, literally, dating.

Cow (L) As the nurturing aspect of the feminine, the cow may come to offer you some mothering. The arrival of cows in a dream may predict prosperity. In its negative connotation, "as big as a cow," a cow may represent obesity.

Cowboy (M) As an archetype, a cowboy boasts the qualities of a tough, rugged, strong man. The appearance of a cowboy in a woman's dream may represent someone who has seduced her with his physique and charm but who will love her and leave her. He may turn out to be a coyote or trickster on a woman's path of self-fulfillment.

Coyote (L) The star of the trickster myths, Coyote brings humor and cunning to force you beyond the boundaries of your self-identity. For women, Coyote can signify a man who seduces, lies, and betrays, forcing a woman to stand in her own power and gain back her self-worth. Similar to the fool archetype, Coyote is spontaneous and wise, offering his coaxing nature to liberate you from your mundane existence. The coyote may also come onto the scene of a dream to call you to travel and explore the world.

Crane (L) The graceful beauty of the crane as a spiritual mediator brings the message of grace into your life. The crane may be delivering the grace or the much-asked-for gifts you have been waiting for to fulfill a promise or dream. (See *Birds*.)

Cross (L) The cross is an ancient symbol with horizontal and vertical lines intersecting that represents the manifestation of spirit into matter. As the structure on which Jesus was crucified, the cross signifies suffering, burden, and martyrdom. A cross that is worn around the neck may point to devotion to Christ or it may mention that you have a cross to bear.

Crow (L) The black crow flies toward the four directions as a guide through life's journey. For the spiritual seeker, Crow can come to represent the spiritual guidance that is available when you attune to nature. The caw of the crow can announce a message of affirmation to a significant question in your life. In general, the crow is a mediator between your conscious mind and your higher self, helping you to navigate in a positive direction. (See *Birds*.)

Crowd (M) Being in a crowd of people may indicate that you are with the masses to witness some social event. It may also point to being just one of the crowd or united with many. A crowd you are a part of may suggest that you are going to witness something in the future that will affect the collective or the masses. It may point to feeling crowded and not being able to find your own space or position in life.

Tom Cruise (L, M) Good-looking, confident, and sometimes defiant, this superstar may appear in a dream as the *Top Gun* hero or as the leader of *Mission: Impossible* to reflect the confidence of the male will. Like Apollo, Tom embodies the ideal image of a real man, too beautiful for words, using his good looks and intellect to get him to the top. He may fulfill a woman's desires as a romantic partner in a dream. As the character Jerry Maguire, he may offer you a look at the desire for success in life, perhaps delivering the message that it all comes together through love.

Crystal (L) See separate listing for *Amethyst; Citrine; Quartz, Clear; Rose Quartz; Smoky Quartz*.

Cup (M) Holding out a cup, the receptacle of receiving, may represent the need to receive the fulfillment of your desire. A coffee mug signifies that you are ready to communicate with someone important to you. A plastic-coated party cup may point to your readiness to experience joy and the celebration of life. A broken or chipped cup may represent internal damage that makes it difficult to fulfill your desires.

Curtains (M) Drawn curtains block the sun or anyone from looking into the house. Therefore, they represent the need for privacy. Drawing open the curtains may signify your readiness for a brighter future. A curtain may veil something you may not be ready to see or expose to the conscious mind, such as a hidden memory.

Cyclamen (L, U) A Christian symbol depicting the Virgin Mary's bleeding from the heart, the cyclamen represents the wounded mother or the bleeding nun. She may comment on the wound of crucifixion on all of humanity.

Daffodils (L) A spring flower, a daffodil reflects cheeriness and sounds forth as the trumpet of joy.

Dairy Queen (M) The fast-food chain that specializes in soft-serve desserts may be visited in a dream to fulfill a wish for immediate maternal nurturing. As the archetype of the mature feminine who is honored, the queen grants all requests and delivers them through her grace and unconditional love. Thus, Dairy Queen may indicate your need to have the treat of royal favor.

Daisy (L) A daisy answers the "he-loves-me, loves-me-not" question. It may comment on love's innocence, or it may signify a period of waiting.

Daisy Duck (L, M) Daisy may come to make a point about a woman's codependent behavior in a relationship and may be a sign to stop putting up with unacceptable behavior from her mate.

Dancing (M) Dancing in a dream may point to liberating the body from complacency or inactivity. It may represent freedom of movement. Dancing with a partner in a dream may fulfill a desire for a more harmonious relationship and a preference to express balance and grace.

Dates (M) Eating dates in a dream may be a comment on the fun of dating as opposed to searching for a committed relationship. Dates also represent virility.

Daytime (L) Daytime scenes in a dream comment on what you are actively pursuing to fulfill your life. Daytime may also reflect the light of consciousness or what is understood or recognized by your conscious mind versus what is unconscious.

Deer (L) Deer come to deliver the attributes of gentleness, sensitivity, and innocence. A deer is sensitive to every rustle in the forest, and a deer in a dream may indicate a need to develop keen sensitivity to your environment or life through shifting from thinking to awareness. The presence of a deer may mean you need to develop a more gentle approach to life or toward your relationships with others. The buck with its branched antlers comes as a powerful expression of masculine strength. He wears the crown of the king and symbolically has associations with Christ. The young buck's strength is in its crown, which, like the branches of a tree, reach into the Upper World for spiritual connection. The doe comes to bring the message to embrace a more passive and sensitive demeanor and the fawn to embrace innocence.

Oscar de la Renta (M) As the signature of a one-of-a-kind woman receiving an Oscar, the appearance of one of this designer's gowns in your dreams may mention that you are ready to express elegance and individuality.

Delivery truck (M) Whether it's UPS or FedEx, the appearance of a delivery truck in the neighborhood may symbolize the arrival of a special gift into your life. It may also point out the need to take your own special gifts out into the worldwide market.

Den (M) Retreating into the den in your dreams may signify a need for some private time away from family concerns.

Dentist (M) A dentist repairs the teeth and thus may remark on the need to drill to the root of a problem that is causing you to lose power in your life. He or she may come to help you with the issue of communicating more concise information or becoming a more effective communicator. A dentist may also arrive with the literal message to take better care of your teeth.

Department store (M) Shopping for clothing in a department store reflects shopping for a new attitude or image of yourself. Shopping at Saks Fifth Avenue, for instance, might represent adopting upper-class values and attitudes about style and image. Trying on clothes at Macy's may represent putting on the attitudes of the middle class. And going through the racks at Wal-Mart reflects concerns about getting the best bargain for your money, with little regard for your image.

Desert (L, M) A desert, with its desolate and arid terrain, represents difficulties, hardships, and a general lack of resources for sustaining life. In a dream, a desert may represent a lack of fertility in life, such as financial difficulties, or even in the body, indicating infertility for the man or woman wishing to conceive a child.

Desk (M) A desk as a piece of furniture comments that your ideas are at work and on work. An oak desk might mean that your ideas about work are solid and strong. Having a desk in the bedroom may comment that your concerns about work are interfering with your intimate relationship or with your sleep.

Detergent (M) Detergents clean dirty clothes and, therefore, may signify the need to clean up your attitude or image. A detergent appearing in a dream may indicate that it's time to clean up a major problem or difficult situation you are facing. A detergent may also symbolize an ingredient that, when added to a situation, may improve your image. (See *Tide laundry detergent*.)

Diabetes (L, M) As a disease caused by a lack of insulin in the body or insulin resistance, diabetes may represent your inability to process and absorb the sweetness of life. It may indicate that you have failed to see or express joy. Diabetes in a dream may also come as a warning sign of the onset of diabetes in real life and, like any other disease that may appear in a dream, should be taken as a serious message to seek medical advice.

Diamond (L) When cut, this multifaceted gem brings the essence and qualities of clarity and radiant light reflected out. It may suggest that you begin to radiate your good qualities and inner light. Set in a ring, it symbolizes a gift of love and marital engagement for a woman. Wearing a canary diamond can represent the possession of a rare and valuable gift of intelligent beauty.

Diamond nuts (M) A bag of Diamond nuts may mention that your radiance will be discovered once your hard shell has been cracked open. You may need to crack open your hard exterior to discover the meat or wisdom you really may have to offer others.

Diana, Princess of Wales (L, M) As the Queen of Hearts, Diana may appear as a humanitarian who brings the attributes of genuine compassion to her duties. She also represents a princess who is wounded and dethroned by ridicule and emotional abuse. In this way, she may appear in a dream to mention a woman's tendency to buy into the Cinderella myth, which discredits her value and worth. Some dreamers have felt that they have had real visitations from Diana from the spiritual realms since her death in 1997. She has brought them her light, compassion, and grace.

Leonardo DiCaprio (L, M) The Romeo of film actors, Leonardo may appear in a dream to take the hand of a dreamer into the chamber of romantic love. He may portray the projection of the perfect lover as youthful and innocent. He may announce the arrival of a soul-mate relationship.

Dice (M) If dice are cast in a dream, this may signify that the circumstances of fate are at hand. It may also indicate that you are taking a gamble. Snake eyes, when the number one shows up on both dice, suggests failure.

Digging (M) Digging in the ground in a dream may ask you to dig up old memories from childhood in order to transform emotional patterns that interfere with your happiness. It may also comment on excavating the treasures within. Digging up bones may point to the excavation of old feelings of grief around previous losses in your life.

Dining room (M) As a room where you may nurture others by serving food, the dining room may present concerns about your family. In your dream, the dining room with its furnishings and serving tools may express a great deal about your attitudes regarding giving and receiving love and nurturing.

Dining room table (M) A dining room table may represent symbolically your ideas about being nurtured and how your ideas may offer others something substantial. Thus, a table that is long with two chairs at opposite ends might comment on the distance that you feel between yourself and another.

Dinosaur (L) Dinosaurs take you into prehistoric experiences and reflect the imprint of your history on the psyche. The dinosaurs' power lingers even after they have become extinct. In other words, a dinosaur may come to represent an old idea, belief, or pattern that still hugely influences you. Even though it may be outmoded or archaic, you may still be clinging to that which thwarts your evolution and growth.

Directing traffic (M) Directing traffic may be a response to feeling that you are in charge of others and directing their destinations. It may also compensate for frustration about not being in control of others' behavior.

Dirt road (M) Traveling down a dirt road may reflect a difficult passage toward your goals on which you may have to face rockslides, potholes, or mud if the weather or your mood changes. A dirt road may comment that you have chosen a path that is a new frontier in that it is unpaved.

Dish-washing liquid, Dawn (M) Washing dishes with Dawn may comment on a revelation or inspiration coming through the simple and mundane acts of life. It may suggest that you just came up with a great idea in the most unusual moment, or it may represent fresh ideas, which may initiate a new beginning.

Dish-washing liquid, Joy (M) Squeezing a bottle of Joy dish soap in a dream may mention the need to put some joy into the simple things in life.

Diskette (M) A diskette holds data, which may be transferred into a computer's hard drive or run without storing it. Thus, metaphorically it may represent information given to you that you can use and incorporate for a time but you don't necessarily have to buy into forever. It also may represent information or ideas that you pass on to someone else.

Diver (M) A diver may appear to accompany you into the depths of your emotions. The diver may come as a guide into the ocean of the subconscious to retrieve some treasure of wisdom for you to bring out into your life. It may point to a professional shaman or hypnotherapist who assists you to enter the labyrinth of your soul.

Diving (M) Diving into the ocean in a dream may represent diving into subconscious memories, which may need to be explored in order to heal deep issues. Diving and gazing at fish may suggest exploring or coming into direct contact with all the abundance and creativity that is available to you through exploring your subconscious. Diving may also appear as a response to feeling submerged.

Doctor (M) Consulting with a doctor in a dream may remedy concerns about your health. It may announce that you may need someone to assist you in diagnosing a health problem. There is an aspect within the subconscious called the inner healer, which brings the power to transform a condition of disease within you that may have created a real disease in your body.

Dog (L) Dogs are man's companions and loyal friends and thus can come in a dream to represent a real friendship. Because of a dog's extreme loyalty to its owner, the appearance of a dog can represent a tendency toward being too loyal to your friends and thus sacrificing yourself and your needs. A dead dog can come to represent the death of a friendship, and the birth of a puppy can come to signify the arrival of a new friendship. A bite from a dog can be a response to an argument with a friend. Dogs as guardians can signify the need for personal protection, or they may comment that you feel watched, as by a watchdog.

Dog breeds (L)

- **Bulldog** (L) A bulldog may symbolize a bull-headed individual who looks tough on the outside but is actually quite lovable.

- **Chihuahua** (L) A Chihuahua may arrive to remind you of a friend or associate with a small ego and a nervous disposition.

- **Dalmatians** (L) In that the Dalmatian is often a companion to firefighters, the appearance of Dalmatians in a dream may point to a tendency to want to rescue others or to put out their emotional fires for them. The appearance of those charming spotted pups from the Disney animated movie may also comment on your need to be everything to everyone. As the carriage dogs for royalty, the Dalmatian may indicate that you have elevated your friends to regal status. Thus the overall message may be that although your friends deserve to be honored, you may need to consider honoring yourself.

- **German shepherd** (L) A German shepherd may appear to let you know that you are on guard or that you may need some real protection from a special friend.

- **Golden retriever** (L) Dreaming of a golden retriever may indicate that you need to retrieve an old friendship or other relationship.

- **Newfoundland** (L) Newfoundlands are renowned as rescue dogs. A Newfoundland may symbolize that you are in need of rescue in a business deal or partnership or in a personal relationship.

- **Poodle** (L) A poodle may arrive to remind you of someone who is well groomed or someone who is just prissy.

Doghouse (M) A doghouse may mention that you feel you have done something to displease your mate. Thus you feel you are in the doghouse or in trouble. A doghouse may represent feelings of shame.

Doll (M) A doll as an outstanding symbol in a dream may be offered to stimulate a childhood memory about the style of mothering you received. It may comment that a woman is a doll, as in very attractive. It also may denote fragility.

Dollhouse (M) Playing with a dollhouse may remark on your idealistic fantasies about having a family. It may mention that your perception about your family constellation is based on childhood concepts and experiences. It may represent a model for working out the real problems in your family in order to find a solution that will address each member's needs.

Dolphin (L) Dolphins bring the spirit of playfulness to your life. They swim in groups, called pods, and thus can reflect the need for a closer connection to your family or social group. Extremely intelligent, they may come to activate your own higher intelligence or higher self that is connected to the universal mind. A dolphin in dreams may reflect shared intelligence and telepathic communication.

Donald Duck (L, M) The wacky, quacky duck of Disney cartoon fame might appear in a dream or a waking dream to signify frustration. With his often-explosive temper, Donald may come to poke fun at your own tyrannical nature. He may also arrive to poke fun at how easily you become frustrated by others.

Doors (M) Doors most often represent openings into new opportunities that may fulfill your desires. A closed door may suggest that you feel locked out emotionally. Being unable to open a door in a dream may suggest that you have missed an important opportunity or that you do not possess the key or tool for opening it. It may also separate you from others or from welcoming others to you.

Doorway (M) Doorways represent open entrances for self-exploration. If the door in your dream is in your own home, it may represent an open doorway to a more intimate relationship with family members. A doorway in a house that is unfamiliar may represent a doorway into the soul. A doorway in a friend's house may suggest having an open invitation to get closer.

Dorothy (Gale) (L, M) Judy Garland, as Dorothy in *The Wizard of Oz,* may represent an adolescent aspect of your personality that is ready to individuate from the values of your family and your culture in general. She may take you on a heroine's journey down the Yellow Brick Road to enlightenment. She may ask that you use your intelligence, open your heart, and cultivate courage in confronting the fears of the shadow of the Wicked Witch of the West in whatever form she takes in your life. She may tell you not to follow any gurus and that you don't have to venture outside your own backyard to find your heart's desire. She represents the spiritually maturing female.

Double ax (M) A symbol of feminine power associated with the Amazon tribes of Greek mythology, this tool offers a two-sided power with both negative and positive qualities. The double ax represents the strength of feminine power or the betrayal of one's power.

Double bed (M) Entering a room with a double bed may point to your desire for sexual intimacy in a committed relationship. It may present your concerns about your relationship as well as your sexual preferences.

Doublemint gum (M) A pack of Doublemint gum may comment on a relationship or partnership with a twin or a like-minded individual. It may point to a couple who are stuck together or partnered in life and in business. It may simply ask you to "Double Your Pleasure and Double Your Fun." (See *Gum*.)

Doughnut (M) Eating doughnuts in a dream may signify greediness and overindulgent behavior. They may describe a character too consumed with money, as in "dough nuts." With a hole as its center, a doughnut may represent feelings of emptiness or a loss of what is central in your life.

Dove (L) The appearance of doves in a dream may point to a love relationship that is bonded and sincere. A dove is also a messenger of peace. In that doves coo, they may bring the power of romantic love into your life. (See *Birds*.)

Downhill (M) Traveling downhill may represent either an easy coast to your destination or that you are heading downhill in your profession, suggesting a loss in your financial worth.

Dragon (L) This mythical creature brings the element of fire as a transforming agent. The dragon can come to represent the power of creativity as well as sexuality. It can signify alchemy and magic. A dragon may also represent someone who has fire breath or who uses his anger to get his way.

Dragonfly (L) This translucent winged creature flies through the window of illusion to offer you an opening to the dream world. It may comment on the condition of Maya, referring to the great illusion of a third-dimensional view of life. Dragonfly mentions the need to cut through life's illusions. The dragonfly is the guide into the astral or spirit world.

Drapes (M) The heavy, protective fabric common to drapes may comment on your concerns about protection and privacy. Closing the drapes may indicate your need to block out the concerns of the world for a time and to retreat. Or it may suggest a need to enter the darkness of the subconscious.

Dress (M) Putting on a pretty dress may point to a woman's concerns about looking feminine and expressing feminine qualities. It may point to your concerns about looking pretty enough. Wearing a tight dress may make the statement that you are feeling cramped by the world's expectations that you look a certain way. A long dress may suggest you lack sex appeal.

Dresser (M) As the place where you usually store underwear, it may reveal hidden underlying beliefs that need to be explored. A dresser may have secret compartments where you may retrieve objects relating to childhood memories. If stuffed too full, it can suggest a need to throw out some old beliefs about yourself.

Driver's license (M) Losing your driver's license in your dreams may comment that you have lost your true identity. It may also signify a loss of freedom to move toward your own goals and destination in life. Your own driver's license appearing in your dream may comment that you are having an identity crisis. Finding someone else's driver's license may suggest that his or her true identity has been revealed to you.

Driving (M) Driving down a road may comment on how you are doing with steering yourself toward your goals and destination. It can represent the journey of life and how the force of your will can take you in many different directions toward eventual fulfillment. Driving east may represent moving toward spiritual goals. Driving south may represent the direction of sexual concerns or personal and psychological transformation. Driving west may suggest moving toward your emotional issues or introspection, and moving north represents accelerating toward your vision. Speeding may comment on carelessness in the pursuit of your goals. Blocking traffic suggests that you are preventing others from expressing their personal freedom.

Drum (M) Delivering a beat, a drum may come to represent your heart. Native American drums may induct you into altered states of consciousness and therefore may signify spiritual attunement. A drum may represent the heartbeat of the earth. A set of drums appearing in a dream may remark on the need to develop a rhythm in doing things.

Dryer (M) Putting wet clothes into the dryer may suggest the need to dry out or air out the emotional issues that interfere with your progress. It may represent dry ideas or those that will not take you far.

Dump truck (M) Usually carrying a ton of dirt, a dump truck may warn that someone in your life is about to dump a load of dirt on you. Thus, it may remark on being the target of ridicule. It may also carry away the negativity in your life. (See *Truck*.)

Dust storm (L, M) As an expression of dirty thoughts delivered, a dust storm may come as a response to a shameful experience.

Dying (L, M) Dying in a dream is rarely literal. It usually represents the death of a friendship or marks an important transition in your life. It also represents a natural cycle of creativity, which is necessary to the evolution and growth of the individual. It may be a response to something catastrophic that affected you deeply and that it may be difficult to recover from.

Eagle (L) Soaring above the clouds, for Native Americans the eagle comes to mediate between Great Spirit and the tribe. In an urban culture, the eagle may signify your spiritual connection to God. An eagle appearing in a dream may express the need to look at your life from a heightened perspective in order to get the overview of a situation or a problem you may be facing. Eagle feathers bring spiritual power to the individual who acquires them. (See *Birds*.)

Earrings (M) Earrings symbolize accentuating your hearing and comment about what you are having to listen to or are willing to listen to. Diamond earrings are worn by the woman who possesses radiant qualities and expresses herself clearly. Sapphire earrings are associated with communicating your vision. Dainty earrings may indicate that you are willing to listen only to the soft-spoken word.

Earth (L) Earth itself comes to signify the manifestation or creation of God. Like the womb of the mother, it offers stability and structure and provides the gifts of plenty. It is that which represents the materialization of thought. Earth sustains all life. It is the ground on which all is built, and it is the playground through which life is enjoyed. Earth can represent the physical body. In your dreams it may represent your concerns about the Earth and her resources. The presence of Earth in a dream may mean simply that you may need to get grounded.

East (L) As the direction of the rising sun, the east points to the source of inspiration, the blessing, grace, and the glory through God's communication. It is associated with the mountain, the highest center of spiritual attainment. Moving in an eastward direction in your dream thus signifies questing for your spiritual connection with the God Source and God Self, as well as entering a new-beginning phase of your life. (See *Compass, Four directions*.)

Eating (M) Eating in dreams represents digesting information. It may express concerns about receiving nourishment or being nurtured by others. Eating in dreams may also reflect literal eating habits such as eating too fast, being too picky, or eating too much.

Eclipse (U) Eclipses in dreams come as a sign of energies available for illuminating the shadows within the subconscious. The sun being blocked by the moon in a solar eclipse brings up the issue of subconscious material that may need to be cleansed and insights that may need to be gained through deep self-reflection. When the moon is blocked by the sun in a lunar eclipse, forces that shadow feminine intuition may be signified. An eclipse may appear as a sign that something may be about to disrupt your conscious life for a time.

Eddie Bauer (M) Good-quality casual wear from Eddie Bauer is the signature of the smart, as well as reasonable, individual who does not need a flashy appearance to feel important.

Eel (L) As the snake of the sea, an eel can come to reflect unseen or unconscious emotional forces. Being bitten by an eel in a dream may suggest that you felt attacked by someone without much evidence of a real assault.

Eeyore (L, M) The pessimistic donkey friend of Winnie-the-Pooh may come to comment on your pessimistic and gloomy attitude. His message is to stop looking for dark clouds where there are none.

Eggs (L, M) Eggs represent fertility and may comment on the rewards gathered from your endeavors. The egg is the symbol of birth and regeneration. A broken egg may represent an opportunity that was destroyed before you were able to benefit from it. Associated with Easter, eggs are a symbol of the resurrected Christ. They may signify good luck. A dozen eggs may represent multiplicity.

Egret (L) A white bird that lives with herds of cows and feeds off the parasites on their backs can come in a dream to represent a symbiotic relationship. The egret may warn of someone who is getting emotionally too close for comfort, or announce a relationship that will benefit you. (See *Birds.*)

Eight (M) Eight is the number associated with personal transformation, infinity, movement, wealth, material gain, cycles, and balance.

Elbows (L, M) An elbow points to your flexibility and ability to reach out. A hurt elbow may comment that you have been overly flexible or have extended yourself to others too much. Being elbowed may comment that you need a gentle urging to get moving or on with things.

Electrical outlet (M) Plugging something into an electrical outlet may comment that you need to get plugged into life or that you need an energy boost to move forward. A short in the outlet may represent blocks in your nervous system or feeling burned out from some negative experience.

Elephant (L) Common to the African savanna, the elephant demonstrates a deep connection to family or clan. Elephants can signify the need for tight family or community bonds. They represent the teamwork through which a project can be successfully accomplished. In India the elephant is a sacred animal that has associations with the matriarch or maternal aspect. It can also represent carrying the heavy burdens of others through extreme loyalty.

Eleven (M) Eleven is the number of spiritual expansion, enlightenment, and spiritual mastery. It may also signify turbulence, chaos, and change.

Elm (L) An elm tree represents elegant beauty.

E-mail (M) Beyond receiving a literal message from a friend, e-mail appearing in a dream may point to a message sent through the psychic airwaves. It may indicate that you need to get your message across quickly.

Emerald (L) A valuable gem whose metaphysical properties are heart-healing and radiant heart expression, the emerald also signifies faith and hope.

Engine (M) The engine in your vehicle can represent the power of your heart. A blown engine may signify that a heart has been blown apart, perhaps by love's betrayal. A blown head gasket may signify that anger has ruined an opportunity and that as a result you won't be going anywhere soon without some major and costly repair. Getting an engine tune-up may point to the need to open your heart after a spat. An engine left running may suggest hesitation.

Envelope (M) Receiving a blank envelope in a dream may point to a hidden message or a hidden agenda. It may also comment that you feel enveloped in some purpose or project. It may represent the condition of your skin as a protective covering. A brown envelope may represent a tan.

Eraser (M) An eraser may comment on the need to clear up some mistakes that you made that may take some diligent action to cancel out. As a play on words, it may humorously be telling you to "erase sir," or stop referring to someone's position as a supreme authority.

Eucalyptus (L) The aromatic leaves of the eucalyptus bring protection.

Europe (M) Taking a vacation to Europe in a dream may represent a desire for historical understanding. In business, it may reflect your opportunities with foreign trade.

Evening gown (M) Denoting elegance and formal attire, selecting an evening gown in your dreams may suggest rising to a special occasion, which requires that you cultivate poise, manners, and a stylish presence. It may signify preparation for meeting a man.

Eveready batteries (M) With its mascot, the Eveready Bunny, a pack of this brand name of batteries may remark your stored-up energy as being "ever ready" to be used; it needs only to be applied. The presence of this battery may also suggest that you are all wound up about something.

Evergreens (L) Evergreen trees such as spruce, cedar, and pines signify eternity and immortality. They express everlasting qualities. In your dream, these trees may comment on the longevity of a relationship.

Exercising (M) Exercising may mention the concerns you have about your physical stamina and the need to get in shape. As a metaphor, it may comment that you need to exercise your rights in a difficult situation.

Expressway (M) Suggesting an avenue of self-expression, an expressway is a fast and easy way to the top. An expressway may mention that you need to express your feelings in order to get the results you want.

Eyeglasses (M) Finding a pair of eyeglasses may point to the need to look more closely at a situation before acting. Broken glasses represent impaired vision.

Eye of Horus (L, U) An ancient Egyptian symbol, this stylized eye represents the all-seeing eye. Associated with Horus, the son of Isis and Osiris who was birthed after the death of Osiris, it is the symbol of the resurrected king. Emerging out of the archaeology of the soul, it comes to signify the enlightened view, all things being understood through spiritual sight of an opened third eye penetrating the principles of higher truth.

Eyelashes (L, M) Eyelashes protect the eyes, and curly eyelashes are desirable expressions of beauty. Curling your eyelashes in a dream may comment on your ability to see your own beauty. It may also mention pulling away the veils of your psychic vision. Eyelashes falling out may point to an inability to protect yourself from seeing something disturbing.

Eyes (L, M) Referring to sight, attention to the eyes may reflect the power to see clearly in a situation. They may also represent third sight or psychic abilities. Blue eyes represent clarity and truth; brown eyes, wisdom and depth. Having something in your eye may be a response to having witnessed a painful situation. Closed eyes may remark on your refusal to see something you should face with both eyes open. Being stared at may reveal feelings of insecurity and shame.

Eye shadow (L, M) Putting on eye shadow accentuates the eyes with color. Eye shadow may mention that you would like to be noticed. Specifically, it may suggest that you wish your eyes were more inspiring or noticed more. On a darker note, it may remark on the shadow of unconscious conflicts about your psychic abilities.

Fabric (M) Selecting fabric may represent looking at the fabric of your life—its textures, patterns, and colors—as reflecting different qualities and aspects of life you may enjoy. Fabric may be used in order to construct some new clothing, which may reflect a new attitude or image you want to embrace.

Factory (M) Working in a factory may signify that you are working in a sweatshop. It may express dissatisfaction with your career, or with doing a monotonous job that's getting you nowhere. A factory may also come as a play on words, commenting that you may have to embark on a "fact-finding" mission about some issue or problem.

Falcon (L) A bird of prey that is used to hunt small game, the falcon comes to bring the power you need to seek out or locate opportunities or new prospects. The attributes it brings are keen foresight and aggressive action to search for and seize an opportunity. (See *Birds*.)

Falling (M) Falling in your dream may come as a response to some failure. It may comment on feelings of loss of control. It may also be a response to falling from grace or falling from your stature in life. Falling dreams may recur when you have lost a significant relationship, or have faced a personal disaster in your career, or have been diagnosed with a particular illness.

Farm, agricultural (M) If a farm setting appears in your dream, it may reflect your concerns about sustaining or contributing to community. A farm with a variety of crops may reflect the variety of ideas that are being cultivated all at once. A farm with one crop, such as corn, may represent productivity or fertility.

Farm, horticultural (M) A place for cultivating plants for beautification of a community environment, a horticultural farm may point to community concerns. You may be creating plans that were inspired by a vision for restoration of the culture through the growth of new ideas.

Faucet (M) Hot or cold water running from a faucet may indicate that you are running hot and cold around some decision or situation in life. It may represent a literal need to drink more water. It may also reflect the flow of life force.

Fax machine (M) In a dream, a fax machine may signify that you are receiving a telepathic message sent from someone through subconscious channels. That it is received on paper brings authenticity to the message.

Feather (L, U) Receiving a feather in a dream may signify receiving spiritual power. An eagle feather is used for sacred ceremonies by Native American cultures and thus may signify the need to bring spiritual dimensions into your life through prayer. A turkey feather is the power of giving and receiving. Owl feathers are for healing and denote wisdom. A feather may also be telling you to lighten up and not take things so seriously, or to lighten your load.

Feet (L, M) Feet represent your connection to the earth and are what one stands on. Injuries to your feet such as a wound may signify an old emotional scar that prevents you from feeling grounded. A broken foot may comment that you are unable to stand on your own two feet or to move forward without support from others. The sole of the foot may mention the soul.

Fence (M) Fences represent the need for good boundaries in relationships. A fence that is torn down may signify the tearing down of the boundaries or barriers in a relationship. A wooden fence keeps others out as well as keeping you from being seen. Thus, it may be commenting that you are hiding from others. A chain-link fence may point to someone who is willing to be seen but still maintains a boundary of safety. A stone or brick wall may signify a solid, impenetrable wall between two people.

Fever (L, M) Having a fever in a dream may indicate a physical illness that you are attempting to clear during the dream state. A fever may also suggest the desire for romance, as in "spring fever."

Fig (L) The fig tree symbolizes carnal knowledge and wisdom. Associated with Adam and Eve, it may represent the fall from grace or shame.

File folder (M) Not being able to locate a file may mention your frustration about lack of organization at work or at home. Or it may express fear and apprehension about work performance. A file folder may hint at the nondisclosure of information. It may also point to important information that you may not be ready to deal with or process at the moment.

Fingernail (L) Fingernails are human claws and thus relate to your ability to protect yourself. For a woman, they may remark on her rage. Long fingernails may mention the need to claw through some great obstacle. A broken fingernail may indicate a loss in the ability to protect your work or a creative project.

Fingers (L, M) The fingers on the hand relate to work and service in the world. They may also be used to point out a situation, to blame, or to accuse. Damaged or hurt fingers may point to difficulties and limitations at work. The little finger relates to memory, communication, daintiness, and the intellect. The ring finger, or Venus finger, relates to contracts, marriage, and other bonds in relationships. The middle finger, or Saturn finger, is associated with structure, form, hard work, and responsibility. The index, or forefinger, is associated with Jupiter and is the finger of authority, God, accusation, or judgment.

Fire (L) Fire is a purifying element that is destructive yet transforms everything eventually. Setting fire to your emotions may act as the cleansing agent of the soul. It can represent the passion that fuels the heart and the sacred ember of your sexuality. A fire in your house may relate to some anger that is destroying the peace at home. Fire may also signify destructive behavior on your part or that of another family member.

Fire engine (M) The arrival of a fire engine may signify that there is a fire to put out at home in order to remedy an out-of-control argument or emotional explosion. It may mention that you need help in letting go of anger. It may also appear as a rescue from a friend who could mediate a heated argument. It may point to an emotional emergency that can transform into a spiritual emergence.

Firefly (L) As mystical little bodies of light, fireflies signify your bright ideas that may arrive to light up the darkness of discontent.

Fireplace (M) A hearth or fireplace in a dream represents a place of warmth, comfort, and passion. It may point to the inner fire or sexual energy, which warms the soul and attracts intimacy.

Lighting a fire in the fireplace may signify preparation for romance.

Fish (L) Fish represent wealth and abundance. A fish can represent a business prospect or an opportunity for financial reward. Being served a filet of sole may represent the opening up of the power of the soul and its wisdom. Eating fish may mention that you are enjoying an abundant life. As an ancient symbol, the fish represents the self or the soul in its wholeness.

Fishing (M) Fishing may represent retrieving the wealth within the subconscious. It may mention the need to be still and just wait for business prospects to bite the line. Once they do, you can reel in the rewards. Fishing can reflect a contemplative experience in which you learn the power and serenity of Zen meditative thinking.

Fishing boat (M) A fishing boat may appear to recommend that you go out and drum up some business prospects. There are plenty of fish in the sea if you go out far enough.

Five (L, M) Five is the number of the conscious female and is associated with the attributes of the goddess, those of compassion, peace, clarity, love, and receptivity. As with the five-pointed star, the number five presents the five elements in the cycle of creativity. Thus, the number five may signify creativity itself.

Flamingo (L) One of the most beautiful of aquatic birds, the flamingo reflects grace as well as beauty. As they flock in groups, flamingos bring the message that group energy can offer an emotional quality of love and support. Their pink color reflects love and beauty. In your dream, flamingos may flock together to inspire you to join with others in the celebration of love. (See *Birds*.)

Flashlight (M) Holding a flashlight may suggest that you are ready to bring to light the answers to questions holding you back. A flashlight may represent a search or a quest for spiritual truth. It brings to light what is hidden in the dark spaces of the subconscious and may suggest that you are searching to uncover the clues to a problem that is plaguing you.

Flea (L) These tiny, annoying, blood-sucking creatures may comment that you should look at how you allow others to sap your energy. (See *Insect*.)

Peggy Fleming (M) This gold-medal-winning Olympic figure skater brought precision, style, grace, and elegance to top-level athletic competition. She may arrive in a dream, particularly a woman's because of her experience with breast cancer, to comment on your ability to manage a difficult situation with grace and dignity.

Flood (L) Torrential water stands for emotions that can flood your life and that may require a great deal of cleanup. The location of the flood can be a key. A flood in the kitchen suggests emotions that reside deeply in your heart and that may relate to your family. It may indicate grief or sorrow. A flood in the bedroom signifies emotional issues around the healthy expression of sexuality. If the flood takes place in the living room, it could indicate emotional tensions in social relationships. Flooding in the bathroom suggests overwhelming emotions that are backed up and blocked from being released easily. And, finally, walking in floodwaters could represent a deep desire to experience your emotions more fully.

Floor (M) A floor may represent the foundational beliefs on which you stand. These are the most precious values. They also represent your primary concerns, such as your security. A wood floor may signify your natural beauty. A marble floor represents a beautiful and hard surface that is not penetrated easily; therefore, it may suggest that your ego will not be damaged if many people walk over you.

Flower garden (L, M) A flower garden represents the variety and qualities of beauty that you demonstrate to the world. Its condition may reflect a lot about how you feel about yourself. If strangled by weeds, the garden may suggest that you have negative ideas about your beauty that may prevent others from responding to you in the way you want.

Flowers (L) Blooming, fragrant, and beautiful, flowers in their many varieties come as reflections of feminine beauty. Each may have different attributes and fragrances commenting on the many expressions of a woman's beauty.

Flute (M) A wind instrument often associated with Native American Indians, a flute may remark on a melodious spiritual experience. A flute may appear to uplift the soul. As the instrument of the Pied Piper, it may warn that there is a seduction in the air that may lead you away from yourself.

Fly (L) Buzzing around your head, a fly may appear as a rude reminder to stop negative thinking patterns. A fly on the wall may come to say that much can be learned by observing.

Flying saucer (U, M) A flying saucer is a vehicle that moves through space with little connection to the Earth. Its appearance in a dream can signify a response to a "too-spaced-out" attitude, reminding you to get grounded and real or back into this galaxy with your goals. In that it signifies the arrival of aliens, a flying saucer can represent feelings of alienation from your friends or from the world in general. It may also represent a real encounter of the third kind. UFO dreams can be authentic experiences with alien beings who wish to communicate with you. They demonstrate that the universe has other inhabitants.

Food (M) As that which sustains life, food can represent the areas of concern that maintain your life and make you feel secure with the world. Food may be synonymous with knowledge, as in "food for thought." Carrying a bag of groceries in your dream may reflect your concerns about taking care of your family's needs and your ability to nurture them properly. Eating food may represent nourishing yourself.

Food processor (M) Processing food may suggest the need to process information that is coming in rapidly as the stimulus from the events of the day or from work. It suggests chopping or puréeing ideas into something more digestible and useful.

Football (M) A very aggressive sport in which you can make a goal playing offensively and defensively, football may thus metaphorically reflect an individual who will do anything to win and achieve his or her goals. Viewing a football game in your dream may be a response to some aggressive behavior in your workplace. It may mention the need to get more aggressive in pursuing your goals professionally.

Harrison Ford (L, M) As Indiana Jones, Harrison Ford may make a special appearance in a dream to excavate the treasures in the Lower World. He may point to the pitfalls of seeking wealth over wisdom. He presents the characteristics of a strong-willed individual who is also compassionate and sensitive.

Forest (L) A forest of trees can signify the peril of a dark crossing through which you may have to face your fears and the tribulations of life. As nature's preserve, the forest can represent serenity and the desire to connect with the mysteries and subtle energies of nature.

Forest fire (L) As a destructive event that threatens life itself, a forest fire may represent the destruction of your life. It might criticize you for allowing anger to ruin your prospects for fulfillment. In that there are many trees around, a forest fire may point to destruction that has affected the lives of many. The transforming quality of fire may represent a need for regeneration of your spirit.

Forest path (L) Traveling by foot on a path through the forest may reveal some lions, tigers, and bears to contend with. It suggests a journey into the darkness psychologically for a time, which may really be a heroic path in the end.

Forget-me-nots (L) Forget-me-nots may simply bring the gift of remembering.

Fork (M) Being offered a fork in a dream may represent being given an important tool that will assist you in fulfilling your goals. A fork as an implement may suggest that you need to pierce some idea and grab it before someone else takes credit for it.

Forklift (M) Used for moving heavy containers or boxes, a forklift may signify the need to shift some ideas around in order to solve a problem. It may move things in and out of a warehouse, which would signify needing to clear out what you have stored inside, such as old memories, ideas, or emotions.

Forty-four (L, M) Forty-four is the sum of twenty-two and twenty-two, the number of a spiritual master or teacher. This number can also represent the sacred union or a divine marriage.

Jodie Foster (L, M) Like the goddess Athena, Jodie displays the trait of a strong intellectual capacity. She attests to the fact that a woman may receive a great deal of recognition for her smarts. Her roles as a scientist and teacher command respect. She may appear in a dream to summon a woman into a professional career where she might use her intellect rather than her beauty.

Foster's Beer (M) Brewed in Australia and in an oversized can, Foster's beer may comment on fostering good cheer or on expressing brute strength. It may point to a foster parent or a substitute parent as well.

Foundation (M) The foundation may represent the cornerstone of your thinking and patterns of belief that may have been formed very early in your life. Foundational beliefs may be personal statements you make about yourself such as "I am pretty," or "I am intelligent." They make your foundation solid, but if they are negative they may arrive in a dream as structural instability in a building under construction.

Four (L, M) The number four represents structure and materialization. Like the four directions, it binds the physical world with the spiritual dimensions. The number four may signify earthbound activity or grounded action. It may point to a need for structure in your life.

Four directions (L) Each direction may signify movement toward esoteric knowledge, spiritual light, and personal transformation. By noticing which direction you are facing or moving toward in your dream, you may come to understand more about the direction of your life course. For Native Americans, the four directions bring spiritual power into manifestation on the earth. (See *Compass,* and *East, North, South, West.*)

Fox (L) Sly and intelligent, the fox may appear to summon you to solve a problem intellectually. Fox, with its beautiful red coat, demonstrates the importance of cultivating beauty or instructs you to consider yourself more beautiful or foxy. Fox is a loner and may arrive in a dream to usher in a time of isolation or retreat.

Saint Francis (U) The patron saint of Christianity who spoke to the animals, Saint Francis teaches respect for nature and all of its creatures. He may mention the sacredness of things, which we often take for granted.

Freeway (M) Riding down the freeway may comment that you have chosen an independent or even irresponsible approach to life. Depending on which direction you are heading—north toward one's vision, east toward spiritual attainment, south toward materialism and transformation, or west toward playful expression—you may find the journey a quick route. A crowded freeway may comment on feelings that others are crowding you.

Freezer (M) A freezer may mention frozen feelings of fear. Keeping things frozen represents the preservation of your ideas or resources until you are ready to use them. On the other hand, a freezer in your dream may also point to frigidity.

Fried wonton (M) A Chinese appetizer filled with vegetables and meat, a fried wonton may signify creating a gift or project that is filled with good things, wrapped attractively to entice a customer.

Friend (M) Friends in dreams may appear to reflect aspects of your own personality. They arrive to bring attention to the traits you share that may need to be examined and embraced. They may also come to mention the need or desire for companionship.

Frisbee (M) Playing Frisbee may comment on tossing ideas through the air with a partner, perhaps about a creative project.

Frog (L) Jumping from lily pad to lily pad, frogs demonstrate the ability to let go and to go on to the next opportunity. In that they are amphibious creatures, they may indicate going through a transformation that demonstrates the ability to evolve from relating through emotions to a more grounded and mature approach. Frogs may also signify a need to cleanse the body.

Froot Loops (M) As a brand-name cereal, eating Froot Loops may suggest enjoying a giddy or colorful conversation. It may also comment that you are acting childish or crazy.

Fruit (L) Fruit in general may represent symbolically the fruits of your labor. As sweet nectar it may signify fulfillment and the sweetness of life. A basket of fruit may be presented as a gift of fulfillment of a wish.

Funeral (M) Attending a funeral in your dream may represent the completion of old psychic or spiritual ties with someone. In rare circumstances it may foretell of a death of someone close such as a friend or relative. It may suggest that it is time to say good-bye to someone you love. If the funeral in your dream is your own, it may comment that you have suffered a significant loss from which it may be difficult to recover.

Fungus (L) Fungus grows in dark, moist places, and its appearance in a dream may signal something that has grown and spread within the subconscious, such as negative emotions. It may also point to disease in the body.

Fur coat (M) As a sign of status, wealth, and sophistication, the wearer of a fur coat may portray an elitist attitude. From a shamanic perspective, wearing the skin of an animal signifies the identity of your power animal.

Furniture (M) Furniture in the rooms of your house represents ideas and values you live with that may be moved around or rearranged. Furniture may relate to a style of thinking you have adopted. Whether modern or traditional, furniture may reflect a lot about your personality.

Archangel Gabriel (U) The angelic messenger who announced the birth of Christ, Archangel Gabriel heralds good news.

Gambling (M) Gambling in a dream may signify leaving important decisions to chance rather than using reason. Losing at gambling may represent ill fate. Gambling could also simply mean that life is a gamble.

Gap (M) The clothing chain the Gap is known for the simplicity of solid colors with style. Putting on clothes at the Gap may comment that you are ready to hit the street solid, balanced, and ready. It may also mention that there is a gap in your life or a separation between masculine and feminine aspects of your soul.

Garage (M) The garage is where you store your vehicle. It also represents the opening to the world. It may represent your psychic field, or what is referred to as your aura, extending out. In that things are stored in a garage, it may also represent the place where you have stored the tools that can be used constructively to fine-tune areas of your life.

Garbage truck (M) A garbage truck may arrive at your front door to comment on your tendency to pick up and carry other people's psychic garbage. It may warn you of a stinky mess in your life.

Garden (M) A garden represents self-expression and reflects the level at which your personality is developed. You may have planted new ideas, hopes, and wishes in your garden, which will bloom in the spring for life's fulfillment. A flower garden may represent the myriad variety of personal expressions that can blossom when cared for. A vegetable garden represents your plans for sustaining life, or it can represent your expectations for the future. A walk through your garden suggests that you are in appreciation of what you have created.

Gardening (M) Tending your garden may reveal the stage at which you are fulfilling your plans for the future. It may mention that you are putting a lot of energy into your dreams, or it can reflect that there is still a lot of work to do.

Garden tools (M) Tools for gardening relate to cultivating the areas of your life or your creative projects. They may suggest that it is time to plant seeds for a new beginning or to cultivate your ideas into a project.

Gatorade (M) This brand-name power drink combines the animal power of the alligator and "aide" in its name. Alligator power represents becoming thick-skinned and aggressive. Thus, if you are handed a Gatorade, you may be receiving the message to "get thick-skinned and tough now."

Gecko (L) The gecko lizard with its loud clucking sound comes to affirm with a big "yes" what you are contemplating or pondering.

Gemini (U) The sign of the twins, Gemini evokes the unification of opposites or two aspects of the personality. In a dream, Gemini may announce someone who possesses a strong intellect and good communication skills but who may be indecisive and flighty.

Gems (L) Gems and minerals, as expressions of beauty and radiance, bring a list of attributes to the dreamer when unearthed within a dream. They may appear as a piece of jewelry or in a raw form to bring essential qualities of light and radiance to the individual who receives, finds, or wears them. Many of these specimens from the mineral kingdom bring healing qualities that attune and balance the mind, emotions, and body. Their appearance in a dream represents your direct connection with the Lower World kingdom of minerals. Gems deliver the gift of healing energy and power. (See *Diamond, Emerald, Ruby*.)

Saint George (U) A knight who gave up his fortune to adopt Christianity and gave unselfishly to the poor, Saint George's appearance in a dream may signify the necessity for self-sacrifice in service. As the dragon slayer, he is the liberator from darkness and evil.

Geranium (L) A hardy flower, the geranium signifies the strength of enduring beauty.

Ghost (M, U) A ghost may bring attention to old relationships that are still hanging around in your thoughts or at psychic levels. The eerie appearance of a ghost may point to an actual visitation from the astral plane of a dead relative or a stranger who invades your consciousness at night.

Mel Gibson (L, M) As the character in *Braveheart,* Mel arrives as the spiritual warrior to reclaim his motherland in a fight for glory. In a man's dream, he may represent someone to emulate, a sincere and strong family man. For a woman, he may arrive to conquer the valley of her sexuality.

Giraffe (L) A giraffe, with its long neck, holds the perspective of having its head in the trees or clouds and can signify working toward high ideals. It can come to bring you the direct message to accept a situation by rising above it.

Giving birth (M) Giving birth in a dream represents giving birth to some project or creative endeavor. It may mention a new friendship. It may also signify the birth of a new aspect of the self that brings new qualities and skills to your personality. A difficult birth may represent problems in delivering a product to the marketplace. A premature birth may remark that you are way ahead of yourself and others and, as a result, your ideas may not have been cultivated long enough in order to be realized.

Gladiolas (L) A bunch of gladiolas represents celebration, joy, and happiness.

Glass (M) A full glass may represent taking in a fulfilling experience that has been offered. A half-full glass may remark that you are viewing an experience as not having met your expectations. In that a glass is a fragile container, it may reveal the delicate nature of a situation or of the person holding it. A shattered glass may mention that you feel shattered by a disappointment in life.

Glass-topped table (M) In that glass is transparent, it may comment on seeing through a situation across the table from you, such as whether another's intentions are sincere. It may mention that you can see what really lies underneath the surface. It may also remark on a fragile or delicate conversation.

Gloves (M) Gloves cover and protect the hands and reveal a lot about how you present what you have to offer to the world. Wearing work gloves in your dream may mention that you are working hard or are ready to work. White gloves represent cleanliness and purity. And winter gloves may signify the need for protection or a well-guarded personality.

Glue (M) Used to bind things together, glue may symbolize a bonded relationship. Glue may suggest that you learn how to bond with someone deeply and emotionally. Having glue stuck on your fingers may comment that you have touched a sticky situation it may be difficult to peel yourself away from.

Gnat (L) A tiny fly that lands on sweet fruit, a gnat appearing in a dream perhaps has a positive message to offer. It may suggest that there is a ripe opportunity to land on. A gnat can also represent a small nuisance or a nagging problem.

Gnome (L) An immortal character whose wisdom comes from age may appear in a dream to escort you on an adventure to discover lost continents or a forgotten time within your own history.

Goat (L) Since a young goat is called a kid, a goat may suggest the need for and importance of nurturing the inner child, the aspect of you that is innocent and divine. It could also arrive to represent your own children or the children of others. A mountain goat may come to lead you on a narrow rock path or precipice, demonstrating your power and ability to make a difficult transition or life passage. Mountain goat brings the attribute of surefootedness.

Gold (L) Associated with monetary wealth, gold is the gift of grace bestowed as wealth upon the individual. It is the prize of all heroes. Associated with the male aspect as the manifestation of the sun, the alchemy of gold brings the qualities of intellect, logic, and strength to the individual who wears it. In the form of jewelry such as a ring, it binds relationships symbolically. As a chain around the neck, gold is linked to the respect of wealth. As a bracelet around the wrist, gold signifies wealth acquired through the use of your hands or through your work.

Gold car (M) Driving a gold vehicle delivers masculine expression. It may announce the identity of an individual who will be of great value to you. It signifies wealth.

Golf (M) Golf is a leisure sport in which one plays either nine or eighteen holes. In numerology, nine is the number of completion and an ending cycle. Thus, golf may mention that you are ready to retire from work or from some sense of duty. It may express a desire for a more leisure-filled life.

Good witch (L, U) Glenda, the good witch in the Wizard of Oz, waves her magic wand to remind the dreamer that the power to get home is within. She may come to represent a spiritual guide who protects the heroine on the Yellow Brick Road to enlightenment. She may point to a friend who is compassionate and wise and who can give you some sound advice. The good witch may also represent the higher self.

Goofy (M) This less-than-brilliant character may point to a naïve aspect of your personality that may be making stupid mistakes. He may come as a response to having missed the point of a situation or event in life. He offers comic relief to your stumblings and may inspire the inner comic to emerge from your personality

Grandfather clock (M) A grandfather clock ticking in the hallway may point to traditional patriarchal influences. It may reflect a passage of time. It may also suggest that you look back into your history to discover the paternal legacy and the genetic influences that relate to your relationship with male authority. A grandfather clock in your dream can also mention that you are driven or dominated by patriarchal values, which may be constrictive and outdated.

Hugh Grant (M) "What becomes of the brokenhearted" may be the message of Hugh Grant. He may appear to mirror a dreamer's lack of confidence, offering comic relief for the individual who is confronted with difficult love relationships. For a woman, he may be the lover whose charm is secondary to his sincere intentions.

Grapes (L) Associated with Dionysus, the vine god in Greek mythology, grapes signify the ecstasy and rapture of love. They may also comment that you need to loosen up and celebrate your life more.

Gray (M) Gray represents lifelessness, a drab appearance and dull ideas. It may mention that you are lacking aliveness. A gray business suit may point to someone with traditional and conservative attitudes about business.

Gray hair (L, M) Gray hair signifies the wisdom that comes with age. It may also comment on your fear of getting older or may reveal that you are worrying too much.

Green (L, M, U) Green brings the qualities of healing into a dream. It may also represent nature's harmony. As it is the color of American money, the color green may represent wealth.

Gremlin (L) A mischievous, nocturnal little monster who comes out at night and performs destructive acts, a gremlin can represent a repressed aspect of the personality that is destructive in nature.

Grotto (L, M) A grotto, as a wet, mossy, and lush environment, may be the setting of a mystical dream experience where nature's dark mysteries may be explored. It may contain the primordial powers that relate to your more instinctive nature.

Grout (M) Used to lay ceramic tile, applying grout in a dream may represent the need to cement in some new ideas or fix the pieces of a new design together.

Gucci (M) The woman carrying an Italian-made Gucci bag may be commenting that she is authentic. She may come as a messenger to nudge you to share the wealth and beauty of the authentic self. The Gucci symbol may also represent an aristo-cratic or elitist attitude.

Guitar (M) Learning to play a guitar may point to a desire to learn music or to embrace your creative side for enjoyment. It may comment that you need more rhythm or to get in tune with things and others around you.

Gum (M) Chewing gum may mention that you are thinking seri-ously about a sticky situation in your life. As it is never allowed in school, chewing gum in a dream may point up your rebellious attitude.

Gun (M) As a lethal weapon in the hand of a shadow character, a gun may express the threat of annihilation. As its shape is somewhat like a phallus, a gun may also represent destructive and aggressive male power. A gun that will not go off could point to your feelings of powerlessness in a challenging situation.

Gymnasium (M) A large indoor space where you may play, work out, or be a spectator may help you evaluate your skills and performance in fulfilling your goals. As a spectator, you may have an opportunity to critique your style and abilities. As a player, you reenact and learn from events of your waking life that required a team effort as well as individual skill. (See *Health club*.)

Hail (L, M) A hailstorm may come to comment that your fears are bombarding you. It may point to a situation in which you felt bombarded by others' expectations or by someone who was attempting to make a point.

Hair (L, M) Hair in dreams represents power. Styling your hair may mention that you are refining your personal power. It may also simply express concerns about your appearance and beauty.

Dyeing hair in various colors may express the powerful attitudes you want to display to the world. Red hair may remark on a fiery and passionate expression of power. Purple hair represents spiritual power. Getting a haircut signifies having your personal power taken away and may be a response to a heated argument in which you felt criticized. Hair falling out in a dream may indicate an emotional response to losing power. It may also mean that you are nervous.

Hallway (M) A hallway or corridor in a dream represents a passageway of self-discovery. It may signify a passage through time. If you pass someone in the hallway, it could represent a brief relationship in the future that will be short-lived.

Ham (M) Carving a ham in dreams may represent slicing into a rich and meaty experience such as a feast with friends or enjoying a special occasion with family. It may mention that someone is acting like a ham or being a show-off. As a pig is a symbol of fertility, a ham may represent the feast of fertility.

Hammer (M) As a tool used for construction, a hammer may mention that it is time to hammer on a point or to stress an idea. As a tool used to pull out nails, a hammer may mention the need to reconstruct your plans or ideas.

Hammock (M) As a resting place between two trees, a hammock may comment on the need for leisure time in nature. It may also point to someone you consider to be lazy.

Hands (L, M) Attention to the hands in a dream may comment that help is on the way. The right hand represents giving and the left receiving. A cutoff hand may mention the inability to give or receive, or to work.

Hangers (M) Clothes hangers help to organize clothing in your closet. They may comment on the need to put away some out-moded attitudes. As a play on words, a hanger may represent "Hang her." Thus, it may point to the fear of persecution for your beliefs or special abilities.

Hang gliding (M) Hang gliding may represent trusting the winds of change to glide you safely to your destination in life. Crashing a hang glider may remark on a loss of faith. It may also represent personal freedom.

Tom Hanks (L, M) As the ultimate "nice guy" who wins the heart of his leading lady with his sharp wit and sincerity in romantic comedies such as *Sleepless in Seattle* and *You've Got Mail*, Tom Hanks may arrive in a woman's dream to coax her out of a mind-set of suspicion and mistrust of men's intentions. In *Splash*, where he brings home a mermaid who saves him and attempts to socialize her, he represents the archetype Poseidon, the ruler of the undersea, who creates sea creatures of his liking. Playing this role in a dream, Tom Hanks may symbolize a woman's male side and may indicate that her wisdom and strong feminine intu-ition do have a place in the world. Appearing in a man's dream, Tom Hanks may offer a model for a strong intellect and an equally strong heart in balance.

Hard drive (M) The hard drive in your personal computer is where information is stored. If your hard drive has crashed in your dreams, it may point to a significant loss of information, which may create lasting problems and great emotional pain. If the hard drive is full, it may reflect feelings of being oversaturat-ed by information or processing all you can handle. It may also point to the need to drive hard to pursue a goal.

Harp (M, U) A harp may appear to summon you to the angelic dimensions beyond the veils of illusion of the third dimension.

It may also comment not to harp on a particular subject for too long. It may point to harmonizing with someone.

Hat (M) Hats, in general, represent the attitudes you wear and explain something about the direction of your thinking. A flowered bonnet may comment on old-fashioned feminine values. A Nike sports hat may point to someone who thinks he can do anything with the right attitude. A Nike cap worn over the third eye may suggest that you use your psychic abilities. A sports cap representing your favorite team may indicate a sense of rooting for yourself and those you love.

Hawk (L) As a bird of prey, Hawk comes as a messenger from above to communicate something important. It may soar as a sign that the spiritual dimensions are operating in your life if you pay attention. It may point to the need for some rapid communication in business. (See *Birds*.)

Healing (M) Receiving healing in a dream may comment on the self-healing potential of the dream state. Healing someone else may express your concerns about someone close to you. It may reflect a soul-to-soul connection that places you in the helper role. It may also represent a deep desire to be a healer in a caregiving profession.

Health club (M) As a place to work out, a health club may present you with concerns about your physical health, your personal fitness, or your physical appearance. (See *Gymnasium*.)

Health food store (M) Concerns about your nutrition, weight, and general health may be reflected if your dream takes place in the setting of a health food store. Dreams express the condition of the body, and important messages that recommend conscious change in behavior patterns that are destructive to your health may be conveyed clearly.

Heart (L) The heart is the symbol of love. It may appear as a sign of love's potential within you or coming to you. It may state "Have a heart." A bleeding heart may comment that you are being too sentimental. A broken heart may be a response to the loss of a relationship.

Heart transplant (M) Receiving a heart transplant in a dream may comment simply that you need a new heart or to become more openhearted. It may mention that your love for someone has been renewed or point to a physical healing crisis that has been remedied through the dream state.

Hedge trimmer (M) Since it trims overgrowth, a hedge trimmer may snip at your natural protective barrier or suggest that you need to refine your ideas a bit. It may refine and shape up your physical appearance or what you present in your own front yard as who you are. It may constructively advise that you shape up physically.

Helicopter (M) With its ability to land on a target and hover in the air, a helicopter may represent the need to look at the whole picture before making a decision in life. It is through objectivity that you may land on target. As a mechanical bird, it represents mechanistic ideas or ideals that may be floating around in your mind.

Jimi Hendrix (M, U) Twanging notes on his steel-string electric guitar, Jimi may appear from the spirit world as a messenger testifying to the spiritual power of music. In a budding musician's dream, he may arrive to inspire you to pursue the vocation. Singing "Purple Haze," he may come to alter your consciousness in order to retrieve a spiritual vision. He represents the mystic or prophet.

Hershey's chocolate (M) Unwrapping a Hershey's chocolate bar in a dream may comment that your desire for love is being fulfilled. In that the brand name Hershey's contains both "her" and "she," it may point to the nurturing principle of the feminine as a source of love.

Hershey's Kisses (M) Eating a chocolate kiss in a dream may describe your response to a loving kiss that came from one of your admirers the day before.

Hexagram (L) A figure with six lines commonly associated with the I Ching, an eastern divination tool, the hexagram symbolizes the order of the universe as applied to human consciousness.

Highway (M) Driving down a highway may comment that you have chosen the high road, a path least traveled, or a path of wisdom and spiritual truth. It may represent a well-traveled or well-paved direction in which many can travel. A crowded highway may represent frustration with others who are moving too slowly, such as in making a decision at work.

Hippopotamus (L) A mammal living in water and on land signifies the mediation between the elements of water, your emotions, the earth and your body. It may comment on a big emotional issue that has affected your health. With its huge body, a hippopotamus often comes to represent the undertaking of a big project in which you may have some mud to wade through before you can complete it.

Hispanic (M) Steeped in tradition and the need for extended family relationships, being among a group of Hispanics in a dream may represent being embraced by your extended family. Hispanic figures may also portray strong Catholic religious beliefs. As a play on words it often refers to "his panic."

Hives (L, M) Erupting in hives in a dream may indicate nervousness, fear, or worry.

Hockey (M) Hockey, a game popularized in Europe, uses a stick to slam a puck into a goal net. Hockey in a dream may comment on a competitive battle in your company or business that might prove dangerous. Playing hockey may also represent an aggressive team that can get the job done.

Hollywood (M) As the land of the stars, a dream whose setting is in Hollywood may comment on your desire for fame and recognition. It may mention that you are thinking about your image and self-concept. It may reflect your interests in the media and in living a more artistic expression of yourself.

Home (M) Your home may contain the concerns about family affairs. Since "home is where the heart is," being in your home in a dream reflects a sense of security and comfort. Wandering through the rooms of the home where you grew up may signify the need to explore the patterns of belief that influenced your personality in order to heal old wounds.

- **First floor** (M) The first floor of your home as a setting in your dream may reflect primary concerns that are essential to your happiness: your family, your social relationships, your safety. If the first floor is a mess, there may be a messy situation within your family that is troubling you. If you are remodeling the first floor, this may reflect changes you are making in your attitude and behavior toward family and friends. In terms of your physical body, the first floor may reflect a concern for your overall physical well-being.

- **Second floor** (M) Often the bedrooms are on the second floor of a home, and the appearance of a bedroom may reflect your concerns about intimate relationships and sexual fulfillment. Finding yourself on the second floor of someone else's house may suggest that you are snooping into his or her personal business.

Hometown (M) Wandering around your old hometown in your dream may suggest that you are still living with your past. It may suggest that you are confronting the emotions, patterns of belief, and attitudes of childhood. Whether living in your hometown was a pleasant or unpleasant experience, this setting will give you a historical review of your early days.

Anthony Hopkins (L, M) A humble and distinguished character actor, Anthony Hopkins has achieved fame and recognition in numerous roles. He may offer the message that you may need to become more humble and honorable. As Hannibal the cannibal, in *Silence of the Lambs* and *Hannibal,* this strong character actor may come as the archetype of the Devil to demonstrate the force of evil in your life.

Horse (L) A horse may offer its power to the dreamer as a vehicle for moving forward in life. Horse brings the attribute of strength to deliver you to your destination. For the hero, the horse carries him to his mission, perhaps over long distances, and thus it may signify the need to travel. A wild horse can represent unleashed and untamed power. Horses may also trot into your dream to indicate the need to stand your ground in a power struggle.

Horseradish (M) Horseradish is made into a condiment that has a pungent taste. It may point to a poignant statement that was made in an important conversation. It may mention that you have made too strong a statement.

Hospital (M) Entering a hospital may represent concerns about your health and even suggest that you need to recover from a serious illness. It may bring attention to the powers of the sub-conscious to heal and bring balance back into the body. It may also signify the need to surrender to being cared for.

House (M) With their many unique features, floor plans, and structural designs, houses represent the complexity of the soul and the boundaries of the personality. Living in a Victorian house in a dream may signify living with outdated beliefs, perhaps about sexuality. Living in a Spanish-style hacienda may reflect a need for extended family.

House frame (M) A house under construction may suggest the construction of a project that has been framed in your mind but has not yet been completed. It may represent the ideas that have been put together as the basic structure of what has been created.

Houses next door (M) Anything that is next to us represents something close to the boundaries of our consciousness. For instance, if you live next to a mansion in a dream it might suggest that you already possess the resources to elevate your status and personal value. You just have to realize it.

Huggies (M) Delivering a box of Huggies disposable diapers may voice the need to embrace a friend or to give a hug. It may also announce a pregnancy or indicate that someone is acting like a baby.

Hunchback (L) A character who has a hunched back may comment on the burdens you carry. A hunched back may suggest that you may have piled too many of other people's problems on your shoulders.

Hunting (M) Hunting wild game can point to the need to hunt down prospects for your business. However, hunting down your animal power may be a negative response to giving up your supernatural or mystical powers. For woman, hunting in a dream may represent that she is husband hunting.

Hunt's tomatoes (M) A can of Hunt's tomatoes may warn you of someone who is on the lookout for a sexy girl and therefore may caution that there is a womanizer in your life.

Hurricane (L, M) A storm of high velocity that can create a great deal of destruction, a hurricane in a dream is often a response to an extreme emotional situation or trauma in your life, which can leave you with a great deal of emotional debris to cope with. It may reflect extreme moodiness.

Hyena (L) With its insidious laugh, the hyena makes light of mistakes in life, teaching you to give up self-torment. Hyenas in dreams can also point to destructive behaviors that are a disgrace to your integrity.

Hyundai (M) The message to the dreamer who is riding in a Hyundai automobile may simply state "High you and I." Thus it may relate to the performance of a partnership or marriage as moving forward in life together.

Ice (L) Frozen sheets of ice metaphorically comment on frozen conditions, which create hazardous areas to move across. Ice can also represent frozen feelings that may need thawing out. Moving on an icy road can thus represent moving through a fearful experience in life in which you might lose control easily. Skating on ice can represent overcoming fears gracefully or performing some risky business.

Ice cream (M) Eating ice cream may comment that you could be suppressing emotions or the need to scream. It may reflect the fulfillment of a childhood or childish wish. It may comment on a refreshing and nurturing experience.

Ice cube (M) A melting piece of ice may point to the melting away of your fears. An ice cube may also mention emotional coldness as in a hard-hearted individual.

Ignition (M) The ignition of a vehicle turns on the engine and thus may reflect your ability to get moving toward your goals. An ignition that fails to start your car may mention difficulties in getting something going.

Impatiens (L) An annual flowering plant, impatiens may point to your "impatience" with waiting for the right moment, for someone else, or for the arrival of some news.

Imperial margarine (M) Imperial margarine spread on a piece of toast may suggest that you are being honored. It may remark on being treated well, like royalty. It may also signify a cheap imitation.

Indian (M, U) A Native American as a character may appear as a guide to living a more spiritually connected life. An Indian may come to bring spiritual truth or teach you the ways of a warrior.

Infinity (U) The symbol of infinity, also know as the lemniscate, which looks like the numeral "8" placed on its side, signifies the eternal cycle of time. Its appearance may help you understand time's illusion and the never-ending story of existence.

Insect (L) In general, bugs in dreams can represent things in life that are annoying or bugging you. But insects may, in addition, come with a specific and important message. A fly, for instance, may comment on negative thinking. And a gnat may mention that the fruits of your labors are ripe for the marketplace.

Intel Inside (M) The computer-processing chip that processes information at a rapid rate may refer to your innate intelligence. It may instruct you to go inside to find the answers. As its power is described in megahertz, it thus may point to the need to process the "big hurts" of your life.

Interior design (M) Remodeling your home in a dream may point to deep psychological work and attitude changes that are in progress. Thus, interior design work represents planning by bringing in new ideas about yourself that may change your self-concept.

Internet (M) Surfing the Internet may express concerns about international business ventures, which depend on linking and thinking globally. It may be a metaphor for an expanded perspective of human consciousness, which sees the universe and every soul as being linked soul to soul, light to light. Surfing the Internet in a dream may represent exploring new technological information or something as simple as shopping from home.

Intoxication (M) An intoxicated or inebriated character in a dream may represent an aspect of your own personality that's in the process of making a spectacle of you. Constructively, it may remark that you are too loose and need to mind your manners.

Intrepid (M) A Dodge Intrepid may be driven by someone who lives fearlessly and with fortitude, and who is able to endure great difficulties and still persevere.

Intrigue (M) A Plymouth Intrigue behind you in a dream may suggest that an individual with secret motives may be tailing you.

Iron (L) Denoting strength and weight, iron may appear as a symbol eliciting the development of an iron will. It denotes strength and an impenetrable force.

Island (M) Being on an island may point to your feelings of isolation or loneliness. It may signify the need to be rescued by someone who cares. An island in a dream may also represent the return to paradise or the primordial garden of innocence.

Israel (M) As a play on words, a dream set in Israel may be telling you that it "is real." A pilgrimage to Israel may reflect your desire for spiritual salvation. As a place where conflict rages between Jews and Palestinians, Israel may also point to a place of spiritual conflict within an individual.

Isuzu (M) This vehicle may arrive at your front door as a warning that someone intends to sue you, perhaps for crossing him or her on the road of life.

Ivory (L) Ivory, as in the rich white tusk of an elephant, represents purity, beauty, and wisdom. Wearing real ivory may evoke protective energies.

Jack (M) Jacking up your car may mention the need to get underneath to see what is wrong with your vehicle or physical body. Thus, it may suggest that you look into the subconscious to discover hidden health issues. As it is used as a tool for changing a tire, a tire jack comments on addressing the emotional issues that have flattened you.

Jack-in-the-box (L, M) Discovering or playing with a toy jack-in-the-box may indicate some startling news or a surprise that delighted you.

Jack in the Box (M) The animated jack-in-the-box character that has popped out of this box sends a powerful sales pitch to fast-food consumers: "Get it fast and fresh from the grill." As the setting of a dream, however, driving through a Jack in the Box may metaphorically comment that you might soon get an unexpected scary surprise popping out at you at the most unexpected time. It may frighten you or make you laugh. It may also indicate that you feel rushed and unnurtured.

Jack-o'-lantern (M) Carving pumpkins at Halloween began as a Celtic tradition on All Souls' Day to ward off evil spirits. The appearance of a jack-o'-lantern in a dream may suggest a need to scare away those ghostly past relationships that are still haunting you. It may symbolize the need for protecting your harvest from evil influences that could steal your prosperity, or it may welcome little visitors who want a treat.

Jacks (M) Playing jacks may be a sign that life is a game in which you are tested as to how much you can pick up at one time. Jacks in a dream may represent greediness. They may also represent new knowledge, ideas, or the thoughts of others that need to be gathered. As a game played mostly by little girls, a game of jacks may remark on female competition.

Jesse Jackson (M) As an American civil rights leader, Jesse's appearance in a dream may point out that you may feel that you have lost personal freedom. He may appear as a guide to help you rise out of oppression and suffering or to fight for equality in some situation in which you felt discriminated against. An eloquent speaker, Jesse may offer some pragmatic advice.

Mick Jagger (M) The renegade extremist lead singer of the Rolling Stones, Mick may represent a shocking and provocative character seeking recognition. He may comment on your antisocial behavior. He may come to deliver the message that to be wild is to be wonderful.

Jaguar (L) Jaguar wanders through the jungles of South America and is sacred shamanic medicine to indigenous shamans of these areas. In a dream, a jaguar comes to initiate and refine psychic power, such as your clairvoyance. Its power offers the initiate the ability to see into the distant past and the present, as well as the future.

Jail (M) Being in jail in your dreams may comment on your lack of personal freedom. It may also come as a response to guilt feelings.

Japanese (M) A Japanese figure in a dream, if male, may comment on performing or parroting business practices based on capitalistic values and free enterprise. If the figure is a woman, she may present a stereotypical image of a woman who is devoted to her husband and serves him quietly with poise.

Jawbreaker (M) Sucking on a jawbreaker may comment that what you have put in your mouth is sweet but too hard to swallow; it may point to a situation that is tempting but too much for you to handle. The name jawbreaker implies breaking the jaw. The jaw represents structure and foundational beliefs.

Jeans (M) Wearing a pair of tight jeans in a dream may suggest that there is something in the genes that feels too restrictive. Your genetic imprints may express deeply seeded attitudes that drive your personality. Jeans may also represent a rugged attitude.

Jeep Cherokee (M) A Grand Cherokee is an off-road vehicle, which may point to the identity of someone who enjoys the great outdoors. The Cherokee Indians, for whom this vehicle is named, may point to someone who is driven by a heritage that is connected to nature, tribe, and community. Thus, pursuing a Grand Cherokee may refer to pursuing Native American spirituality as a path.

Jesus (U) The dreamer who has an encounter with Jesus has been touched by the Son of God and a great teacher. Jesus may call you to express unconditional love and Christ-like qualities. He may come to renew your commitment to Christianity. As the simple carpenter, he may remind you that anyone may enter the Kingdom of God and that the meek will inherit the earth. He may come to release you from the burdens and suffering of the world by offering his salvation.

Jewelry (M) Jewelry accentuates your appearance and, depending on where it is worn, may reveal a great deal about your wealth and radiant qualities. It may be a symbol of beauty and of protection. (See *Gems*.)

Jewelry store (M) Entering a jewelry store in a dream may reflect concerns about expressing your radiant qualities and self-worth. Shopping for fine jewels may comment on your readiness to embrace your true value.

Joan of Arc (U) Sainted for having liberated France, Joan may appear as a martyr who sacrificed herself for her spiritual beliefs. She may appear to the woman who needs to develop valor and courage to face fire, if necessary, to preserve her spiritual freedom. In that she was burned at the stake, Joan of Arc may also come to assist you to relinquish martyrdom in favor of spiritual liberation.

Saint John the Baptist (U) The arrival of John the Baptist from the Upper World might award you with spiritual salvation through baptism. He may bring cleansing from original sin. And he may signify the return to innocence and purity.

Magic Johnson (M) As a basketball All-Star, Magic may come to announce the magic of success that is attained by playing the game of life by the rules. He may point out that by developing your true skills, you may look like a magician to others who may want to emulate you. He may also comment on the power that magic plays in slam-dunking the opportunities of life.

Michael Jordan (M) As the warrior who uses no weapon, Michael may appear in a dream to signify the need to win. He may bring the message "Just do it" to end your procrastination. He emanates a charismatic style of relating and is truly a tall man. He may represent a humanitarian who promotes the wholeness of children.

Journal (M) Writing down your secrets and personal process in a journal in a dream may demonstrate a need to explore your personal life and feelings. If someone has read your journal, it may signify that personal information about you has been exposed, and it may comment on your feelings of betrayal.

Judge (M) A judge may represent the critical and judging aspect of your personality. He may comment that you are passing judgment on others or on yourself. He may come to settle a dispute and to demonstrate fairness.

Juice (M) Drinking juice may comment that you are getting "juiced up" about something. It may simply represent good energy. Tomato juice represents savoring the energy of a beautiful woman. Drinking papaya juice may represent having a rich experience that leaves you feeling like you are in paradise.

Juicer (M) As an appliance, a juicer may mention that you may need to liven things up a bit or to produce more energy and enthusiasm to achieve your goals. It may also suggest that you have had the life squeezed out of you.

Jungle (M) As a thick tropical forest, a jungle may signify density and mystery that you must penetrate in order to liberate yourself finally from an overgrowth of influences in your life. It may represent a wild environment with prowling animals or threats at every turn.

Jupiter (U) Expansion of the spiritual side of life is the message of Jupiter, the planet of spiritual attainment and rewards. Jupiter's influence brings about potent energy within a dream that may catalyze spiritual growth. It offers liberation from the limitations of life and announces a time when any idea may come into manifestation. It is a sign of financial good fortune.

Kangaroo (L) Native to Australia, this marsupial's appearance in a dream can represent the mothering aspect when carrying its baby in a pouch. It can represent the need to incubate an idea or project for a long period of time. The leaping movement of a kangaroo comes to signify springing forward with an idea or making a leap of faith.

Keys (M) A set of keys represents the way to open a door of opportunity. They may point to the keys of knowledge or the tools of your trade. Losing your keys may suggest that you have lost the main idea in the solution to a problem.

Nicole Kidman (L, M) Whether a courtesan or a witch, Nicole may arrive as a sharp, brassy woman who will do anything to get her way. Demonstrating wit as well as charm, she may arrive to represent a woman who has won the love of her leading man just by being herself.

Kiss (M) Receiving a kiss from an admirer may indicate your desire for intimacy and love from someone special. A kiss may also represent a special blessing.

Kitchen (M) As the place where food is prepared, a kitchen may house your feelings about nurturing or mothering your family. It also may signify the heart chakra, from which you express love.

Being in the kitchen when the light dims or goes out may comment that you have let a light in your heart go out.

Kite (M) Flying a kite may mention an uplifting thought or idea that others may notice as remarkable. It may suggest an idea that will take flight in the future. Or it may remark, "Go fly a kite," as in "Get lost."

Knee (L) Knees represent flexibility in moving forward. A knee injury may mention that you may have been moving too quickly or not quickly enough to fulfill a desire. Being on your knees may represent bowing down to some outer authority. Walking on your knees may humorously state that you are acting like a coward. To kneel down may also signify the act of giving honor.

Knife (M) Used to cut, slice, chop, or stab, a knife may represent a tool for cutting away or disconnecting from negative influences. It may also represent a weapon, which may pose a threat. It may comment that you feel wounded. The shadow villain who appears with a knife in a dream may direct you to explore some early betrayal that threatened your emotional well-being.

Knot (M) A knotted rope represents a bond or tie that is lasting. To tie the knot comments on the commitment in marriage. A knot may also represent an entanglement that is difficult to get out of.

Koala (L) This little animal comes to bring the qualities of gentleness, innocence, love, and wisdom. It lives high in the branches of eucalyptus trees and is nocturnal, making mention of its mystical qualities. It brings the message of living high and feeling protected and may point the need to hide out and rest for a while.

Kool-Aid (M) The sugary-sweet drink, a favorite of children, may represent the desire for the sweetness of life. It may also comment that you need some good help from someone. The presence of Kool-Aid in a dream may be a response to a sickeningly sweet situation in which you felt oversaturated by someone's charm.

Lace (M) Lace is a symbol of a delicate and beautiful manner. It denotes femininity and politeness. Laying a lace tablecloth on the table comments on preparation for some old-fashioned nurturing by a female companion.

Ladder (M, U) The tool for ascending into the Upper World, the ladder is a symbol of the spiritual bridge between heaven and earth. Each rung represents acts of goodness or spiritual truths that one must master in order to ascend into the light. The ladder may also represent the ladder to success and your financial goals.

Ladybug (L) A fiery red insect, the ladybug may be a sign of a woman's own rage, which can gnaw away at or destroy opportunities of growth. It may fly in to ask the question, "What is bugging the lady?" As it eats aphids, it offers protection to your beauty.

Lake (L) A place that offers serenity, a lake represents smooth sailing and may be a sign that you need to embrace experiences that include withdrawing from the rat race. A lake may appear in a dream to summon you to take time for rest, for recreation, or to contemplate and reflect upon life's meaning.

Lamp (M) A lamp brings light into a room and thus points to the illumination of concepts or ideas or anything hidden. In the bedroom, it may illuminate issues about intimacy. In the kitchen, it may light up your heart.

Lane (M) Commenting that you may need to change lanes or change your mind or thinking from right to left or left to right, a lane represents one-sided thinking. The right lane represents masculine ideas and attitudes, and a left lane represents more feminine values, such as intuition and sensitivity.

Lapis (L) Called the philosopher's stone, deep blue lapis enables you to communicate your depth and wisdom and esoteric knowledge. Presented in a dream, lapis may signify your readiness to deliver your wisdom through writing or public speaking.

Laundry basket (M) The container for carrying laundered clothes may express your readiness to bring out new attitudes proudly. A laundry basket may also carry those negative attitudes to the washing machine to be cleansed.

Laundry detergent, Cheer (M) This laundry detergent may present a simple message urging you to clean up a bad attitude and put on a more cheerful face. It may also represent some good cheer about to arrive in the form of a celebration.

Laundry room (M) Entering the laundry room in a dream may signify the need to examine the attitudes and core beliefs about your self-image. You may be ready to launder the old beliefs in your life.

Lawn (M) Grass in your front or backyard may represent the exterior carpet that you lay out to welcome others and thus reflects your presentation to the world. If it is overgrown with weeds, a lawn in a dream may comment on a negativity that may repel others. A lawn may represent the energy field that extends out from the body known as the aura.

Lawn chair (M) Moving a lawn chair may signify working with an idea or concept that will give one more leisure time in the end. It can remedy frustration around not getting enough rest.

Lawn mower (M) Since it's used to cut your lawn, a lawn mower may appear in a dream as a tool for manicuring your exterior presentation or the image you project to the world. It may comment on cleaning up your appearance in order to make a good presentation to the public. It may be time to trim away an overgrowth of problems in your life.

Lawyer (M) Consulting with a lawyer in dreams may comment on the state of your legal affairs. He or she may point to the need for sound legal advice. Or the lawyer may represent the defending aspect of the personality and thus may point to your defensiveness.

Lay's potato chips (M) In that it is difficult to lay down a bag of Lay's potato chips, the appearance of these chips in a dream may point to your overindulgence in fatty foods or to any other overindulgent behavior.

Lead (L) This heavy metal can come to suggest that you have become lead-footed, commenting on your tendency to procrastinate. It may signify carrying a heavy burden. Lead may also suggest that you have been poisoned by another's influence or that you have poisoned your own mind by pressuring yourself too much.

Leash (M) Holding a leash may suggest that you are restraining someone from exercising his or her personal freedom. It may represent the restraint of your own behavior in public.

Leaves (L) Green leaves reveal the opportunity for new life and growth whether it is in work, family relationships, or play. Fallen leaves can represent lost opportunities, missed chances, a loss in life, or the falling away of something emotional from the past. Burning leaves can represent transformation of life's opportunities.

Lei (M) A lei, the Hawaiian gift of aloha, is a blessing of love, a welcoming, and an embrace. It may point to being given a gift of little monetary value but of great acknowledgment.

Lemon (M) Sucking on a lemon in a dream may represent that an opportunity has gone sour. A lemon may also comment on something of inferior quality, as in having been sold a lemon.

Lemonade (M) Drinking lemonade may point to receiving a remedy for failure. Encountering children selling lemonade on the street in a dream may express the need for innocence and playfulness in turning your failures to success.

Leo (U) "Being the best that one can be" is the message of the constellation of the lion. Leo summons you to embrace yourself by demonstrating great pride and self-esteem. It may provide lessons that test your willingness to go after what you desire and deserve.

Leopard (L, M) A leopard showing its spots arrives with the message that it is time to come out of disguise and show off your abilities. A leopard in a dream may also signify the disclosure of some hidden information about someone else. As a shamanic medicine, Leopard delivers the ability to heal a serious physical illness through its magical shamanic powers.

Lettuce (M) Eating leafy lettuce may indicate that you are enjoying your money. In a salad, lettuce may suggest pooling your money with several others in order to produce a product. It may also signify the mix of healthy ingredients in your life.

Carl Lewis (M) This Olympic track and field athlete won the gold medal for a record broad jump and again in the hundred-meters in Barcelona in 1988. His appearance in your dream may signal your ability to run the distance to achieve your purpose.

He was, however, disqualified for taking steroids in a later track and field event, so he may also enter a dream to warn you away from cheating to achieve your goals.

Libra (U) A sign of balance and harmony, Libra may call you to embrace equality in your relationships or inspire harmony. It may signal you that lessons about justice are on the horizon. Libra is also the sign of partnership and marriage.

Light (U) Light in a dream may be a sign of a transcendent experience of a divine origin. It may bring spiritual clarity, clear vision, and lucidity to the dream. Being touched by the light may bring about a deep emotional cleansing, a spiritual opening, and even a physical healing.

Lightbulb (M) A lightbulb may appear in a dream as an outstanding symbol for an important idea. A burned-out lightbulb may represent a forgotten idea or feeling creatively blocked.

Lightning (U) Lightning may represent God's power piercing the earth. It may signify an awakening to God's power. In Christian symbolism, lightning may signify God's wrath coming down from the heavens. It may also represent the power of the light spearing the earth, manifesting spirit into matter.

Lilac (L) The fragrant lilac stimulates intuition and dreams.

Lily (L) Lilies represent virginity and resurrection. The cala lily is the symbol of naked innocence.

Limousine (M) A limousine may announce the arrival of a VIP. If you are entering a limousine in your dream, this may comment on your value and point to elevation of your status in the world.

Lincoln Continental (M) A symbol of status in the 1950s, a Lincoln may indicate achievement through honesty and integrity.

It may also be the mark of an older, loyal, honest, and trustworthy individual.

Linen closet (M) Sorting linens in a linen closet may represent managing money. It may present your concerns about comfort and attaining an elegant lifestyle. Thus, the linen closet may represent a place where the good things of life are stored. Or it may point to where we store our purest intentions.

Lion (L) A lion carries self-esteem, self-love, and pride. With its loud roar it vocalizes significance demanding honor. As the king or world redeemer, the lion denotes bravery, courage, and social responsibility. In its contrary aspect, it can come to warn against egocentrism, an inflated sense of pride, or self-aggrandizement.

The Lion King (L, M) Simba, the Disney mythical hero, has emerged as a modern popular archetype of a king who must transform the painful loss of his father into a heroic journey. In a dream, Simba can come to demonstrate the need to mature and embrace the positive aspects of your own father in order to battle and overcome temptation or corruption. *The Lion King* represents the return of a true king to power so that balance in the world can be restored. He may suggest that you are wishing or seeking to use your strength to pursue something for the good of all.

Lips (L, M) Lips signify passionate and sensual expression. In a man's dream, full lips may announce a seductive woman. Thin lips may point to an individual who is tight-lipped and lacks passion.

Lipstick (M) Putting on lipstick may point to concerns about your beauty. It may also suggest that you are ready for a kiss or are willing to speak passionately.

The Little Mermaid (L, M) As an adolescent mermaid who gives up her voice to the sea witch, the appearance of the Little Mermaid in a waking or night dream may suggest the need to conquer subconscious patterns that prevent the expression of feminine wisdom. She may indicate to the female dreamer that it is time to grow legs and go out into the world equipped with her vision.

Living room (M) The living room in a house is where you entertain and interact with friends and family. Therefore, a dream taking place in the living room may reveal your attitudes about close social relationships.

Lizard (L) The appearance of a lizard delivers the ability to see many dimensions at once. The view of life as a dream is one that the lizard carries to the individual who needs to expand his or her thinking regarding the greater meaning of life. As the lizard is sometimes difficult to see, it reflects unseen dimensions of the world. A chameleon, for instance, can represent maintaining a level of invisibility or may comment on being in camouflage. Its appearance can also be a response to not noticing the obvious. As a prehistoric reptile, a lizard may come to mention the need to explore your prerecorded history in order to greater understand your present attitudes and beliefs.

Loading dock (M) Arriving at a loading dock in a dream may represent needing to retrieve the fruits of your labors or the cash from a large sale. It might also represent needing to unload some heavy burden from your shoulders. A loading dock may deliver the goods on someone you mistrust.

Loch Ness Monster (L) The Loch Ness Monster, a legendary creature who lives deep within a mystical lake, might appear as a hidden talent you may feel insecure about using. The monster may represent a talent or idea you believe others will invalidate or that will not be understood.

Lock (M) A lock secures a door and thus may represent your concerns about safety and security. A door that won't lock may indicate that you are too open and that you may feel frustrated about keeping others out of your space. A combination lock may point to secret knowledge that unlocks a special door to power and understanding.

Logs (M) Logs stacked next to the fireplace may represent the fuel for sexual satisfaction; they represent desire. They are a symbol of Yuletide cheer and any experience that warms the soul and heart.

London (M) With its historical associations, arriving in London may signify a port of history where you might explore the art, culture, and traditions of a patriarchal society. Representing living among the royalty, London may signify embracing your sovereign power. As the port of entry into European commerce, it may signify concerns with the European trade market in your own business.

Los Angeles (M) Driven by the entertainment industry of Hollywood, the City of Angels may be the setting for your desire to express your uniqueness. It may reflect concerns about your self-image, or it may point to the desire for a more casual and colorful lifestyle. Known for its crowded freeways, a dream set in L.A. may express the pitfalls in choosing the life you desire. It may also mention that you are living among angels.

Losing one's car (M) Not being able to find your car may represent losing your connection to your body, reflecting that you frequently may be too spaced out and ungrounded. Not having a car in a dream may prevent you from finding your way home to wholeness.

Lost (M) Being lost in your dreams may signify that you have lost your true purpose in life. It may point to soul loss or your disassociation from an important aspect of your personality. If the theme of being lost recurs, it may point to a need to seek guidance spiritually or psychologically.

Lotus (L) The lotus is the highest-vibrating flower essence. It signifies enlightenment through love.

Louvered doors (M) Louvered doors allow the air to circulate. They close out your vision but not other senses. Louvered doors in a dream may represent the ability to sense an opportunity without seeing it, or hearing something you should not have heard. They may mention your frustration around a lack of privacy.

Love seat (M) A love seat in a room represents a cozy place for two. A love seat is a comfortable seat for intimate sharing and conversation. It may also express a desire for intimacy or compensate for loneliness.

Lynx (L) A mysterious cat that is rarely seen may come to help you find something hidden from view or that has been kept secret. It must be uncovered to ensure your psychological health and well-being. A lynx can also come to say that you have been protecting a secret too long.

Lysol cleaner (M) With its fresh pine scent, Lysol may comment on the need to clean the house of the soul. Pine brings everlasting life. It may mention that you are trying to cover up a bad odor caused by your negative thinking.

Madonna (L, M) As the sexy "material girl," the recording star Madonna emerges as the sensual and beautiful Aphrodite who wins the prize of the golden apple in the competition among the other goddesses on Mount Olympus. She may appear in a dream as a goddess expressing her sexuality and divine beauty. Her performance in a dream may coax you into vocalizing a confident tone and beautiful presence.

Magenta (L, M, U) Vibrant and deeply pink, magenta expresses the qualities of love and sensuality combined.

Magic wand (M) A magic wand may be offered as a magical solution to a problem. It may mention the need to use your creative power to bring a miracle into your life.

Magnet (M) A magnet in a dream may suggest that you begin magnetizing the right opportunity or relationship. It may represent a sexual attraction. A magnet might describe a character who is successful in magnetizing good fortune.

Makeup (M) Applying makeup in your dreams may comment that it is time to "make up" with a friend or partner after an argument. It may also express a woman's concerns about looking beautiful. (See *Blush*.)

Mandala (L) A mandala is an intricate design made up of intertwining elements in a pattern that brings together spiritual forces of energy. In a dream, a mandala represents unification. Sometimes displayed as pictorial representations that weave a story of creation or that represent the phases of life in a scheme of transcendence, a mandala represents the evolution of ideas.

Mango (L, M) A luscious exotic fruit, a mango may be served as a representation of sexual enticement. As a play on words, it may signify "man go," as in "Get going" or "The man is going."

Mansion (M) Moving into a mansion may signify that you may have obtained a great deal of wealth and are moving up in status. A mansion may also represent an individual with an old soul who has incorporated many lifetimes of knowledge into this life.

Marigold (L) The marigold represents the divine Mother's wealth bestowed on the dreamer.

Marketplace (M) A marketplace is where you might shop for the items you need or desire and may represent your concerns about getting a bargain. In a dream, the marketplace may also reflect your beliefs about prosperity and whether what you produce will have a market. It may mention that you are selling yourself short or that you feel you are treated as a commodity.

Bob Marley (M, U) The King of Reggae whose early death from brain cancer robbed the world of an extraordinary political voice and prophet, Bob may reappear from the spirit world to tell you to "stand up for your rights."

Marriage (M) Getting married in a dream may represent the sacred marriage between the male, the logical and expressive aspect, and female, the intuitive aspect of your soul. The state of being married may comment on a creative project that fulfilled some longtime wish or desire. Dreaming about marriage may also symbolize your readiness for matrimony.

Mars (U) Made of fire and gas, Mars is the passionate flame bearer that may signal a time for aggressive action. It is characterized by masculine ideas and ideals. It carries a great deal of new vital energy for accomplishing your goals. The appearance of Mars in the dream of a woman may signal a new male influence in a partnership or a romantic relationship.

Mars bar (M) As chocolate signifies love and sensual pleasure, a

Mars bar may announce a powerful and assertive yet loving man in your midst.

Mascara (M) Smearing your mascara may be a response to having been smeared by some gossip. Since mascara enhances and brings attention to the eyes, it may comment on a woman's beauty.

Matches (M) Striking a match in a dream may comment on the suitability of a new relationship. It may state that the person is a perfect "match." In that when struck they light a fire, matches may mention that you are feeling passionate. Or they may comment that it is time to light a fire under yourself and get motivated.

McDonald's (M) As a fast-food chain with a high appeal for children, McDonald's may symbolize the need to feed and entertain the inner child. As McDonald's food tastes good but may not necessarily be good for your health, it may point to overindulgent behavior as well as a fast-paced lifestyle, both of which may threaten your health. McDonald's golden arches signify the gateway to temptation rather than to wealth.

Meadow (L, M) A meadow, with its lush green grass, may point to opening emotionally. It may represent an expanded peaceful space, which may promote inner healing. To romp through a meadow may point to liberation from the pain of a difficult passage.

Meat (M) Cutting into a piece of meat in a dream may comment that you are cutting into the meat of the matter or the situation at hand. Thus, meat signifies content that is rich in meaning and has substance.

Mechanical objects (M) Mechanical objects may represent mechanical or robotic thinking. A mechanical failure may mention that your thinking is faulty and dysfunctional. It may point to a difficult or complex problem that needs to be manipulated by your mind.

Megaphone (M) A megaphone mentions that it is time to speak up and broadcast your feelings so that they can be heard. It may also point to an announcement from your higher self.

Mercedes (M) A finely crafted German vehicle, its status may point to wealth and real, long-lasting value.

Mercury (U) Like quicksilver, the planet Mercury may open new lines of communication in business or signal a time for working out problems through effective communication. The ruler of technology, Mercury may summon you to think ahead and join the global communications network through innovative ideas or entrepreneurial business ventures. The writers' planet, Mercury may announce a forward thrust to pursue creative writing or public speaking.

Mercury (L) Also known as quicksilver, mercury represents swift movement and may signify the need to communicate something in a hurry. Silver is the metal of intuition. It may come as a sign to begin communicating your intuition without hesitation.

Mercury Cougar (M) As Mercury is the planet of communication and the cougar the shamanic medicine of a spiritual teacher, the arrival of a Mercury Cougar at your front door in a dream may bring a sage into your life. It may signify a call to become a spiritual teacher or mention a communication from a higher power.

Metals (L) The resources of earth's bounty include precious metals that, when refined into various forms, lend their properties in dreams bringing special attributes and gifts for your fulfillment.

Each one of its unique characteristics may signify levels of strength at the foundation of your personality.

Meteor (U) A meteor shower may represent a cosmic event that causes you to look up rather than toward the mundane. It may announce some natural fireworks in the air, such as a romantic encounter. In that a meteor fizzles when it hits the earth's atmosphere, it suggests the destruction of idealized states.

Mexican (M) A Mexican character may suggest adopting a passionate and rich lifestyle that celebrates life through a colorful cultural experience. He or she may mention the value of hard labor in supporting your family.

Archangel Michael (U) As the angel of mercy, Archangel Michael offers the sword of truth to cut away connections with the dark side of life. As the heavenly steward whose role is to protect earth's sacred ground, he unifies heaven and earth. Michael's appearance in a dream may signify valor, truth, and protection from the spiritual dimensions.

Mickey Mouse (L, M) The Disney character who won the hearts of millions for three generations represents a special helper and charming messenger to bring you back to the magical kingdom of creative imagination. He may be a mouse, but he is a wise man. He brings with him the wisdom of childhood, imagination, play, lightheartedness, and fun. As the sorcerer's apprentice, he teaches that creativity and magic are to be respected and controlled and are not to be taken lightly. His message is "Magic is real."

Microphone (M) Holding a microphone in a dream may point to the need to speak up so that you might be heard. It represents the amplification of your thoughts and ideas. It may represent a desire to be listened to.

Microwave (M) A microwave may signify a way to produce something quickly such as a new product or idea. It may also represent a quick fix. It may point out your frustration at not having time to prepare.

Military maneuvers (M) Witnessing the military in action in a dream may comment that you feel you are living on a battleground, perhaps with some relationship or at work. It can also represent that you may have battle scars from childhood that you need to take a look at more closely.

Milk (M) Milk nurtures young and old alike. Carrying a container of milk may mention that you are about to nurture someone close to you. Spilled milk may comment on feelings of losing love or compassion from others. Or it may represent an honest mistake.

Mines (L) Mines represent the entrance into the subconscious, which you can explore to discover the jewels, treasures, and other resources within. Entering a coal mine may represent a dangerous journey through your own soot or darkness in order to transform it into fuel for the soul.

Minivan (M) A minivan parked outside your home may announce a new little arrival who may make it necessary to get a new vehicle with more room. It represents family values and your concerns about meeting the needs of your family. It may refer to the frustrations in having to taxi family members around.

Minnie Mouse (L, M) As Mickey's sweetheart, Minnie is a modern feminine archetype. Demure and sweet, she stereotypically expresses the receptive side of the female gender. She may come to characterize a cooperative complement to the masculine aspect, Mickey. When paired together they may represent the balance and harmony of feminine intuition with masculine will.

Mirror (M) A mirror may reflect back to us our beautiful qualities so that we can appreciate them and embrace ourselves. It may point to an individual who is a real mirror for you and who will reflect both personality flaws and positive qualities. It may mention that it is time to look within, to appreciate your beauty, or to love yourself more. A shattered mirror may comment that your image has been shattered.

Mole (L) Living underground, the mole is a guide to the Lower World and teaches you to burrow deep into the earth to get grounded and connected to the earth. It may come as the guide into the many passageways within the subconscious.

Moles or beauty marks (L, M) Moles, sometimes called beauty marks, may appear as something dark on the skin or surface. They may represent a dark secret that has surfaced. Moles may point to a woman's accentuated beauty. They can also represent growth.

Monkey (L) Monkey may arrive to warn of a mischievous prankster at work who may make a mess of things. It points to primal emotions that need to be expressed more freely, perhaps those associated with childhood. Monkeys teach us about the importance of family relationships and group interactions. In that they swing on trees, they may point to exploring branches of knowledge.

Monopoly (M) Playing Monopoly with a close friend may recommend not to monopolize the conversation. It may also point out the part you play in a business deal with a lot of money at stake. It may warn against making a game of making money and may mention boredom with capitalistic values. (See *Board game*.)

Moon (U) In the twilight sky the moon represents the lunar or feminine. Unveiled as feminine expression, it represents intuition, vision, and mystical knowledge. As a symbol of fertility, the moon's four phases express the cycles of the creative process. The waxing moon signifies planting new seeds for new beginnings. The full moon represents the harvest obtained from your ideas and actions, and the waning moon the ending of the fertile cycle or old age and wisdom.

Mop (M) Used to clean floors and mop up water, a mop in your dream may point to a process of cleaning up after an emotional storm in your life such as in an argument or a disappointment. It may also point to tears of sadness that may need sopping up.

Morning glory (L) The morning glory points to awakening God's gift of glory and a brand-new day.

Moses (U) As one of the most recognized prophets in Judeo-Christian religion, Moses led the Israelites out of Egypt to the promised land. He may arrive as a spiritual teacher who teaches humanity God's laws and moral values. He may mention that you have broken one of the Commandments.

Mosquitoes (L) Mosquitoes attacking your body might arrive in a dream as a response to negative influences in your environment. They may point out that someone is feeding on your life force and leaving a swelling irritation. A mosquito may appear to advise that you stop letting others suck your blood. (See *Insect*.)

Moss (L) Growing in damp, dark places, moss may represent subtle emotional growth that was incubated without much effort or intention. Associated with shady spots, moss may comment on someone with a mysterious nature. On a tree moss may comment on something that grows on you with time.

Moth (L) Since they are attracted to the light, moths come as messengers of personal transformation, summoning you to blossom closer to spiritual light. They may represent the transformation of the soul.

Mother Mary (U) Mary's appearance in a dream brings the presence of genuine compassion and divine love. She may arrive to the dreamer who is in need of the qualities of spiritual nurturing and maternal care. In that she is depicted as a virgin, she may reflect purity and untainted desires.

Motorcycle (M) Driving a motorcycle signifies riding forward with an independent sense of power and demonstrating it to all around you. It represents personal freedom. A Harley-Davidson might comment that you are riding forward with the son of David, the king of the Jews. Thus, it rides with the power of the Messiah.

Mountain climbing (M) Scaling the side of a mountain can represent the hard upward climb to your spiritual center. Climbing a mountain may also point to a peak spiritual experience, or be a signal of a difficult climb to the top professionally. Mountain climbing indicates a portal into the Upper World, where you can receive spiritual light and truth.

Mountain range (U) Mountainous regions with high peaks as a setting may point to inspirational experiences that bring awe and majestic beauty to your heart. Traveling through the mountains may suggest that you are appreciating men. It can also represent moving through issues with men who may be too logical or rational for your taste.

Movie theater (M) The need to view your own autobiographical movie may place you in a seat in the audience at a movie theater. Dreams review our concerns and the events that demonstrate the patterns we play out. A theater may mention that it is time to view the dramas and comedies of your life and to begin the process of self-exploration. It may also point to a desire for more entertainment.

Moving truck (M) The arrival of a moving truck at your front door may be a direct message to move out of an old environment, mentioning that a change is needed. Metaphorically, it may reflect a change that liberates you and will expand your horizons. (See *Truck.*)

Mr. Clean (M) Mr. Clean household cleaner may whiz around like a cyclone to deliver the message to clean up the messes in the family, such as any dysfunctional patterns. It may also announce the arrival of a man who believes he is impeccable. (See *Cleanser.*)

Mrs. Butterworth's (M) Mrs. Butterworth's pancake syrup, known for its rich, buttery flavor, may be poured in a dream to represent your self-worth. Butter churned from cream may symbolize the turning of nurturing to gold. Thus, your life may be enriched through nurturing others.

Muffin (M) "Muffin" is often a term of endearment for children and the happiness they bring.

Mulan (L, M) "When will my reflection show who I truly am inside?" may be the message of the Disney character Mulan. She represents the woman-warrior archetype who emerges out of her loyalty to traditional values of family into her own authentic self. She thus asks a woman to "be authentic" and true to herself.

Music (M, U) Listening to a familiar song may bring inspiration and a message. It may comment on the need to return to a state of harmony in any given situation. Lively music may ask you to get up and dance to the music of life.

Mustache (L, M) A man with a mustache may appear in a dream as a suave and sophisticated individual or a smooth talker. Bringing attention to the top of the lip, a mustache signifies the power a male authority figure has through his verbal expression.

Mynah bird (L) The mynah bird comes as a guide to abundant living. Usually paired, their appearance in a dream may comment on a partnership that will bring rewards. In that they are noisy, they may point to bickering or arguing in the background of your life. (See *Birds*.)

Nail polish (M) Nail polish brings beauty and expression to a woman's hands and to her feet. Thus, putting on nail polish in a dream may comment on your getting ready to express something beautiful through your work.

Nails (M) Nails are used to hold wood together in a construction project. Thus, they may remind you to nail things shut with regard to a business deal. They may also symbolically represent feeling crucified; they offer the message to quit being a martyr.

Naked (M) Being naked in public is a common dream experience that may point to a situation in which you felt overexposed in a social situation. Perhaps your true feelings came through. Being naked may mention that you have been stripped of your persona or any false identity you cling to. It may also represent authenticity.

Nana (L, M) The loving nursemaid Saint Bernard in *Peter Pan* may represent the nurturing, compassionate care of a loving friend who might be willing to rescue you from emotional harm. She may represent loyalty.

Napkin (M) Unfolding a napkin may comment that you are preparing to receive nourishment or something good. For a man, it may also comment that you may need to protect your genitals from a smothering mother type. A napkin may also simply reflect neatness or tidiness.

Nashville (M) Walking around in Nashville, Tennessee, with a suitcase in hand in a dream may reflect your aspirations to hit it big in the country and western music scene. It may mention that you are experiencing another "somebody done somebody wrong song" in matters of the heart. It may bring attention to an individual who is characterized as a vagabond or a wanderer.

Natural landscapes (M) Natural regions and settings in a dream whether they are mountain ranges, valleys, or deserts, are dreamscapes that bring out the landscape of the soul for conscious understanding. Mountain ranges represent the masculine, valleys the feminine, and desert the soul.

Nature preserve (L, M) Enjoying the beauty of a nature preserve may represent concerns about the protection of your sacred space or your sacred authentic nature from the litter-filled experiences that pollute or damage your beauty.

Neck (L, M) The neck supports the head and thus may be vividly portrayed to signify strength and tenacity. A long neck may signify high ideals. A short neck may represent a stout or brave individual. A whiplash injury may be a response to a crippling clash with someone. The neck may also represent crucifixion in that Jesus' head hung down on the cross.

Necklace (M) A necklace or pendant may point to what you may want to communicate. A string of pearls may represent wisdom and spiritual, enlightening conversation. An amethyst pendant may represent communicating from your intuition and from what you envision. It may bring attention to the heart if it is hanging low around the neck.

Nest (M) Observing a bird building a nest may comment on a need to prepare for a new birth or the delivery of a creative project that is spiritually inspired. It may also predict a literal move or change in environment. A nest may also simply announce spring.

Net (M) Used to catch a lot of fish at one time, a net in a dream may represent reaping the harvest from out of the subconscious or through some creative project. It may also represent an entanglement or a trap. A net may also mention the Internet or World Wide Web as being lucrative business networks.

Paul Newman (L, M) Known for his powerful yet sensitive leading roles, Paul Newman may represent a "new man" entering a woman's life. In his later years he has been recognized for his generosity and fund-raising for children's projects. He thus is like the archetype of the Hierophant, who brings community-mindedness into action as a benefactor to the disadvantaged.

Newspaper (M) Thumbing through the newspaper in a dream might point to a need to catch up on the news around you. The contents may have an important literal message for you. Bold headlines may emphasize messages from your higher self.

New York (M) Wandering through the streets of New York in a dream may suggest that you have entered the busiest and largest marketplace in the world. A cultural, investment, and political hub, it may reveal concerns with becoming a success in the theater, publishing, international affairs, trade, or commerce. A dream set in New York may also express concerns about crime or feeling overcrowded.

Jack Nicholson (L, M) Embodying the charm of the Devil, Jack may appear in a dream to demonstrate the dark side of a man's personality. As a character, he uses seduction and charm as a means to an end. For a man, he may warn that you are overrun by temptation. In a woman's dream, he may come as a charming, lecherous man, snake-charming a woman into desiring him and then leaving her to do the same to others.

Nighttime (L) If a scene in a dream takes place at night, it signifies exploring what is hidden or shadowed in the subconscious. Nighttime may reflect your unconscious concerns versus your conscious concerns.

Nike wear (M) Whether it is a shirt or sneakers, Nike sportswear says simply "Just do it." The message is to be a winner and to stop procrastinating.

Nine (L) Nine is the number of completion of patterns and karma. It may mark the finish of a cycle, perhaps in business or in a relationship, or comment on the termination of destructive patterns.

North (L) North, as one of the four directions, offers entry into the great mystery of the universe. It points to the void in which there is no time and no space. It is the place of your vision and of illusion. Moving north is moving toward knowing universal truth. It is the direction of wisdom and depth. (See *Four directions, Compass.*)

Nose (L, M) A nose is associated with the sense of smell. As a metaphor, it expresses the ability to investigate or to do research. Someone with a big nose may represent a snoop who might attract suspicion. A character with a crooked nose may warn of something crooked going on. A runny nose may point to the release of grief or state that you are snooping around too much.

Notebook (M) Losing your notebook in a dream may comment that you have lost important ideas or knowledge. It may represent anxiety and fear about losing important notes that would impact your grades in school.

Notepad (M) A notepad used to jot down important information may remind you to make a mental note of something that is going on. It may represent a suggestion.

Numbers (L, M) Numbers and computations in dreams present esoteric solutions to problems. Phone numbers or numbers on checks, for example, may be added and their sums used to decipher a message. For instance, "333" may represent the power of the trinity, and its sum, nine, represents completion. Therefore, the meaning may be deciphered as the completion of psychological issues in relationship to your spiritual power. Numbers may also point to the ages of the dreamer that point to subconscious secrets.

Nun (M) A nun may represent the qualities of spiritual devotion and chastity. She may comment that you are disconnected or have suppressed your sexuality.

Nurse (M) A nurse may appear to give care and nurturing that are healing to the soul as well as to the body. As the feminine archetype of a caregiver, she may comment that compassion is the greatest healer.

Nursery (M) Roaming through a plant nursery may mention a period of personal growth. It may caution you to select only the best experiences for your growth, which will develop into beautiful expressions you may want to present to the world.

Oatmeal (M) A food associated with stick-to-the-ribs nourishment, oatmeal may signify being given something that is considered good and that will last. Oatmeal may represent good mothering.

Observer (M) Being the observer in your dream is the most common role of the ego. It allows you to view the elements of your life and gain perspective. If you are frequently the observer and seldom take action, it may point to feelings of isolation and may mention that you are being too passive or disassociated from things.

Obsidian (L) This black volcanic stone assists you in penetrating the deep layers of the subconscious in order to excavate and reflect on the shadow forces. It can assist you in grounding your physical body. In that it is volcanic glass, obsidian generates inner power.

Obstacles on the road (M) Obstacles on the road block or slow your progress toward your goals. Rocks may represent hard structures of negative thinking that may get in the way or make for a rough ride.

Ocean (L) Demonstrating the realm of the subconscious in dreams, the ocean is the origin of creativity and all of life. Swimming in the ocean reflects your readiness to experience the vast potential of the subconscious forces that may drive your personality. The sea appearing in a dream may signify that you are in a creative process that will expand your thinking. A calm sea expresses the emotional quality of peace and serenity. A stormy, choppy sea expresses emotional currents that may force you to go deeper into your feelings. Waves, big or small, represent the creative power and potential that can be ridden as opportunities to manifest what you want. They can represent realized potential and understanding brought to shore.

Octopus (L) A scavenger of the ocean depths, this creature comes to take you to the bottom of your subconscious feelings to clear the debris from the sandy floor. An octopus, with its eight legs and tentacles, may be revealing the psychic hold one may have over another that may hold you back. Psychic connections to family or loved ones may be debilitating unconscious agreements that imprison you much like being in the arms of an octopus.

Rosie O'Donnell (L, M) The Queen of Nice, as she is called by fans, may appear in a dream to nudge you to stop placating and to "tell it like it is." She may demonstrate that there is more than one body type for a woman and thus may appear to the woman who is obsessed about her weight to say, "You're beautiful as you are." As a successful single mom, she brings the importance of motherhood and the nurturing aspect of the personality to a dreamer who wonders if her role as a mother is important enough.

Office building (M) Entering an office building in your dreams may represent concerns about work and your career. What floor you arrive on may represent the degree of success and recognition you expect from your accomplishments in the work world.

- If the first floor is in an office building, you may be at the beginning of your career or beginning a new career.

- The second floor of an office building may materialize to help express your desire to become a partner rather than jut an employee.

Old Navy (M) Moderately priced clothing for the teenager, Old Navy clothing may comment on a youthful attitude. Old Navy may suggest old militaristic values that are placed on the young psyche. It may also connote setting off to sea or "see."

Olive (L) Eating olives in a dream may indicate an enjoyment of Greek philosophy. As a play on words it may be saying "Oh, live."

Olive green (L, M) Olive green represents achieving peace through nature. It signifies the wisdom within nature.

One (L, M) The number one represents the self and self-exploration. Appearing on a door, it may open to your first opportunity toward fulfilling your dreams. It may mention to look to yourself for the answer. Relating to the connectivity to God, it may represent oneness. The number one also denotes wholeness and new beginnings.

Onyx (L) Grounding the structure of the mind, this black, shiny stone may be worn as a piece of jewelry. It lends the attribute of balance of the mind.

Opal (L) A fiery gemstone that combines the elements of fire and water, an opal brings the element of fire to ignite your passionate feelings and bring them to the surface of the conscious mind. It stimulates sexual desire and drive.

Orange (L, M) Peeling and opening an orange in your dreams may represent exposing the segments of yourself at the core. A navel orange may relate to the navel chakra, from which you assert your personal authority. Since orange is the color of stability and authority, wearing orange clothing in a dream may mention your boldness. It is the color of the will and thus coaxes assertive action.

Orchid (L) The tropical orchid represents branches of mystical knowledge. It may mention a woman's delicate nature.

Oreo cookie (M) Dark on the outside and white on the inside, Oreos in a dream, may comment on an African American who holds Caucasian values and attitudes. Eating the cream center of an Oreo may symbolize enjoying the insides or the good traits of someone close to you rather than paying attention to how he or she looks on the outside.

Orgy (M) Witnessing an orgy in your dreams may comment on loose sexual morals or the desire to let down your hair and express some sexual freedom. It may reveal normal sexual conflicts, which may be repressed in your subconscious.

Oriental rug (M) An Oriental rug in the living room of a house may represent the mythic layers at the foundation of the soul. It may reveal a motif that reveals patterns or an intricate story about your soul's history.

Ostrich (L) An ostrich may come to comment on your tendency to bury your head in the sand as avoidance behavior. The ostrich egg might represent a gift of fertility or a large prize that has been won. (See *Birds*.)

Owl (L) The owl represents the wisdom that comes from seeing within the mysteries of the darkness. It is associated with the feminine power of the crone or wisdom teacher. It is associated with the wisdom of dreams and the knowledge of dream language. Owl may also come to announce a death, either a literal one or, more often, a symbolic death as an important transition in life. On the shoulder of Athena, the goddess of commerce, Owl signifies the wise woman who is intuitively driven in business.

Pager (M) Pagers transmit an urgent message to communicate to someone and may mention that someone is trying to get through to you. Being paged by your mother in a dream may point to frustration about being intruded upon.

Paint (M) Painting a house interior in a dream may comment that you are creatively freshening up your inner environment. It may signify a more positive or fresher outlook on your life.

Paintbrush (M) A paintbrush in a dream may represent tools you have acquired to put the final touches on some project that is under construction. It may be awarded to you to mention your desire to express your artistic talents.

Pajamas (M) Being in public in your pajamas may mention that you are walking in the world asleep or unconscious regarding some important, real situation. It may represent the desire and readiness to get some rest.

Palm of the hand (L) Attention brought to the palm of a hand may mention that you hold all the knowledge you need in your own hands. It may also represent a fortune or a forecast for the future. Or it may hold the secrets of your life potential.

Palm Pilot (M) As an instrument that stores important information about others, a Palm Pilot might be compared to a little black book. It may appear to comment that everything is in the palm of your hand. It may indicate your anxiety about staying connected to those you come in contact with.

Pampers diapers (M) Being given a box of Pampers in your dreams may comment that you are ready to receive some special attention and pampering.

Pancakes (M) Also called flapjacks, pancakes may represent a product that can be delivered quickly. It may also represent a stack of work you might derive pleasure from cutting into.

Pansy (M) A pansy points to receptivity or gullibility.

Panther (L) Black Panther prowls through thick vegetation, eyes keen, seeking out that which lurks in the shadows. In a dream, the black panther comes to warn and protect against evil or malevolent forces in your life. It presents the ability to distinguish truth from fiction and to trust no one other than your own discerning eye.

Pants (M) In a dream, putting on a brand-new pair of slacks may mention trying on a new attitude of manhood. A woman putting on men's slacks may point up her tendency to overidentify with male qualities in order to feel successful in the world.

Paper bag (M) A paper bag used to carry groceries may comment on having left somewhere with a bag of goodies. In other words, it may represent your ability to bring nourishment home. An empty bag may represent a fruitless venture. Packing a lunch bag may represent the readiness to return to school or to go to work.

Paper clip (M) As a paper clip holds paper together, an unwound paper clip may signify that you may be feeling scattered or behaving in a scattered way. An intact paper clip may signify that you're wired up or looking "together." It may also mention that you may need to hold things together in your life. Thus, the message is "Put things together."

Paper plate (M) Convenient and disposable, a paper plate may signify the rewards that may be received from a one-time offering such as a grant or inheritance.

Paper towels, Bounty (M) Using paper towels to clean may reveal some sticky mess that needs mopping up before you can prosper. A dream character carrying a roll of Bounty paper towels may signify that it is time to absorb the bounty of life's gifts, whether they are material or inspirational.

Parachuting (M) Jumping out of an airplane with a parachute may comment on a risk you have taken recently that ended in a soft landing. It may represent the desire to do something daredevilish. It may also suggest that you are "up in the air" about an important decision.

Paris (M) Sitting in a café in Paris in your dreams may represent being in a place where romance is in the air. Speaking French may mention that you are having romantic feelings.

Park (M) A dream beginning in a park may represent concerns about your recreational life. As a place in nature within a city, a park may signify the need to taste the elements of nature as a break in routine.

Park Avenue (M) Associated with the upper class of New York, being on Park Avenue in a dream may denote status and success in the big city or in the marketplace.

Parking lot (M) Mentioning the lack of movement in your life, a parking lot may represent your inability to get going toward your goals. Not being able to locate your vehicle in a parking lot in a dream may comment that you have lost connection with your physical body, pointing to the need to get out of your head and into your body. This may be because you have parked too close to the issues of others and lost touch with yourself.

Parrot (L) This colorful and talkative tropical bird may bring the message to communicate in colorful language and to deliver a persuasive oration. It may reveal that someone is imitating you. (See *Birds*.)

Patagonia (M) As high-quality all-weather adventure wear, Patagonia clothing may point to an executive personality who also enjoys the adventure of the great outdoors.

Pathfinder (M) Driving a Nissan Pathfinder in a dream may suggest concerns about finding the right path in life, professionally or spiritually.

Pattern (M) Fumbling with a dress pattern may remark on difficulties with constructing a new attitude to wear. It may mention that you are looking at patterns of behavior or modeling or emulating another's patterns.

Peach (L) A peach may appear as an outstanding symbol in a dream to announce the arrival of a beautiful woman. It may also mention that everything is "peachy" or just great. In that it has a large pit, it may point to that sadness that is at the core.

Peanut butter (M) Eating out of a jar of peanut butter in a dream may result in your words coming out all wrong, thus it may mean that you are having difficulty communicating effectively. Peanut butter may also represent the product of two people's hard work, as peanuts come two to a shell. It may also indicate that you are working "for peanuts."

Pearl (L) An expression of beauty and the symbol of enlightenment, the pearl can signify something of beauty formed out of an earlier emotional irritation. A string of pearls adorning the neck of a woman might represent the expression of her wisdom. The gift of pearls is in recognition of a woman's worth and value.

Peas (M) A cup of peas offered to you signifies a little peace of mind.

Pegasus (L) The flying horse and close companion of Hercules arrives from the mythic dimensions of the Lower World to express the winged power of spiritual flight. He is the power that can accelerate you through the spiritual dimensions on your quest for significance and honor through God's grace. He provides rescue for the hero threatened by Hades.

Pen (M) A pen may express the desire to write or be a writer. A ballpoint pen that has exploded may suggest that your words have made a permanent mess of things. A pen may represent a permanent contract or relationship.

Pencil (M) A pencil may mention that you are making a temporary impact with your words in a situation. A number-two pencil may signify a relationship that will not last or that may be erased soon.

Penis (L) As the symbol of masculine power, a penis on a woman in a dream may mention the power of her masculine aspect and her androgyny. A small penis may suggest that the man has little power or virility and thus is wimpy. Having your penis exposed in a dream may comment on your preoccupation with sex or with power.

Pepsi-Cola (M) With its product motto "the Joy of Pepsi," Pepsi-Cola appearing in a dream signifies consuming good energy. "Pep" can suggest vigor and exuberance, and "si" can mean having sight. Combined, these may represent seeing good energy that is uplifting. In that Pepsi is the top-selling soft drink in Europe, surpassing sales of Coke, it may represent a business enterprise that will succeed in the European trade market.

Percolator (M) Listening to a percolator in a dream may recommend letting things or ideas percolate for a time before taking action. It may also comment on something brewing in the background.

Peridot (L) This yellow-green stone brings a soothing and relaxing vibration for the nervous system that is stressed and overtaxed.

Pewter (M) Pewter ware is considered old or antique and may signify holding on to outdated ways of serving others. It may also represent a gift from the past that will not tarnish.

Michelle Pfeiffer (L, M) As an angel of perfection, Michelle may come to represent the perfect woman whose innocence and manner bring quality and value to a woman's worth. She is the archetype of radiance of a common and uncommon nature. She is a woman who is congruent with the statement "Reflect the inner light and shine." She may express a woman's need to pay attention to her image.

Pheasant (L) A pheasant signifies motherhood. It points to life-giving gifts from your relationship to your mother. Hunting a pheasant in a dream may represent killing off your attachment to your mother. (See *Birds*.)

Phoenix (L) Rising up from the ashes, the phoenix represents a personal transformation through death and rebirth. It may fly into a dream as a response to events that dismember the ego and bring about a strengthening of the soul and spirit of the individual.

Piano (M) A piano may represent integrating the right and left through creating a harmony between your intuition and your logical side. It may also represent the integration of light and dark. Ebony and ivory may mention that both aspects of the soul can come together into something melodious. A piano appearing in a dream may also simply comment on a desire to enjoy music.

Pickup truck (M) Associated with the masculine ego and male power, a pickup truck in a woman's dream may signify that she is about to be picked up by a man. The truck may arrive at your door to state that it is time to get more directly into your power and accelerate forward toward your goals.

Picture frame (M) Straightening a framed picture may signify that you need to balance out a concept in your mind. A picture frame may suggest the need to set a framework or explain the perimeters of your vision in order to convey an idea clearly.

Pillow (M) By caressing the head for sleep, a pillow may signify the need to rest and stop the mind from thinking so much. It may symbolize something that has brought comfort to the mind.

Pills (M) Swallowing or taking a pill may represent an unpleasant experience that may have been difficult, as in "a bitter pill to swallow." A pill may express the need to sedate yourself or may remark on feeling ill.

Pillsbury Dough Boy (M) The appearance of the Pillsbury Dough Boy in a dream may announce someone who is perhaps cooking up a big surprise, such as bringing some "big dough" or money into the house. The Dough Boy may also signify that a guy is a real softy or softhearted.

Piloting (M) Being in the cockpit of an airplane may represent being in control of your destination in business or in life in general. It may indicate your competence and confidence in handling the responsibility of making all the decisions. Crashing an airplane may point to the failure of a business venture.

Pimples (L) Pimples, as eruptions on the skin, relate to emotions that are coming to the surface. They may mention that your beauty is blemished. Pimples may also erupt from worry.

Pink (L, M, U) Pink represents love, femininity, beauty, and childlike innocence. It is associated with feminine qualities.

Pink Panther (L, M) The intriguing detective who originated in the Peter Sellers' movie and later was developed as a cartoon character represents the act of stumbling upon the truth quite accidentally. He may point to a snoop who is digging around in your personal business.

Pink tourmaline (L) Pink tourmaline offers heart-opening and -healing qualities that can fix a broken heart or crack open the hard-hearted. Its message in a dream is "You can love again. (See *Gems.*)

Pins and needles (M) Pins and needles can appear together in a dream to show that you may be eagerly awaiting some good news. They represent anticipation. They may also suggest that you have been stuck by an unpleasant situation. Or pins and needles may be holding something together temporarily.

Pipe (M) Smoking a pipe may be associated with paternal nurturing or patriarchal values. A pipe may also suggest that something smelly is arising out of a serious discussion.

Pisces (L) Ruled by the emotions and intuition, this is the astrological sign of the mystic. It may influence dreams by making them more vivid and magnifying what is in the subconscious. Pisces may point to a very sensitive individual.

Pit (M) A seed of a fruit, a pit may comment on hard experiences that require effort to penetrate in order to germinate new life. A pit that appears in your dream may humorously comment that you feel that life is the pits.

Place mat (M) Putting a place mat on the table may signify that you are welcoming someone new into your space. It may also mean that you are welcomed at someone else's table.

Places (M) The places in our dreams are the backgrounds against which we play out the scenes of our life. In general, being outdoors represents our conscious concerns and being indoors reflects deeper and unconscious concerns.

Plaid (M) Plaid clothing may point to conservative Ivy League attitudes that may be in conflict with your wild side.

Plains (L, M) "Wide open with clear sight of what's coming into your life" can describe the experience of living on the plains. It can also represent a simple life with the bare necessities offered and simple, straightforward values to follow. Plains may also represent the plain truth.

Planets (U) The planets represent powerful archetypal energies that may influence your personality and your life. As heightened power, they bring their individual attributes to you to strengthen your character. For instance, Venus offers the qualities of love and beauty and Mars the initiative to move forward. The planets may also signify bodies of knowledge, each offering different lessons to your life. For instance, Saturn teaches you about materializing your goals and offers lessons about structure, rules, and regulations. (See entries for individual planets.)

Planting (M) Planting seeds may comment on the planting of ideas or wishes for further cultivation and for future harvest. It may represent new beginnings.

Plants (L, M) Plants in a dream signify the power and mysteries within nature and nature's ability to regenerate and blossom forth. Plants may also indicate growth—emotional, physical, psychological, and/or spiritual. Their green color may symbolize healing power. A potted plant may reflect what is contained within the self as offering potential for new growth.

Plants, broadleaf (M) With its sturdy structure, a plant with broad leaves may represent a broadening of your perspective. They may also indicate that you have just had a huge growth experience emotionally and psychologically.

Plastic (M) Plastic appearing in a dream may point to artificiality or a plastic persona. It may comment that you are not being natural or are not living an authentic life. A plastic shopping bag may comment on impulse-buying behavior.

Plate (M) Used to serve food, a plate may represent the receptacle for receiving and welcoming food and nurturing. Breaking a plate may signify that your ability to accept what life has to offer has been damaged, perhaps by your feelings of unworthiness.

Playing (M) Playing a game with children may mention a wish or need to become more playful. Playing a board game may comment that you are bored with life. Playing in the water represents turning an emotional issue into something fun and liberating.

Pliers (M) A tool used for pulling things out or apart, a pair of pliers may appear in a dream as an outstanding symbol urging you to pull out the details of a situation before proceeding. Or a pair of pliers may represent needing to pull something out of the way. It may comment "Get a grip."

Plum (L) With its purple color and plumpness, eating a plum may denote savoring your youth. It may also mention that you feel too plump or fat. In comparison, eating prunes may represent concerns about old age or looking old. Prunes may also comment on the need to eliminate constipation.

Plumber (M) A plumber may fix a leak or unblock the pipes that direct the flow of energy in your body. He may represent the power of the subconscious to repair problems in your energy system that may eventually affect your health. He may also help you deal with your emotions.

Plumbing (M) Dreaming about the plumbing in your house may represent the channels for moving energy throughout the body. Clogged plumping may signify emotional blocks, which may back everything up. Leaky pipes may signify the leaking of the life force in the energy system of the body. In a dream, plumbing may also diagnose heart or digestive problems.

Pluto (U) The smallest and most distant planet, Pluto brings about transformation at a soul level. Pluto may appear in a dream to announce a period of deep inner work or the need to let go and dive to a new potential. Pluto is the planet that ushers in deep initiation through a heroic journey of death and dismemberment. Pluto's appearance may tell you to look at the shadow aspects of your psyche and personality.

Police car (M) The arrival of the police in your dreams may signify your need to keep the peace. A police car may symbolize an internal authority that helps to resolve your inner conflicts. It may also suggest that you let go of guilt and self-judgment.

Polo (M) An equestrian sport played predominantly by men, playing polo in a dream may indicate that you have entered an arena dominated by male ideals. It may point to the fact that you have given up your individuality to fit into a man's world.

Pond (L) Being near a pond in your dreams can represent taking time to reflect on things or on life's meaning. A pond could represent the desire for more leisure and quiet.

Pontiac Grand Am (M) The Pontiac named after the Pontiac Indians of the American plains may point to a fighting Native American spirit driving your intentions forward. The Grand Am may suggest that you view every morning as a new beginning. Thus combined, it may state, "It's a grand morning for going to battle for your beliefs."

Pool (M) Table billiards and pool are games that require skill, concentration, and strategy. Thus, dreaming about playing pool may comment on a strategic plan of action that will sink a deal. Associated with gambling, playing pool may warn that someone is literally playing dirty pool.

Popcorn (M) Eating popcorn may comment that you feel puffed up in a situation. Popping popcorn on the stove may mention that you are cooking up explosive thoughts in your mind. Popcorn may also indicate opening fertile potentials that are encapsulated within.

Pope (M) Being in an audience of the Pope may mention that you are in the presence of a spiritual authority. He may represent the ultimate authority on spiritual matters and may fulfill a desire to be led spiritually.

Poppy (L) The poppy signifies unconsciousness and awakening through your dreams.

Pornography (M) Finding pornography in the closet in a dream may point to a desire for sexual satisfaction. It may also mention shameful feelings about your sexuality.

Possum (L) A nocturnal animal associated with the lunar aspect, the possum can point out behavior that is too passive. It may mention the need to let your ideas or projects remain dormant for a time or to keep a secret you are incubating in your mind. In other words, learning how to play dead can be an effective approach. "Wait till the time is right" is the message of the possum. It can also arrive to advocate using a passive approach to a difficult relationship in dealing with a more aggressive individual.

Postage stamp (M) A postage stamp put on a letter may point to the cost or value of the message sent or received in a dream. It may represent the payment of dues.

Potato (L, M) Because potatoes are considered the poor man's food, eating mashed potatoes may signify concerns about your economic status. Digging up potatoes may mean that you are working very hard for very little money.

Power plant (M) Visiting a power plant may mention the need to get to know or realize the source of your power, where it really comes from. A nuclear power plant may comment on a destructive potential in your immediate environment that could easily destroy your life.

Power Ranger (M) A popular toy appealing mostly to boys and based on the children's cartoon, the appearance of a Power Ranger in a dream may comment on the freedom to play with your own power. As a play on words, it may accentuate the belief that power equals "our anger." It may also reveal an inner conflict about accepting your spiritual power.

Prairie dog (L) Prairie dogs live in underground communities and may signify a group or community of individuals who represent a counterculture. Their ideals may be different from the norm. A prairie dog may come to summon you to bond and commit to community life.

Praying mantis (L) This unusual insect's appearance may mention that it is time to start praying for something. As the female of the species viciously devours her mate, a praying mantis appearing in a dream may signify an aggressive female whose intention is to kill a man's ego.

Pregnancy (M) A pregnant woman may arrive in a dream to announce a special event or opportunity on the horizon. Your own pregnancy may suggest that you are incubating a new creative phase or project that will be ready to be delivered soon. (See *Birth*.)

Elvis Presley (M) As the King of Rock 'n' Roll, Elvis may make a return appearance on the stand of your dream to get you moving or to demonstrate the need to get passionate about your work or relationship. His gyrating hips may mention that it is time to loosen up a bit. He may mention that you are about to gain the highest honor and recognition for your artistic achievement, or that you are about to be treated royally. In a woman's dream, he may announce a new flame.

Priest (M) A priest may appear as the mediator between you and God. He may bring spiritual advice or preach to you about being more spiritually aligned with God. If his back is turned to you, a priest may indicate the turning away from the world in favor of a spiritual purpose.

Prime rib (M) Eating prime rib may represent a rare and meaty experience that will have rich rewards.

Principal's office (M) Being sent to the principal's office may express worry and concern about your behavior or fear of punishment by an outside authority. It may also represent repressed childhood anxiety.

Printer (M) Having a problem with printing out information may express your frustration about communicating what is on your mind. You may also be experiencing frustration with bringing what you know into a form that may be understood by others.

Prism (L, U) Since a crystal prism refracts sunlight, it may signify radiant light that arrives from the Upper World to infuse light into your mind and into your life. A prism may point to the many facets of the personality or the soul. As it creates rainbows, a prism may represent a tool for creating a bridge into another dimension of spiritual experience.

Prison (M) Being in a prison may comment on feelings of being persecuted or punished for doing something wrong. A prison may also mention that you are imprisoned by your own thoughts or beliefs. Since a prison represents lack of personal freedom, it may point to a relationship that restricts your freedom, such as a bad marriage.

Pruning shears (M) As the tool used for trimming dead branches, pruning shears may point to receiving the tools for cutting off an overgrowth of ideas. It may also mention the need to prune extraneous things out of one's life.

Public speaking (M) Being in front of a large audience and speaking may mention that you are overcoming your fear of public speaking. If the microphone is not working, it could suggest that there is a fear of not being heard. If the audience is unruly and they appear not to be listening, your dream may be expressing the fear of not having command over your audience.

Pulling (M) Pulling on a rope in a dream may express a desire for or frustration about rescuing someone, perhaps a friend or relative. It may make mention that someone close to you needs your help. Pulling may also comment on bringing something important closer to you, or it may point to a tug-of-war in some relationship.

Purple (L, M, U) Purple is the color of spiritual vision and royal valor. Purple embodies qualities of intuition, psychic power, and clairvoyance. Purple is also the color of the mystic.

Pushpins (M) Stepping on a pushpin in a dream may mean that you have been stuck at work too long. As it is used to put important messages in front of your face, a pushpin may suggest that you look at what is in front of you.

Puzzle (M) Putting together a jigsaw puzzle may point to fitting the pieces of some big problem together, a problem in which there are numerous issues to resolve. A puzzle may indicate that the big picture may not come together without some patience and persistence.

Pyramid (L) With its three sides and apex pointing upward, this symbol signifies spiritual power. The pyramids of Egypt were erected in service to the gods and were used as burial tombs of kings to ensure their immortality. A pyramid points to the embodiment of spiritual power and the understanding of the immortality of the soul. It may announce a spiritual initiation that will help you develop a spiritual commitment.

Quail (L) This herding bird with an antenna crown signifies group movement, such as a team moving forward together with a project.

Quartz, Clear (U) As a transmitter and receiver of light, the sacred geometry of quartz crystals may bring you higher knowledge by opening the channels to the Upper World. Clear quartz may symbolize clarity. A quartz crystal excavated in a dream may activate new psychic abilities.

Quasimodo (L, M) The main character of *The Hunchback of Notre Dame,* Quasimodo represents someone who has taken on the burdens of the culture and who has been exiled because of his shame. In this way, he is the culture's disowned projection of imperfection and shame.

Queen- or king-size bed (M) Lying on a queen- or king-size bed in a dream may point to being or feeling honored in your intimate relationship. It may also compensate for not having enough space in your relationship.

Raccoon (L) Raccoon will do whatever is necessary, go anywhere, do anything, in order to gather its resources. Raccoon can teach you how to become resourceful in taking care of the needs of your family or community. It may come to coax you out of complacency and into action to accomplish a task. Raccoon's message is "Be resourceful." As it has dark bands around the eyes, it may mention to see with your own two eyes the opportunities around you.

Radiator (M) As the mechanism that cools down the engine, a leak in the radiator may point to an inability to cool down after an argument. In the physical body a radiator in a dream may represent the thyroid gland.

Radio (M) Turning up the radio may represent turning up your own radar signal to hear something that may be going on in closed quarters. It may also simply refer to a desire to enjoy music.

Rain (L, M) By releasing emotions that block thinking, rain offers cleansing from emotional tensions in the air. Rain can further represent the release from sorrow or grief and point to the healthy expression of emotions.

Rainbow (U) With its multicolored rays refracted by the sun, the rainbow offers a bridge into the spiritual dimensions. Associated with magic, it leads you to the pot of gold at its end. It often comes in a dream as a sign of spiritual fulfillment and good luck.

Raisins (L) Enjoying a box of raisins may comment on enjoying old age. It may refer to the ideas or beliefs you were raised with.

Rake (M, O) Raking leaves may point to what has died and must now be cleared away to reveal greener grass and make way for new growth. It may signify clearing out old prospects in business to make way for new ones.

Ram (L) The ram with horns coiled as a helmet against its head pushes through obstacles aggressively in a warrior-like fashion. He can announce the need to go to war, so to speak, in order to achieve your mission. The ram's fiery nature may represent an arrogant masculine trait in an individual.

RAM computer memory (M) Insufficient RAM in your personal computer in a dream may signal that you have forgotten something important. It may reflect absentmindedness or forgetfulness.

Ranch (M) The environment for raising livestock as a setting may point to concerns about right livelihood. It can represent a productive place that can generate a good income. It may apply to raising money for a good cause. Or dreaming about a ranch may mention that you need to invest in the stock market or take stock out of something that might bring in substantial rewards.

Range Rover (M) As a play on words, Range Rover may translate to "our anger over." It may pull up beside you on the highway of life to reflect back to you that your anger may be out of control. It may mention that it is time to let it go in favor of love.

Raven (L) A bird associated with magic, Raven comes to show you the magical potential in life, which can be used to manifest your dreams. It can also demonstrate the karmic lessons associated with using black magic or bad magic as a way of controlling others. If Raven appears in a dream, he has come as a sorcerer bringing supernatural powers to you. (See *Birds*.)

Rearview mirror (M) "Look at what is behind you" may be the meaning of looking through the rearview mirror of your car. A broken rearview mirror may point to the inability to see your history or the memories from the past clearly. It may also offer a clear view of anyone else in your psychic field you may not have been aware of consciously.

Receipt (M) Dreaming about reading a receipt may comment on worrying about expenditures. It may suggest that you may have received a costly lesson. A receipt may also represent proof.

Red (L) Red brings fiery, passionate qualities into expression. It may represent creativity. Red may also comment on your anger and the expression of your rage, as in "seeing red."

Red road (L) As the path of Native American spirituality, choosing the red road may bring you to spiritual fulfillment through a divine connection to nature.

Keanu Reeves (L, M) Like Parsifal questing for the Grail, Keanu Reeves is the knight who must find his glory through the tests and trials of his worthiness. His appearance in a dream may signify the challenge ahead in fulfilling your destiny.

Referee (M) A referee as a character in your dreams may point to some problem that needs mediation. He may ask you to follow the rules of the game in any of your social interactions. His appearance may be a response to your own intervention in the arguments of others.

Refrigerator (M) As an outstanding symbol in a dream, a refrigerator may represent frigidity or fear of sexual intimacy. Going to a refrigerator that is empty may point to feeling unnurtured in your relationship. Your partner may be too cold.

Reindeer (L) The reindeer's sensitivity, poise, and nobility are attributes that may influence your character. A team of reindeer can represent a team of leaders delivering products or gifts to the world. Its mystical association with Saint Nicholas or Santa Clause associates reindeer with one who brings gifts and fulfillment of the deepest wishes.

Rental car (M) Driving in a rental car may represent a newly adopted self-image or status symbol you are trying on for size. For example, renting a Dodge Neon may suggest that you may want to stand out from the crowd for a change.

Repairing (M) Dreaming about repairing something may comment on the need to fix an area of your life. Repairing a vehicle in a dream may represent the need to heal physically as a priority. Repairing plumbing represents facilitating the flow of energy through the body by unblocking the flow or fixing some leak.

Restaurant (M) Eating in a restaurant may point to concerns about being nurtured in a social situation. Being in a restaurant and waiting for hours to be served may come as a response to a frustrating experience around getting your emotional needs met.

Rhinoceros (M) A rhino brings the message to charge ahead in order to break through the barriers that are in the way of achieving your goals. It may call you to incorporate a more aggressive method or attitude to get the job done. Rhino never takes no for an answer, achieving results through his sheer brute force.

Rice (M) As rice feeds half the world's population, it represents the sustenance of life. Rice thrown at a wedding symbolically blesses the marriage with health, wealth, and happiness. It is a symbol of fertility.

Riding (M) The act of riding a horse may represent moving forward with your personal power to your destination. It may comment on being valiant or on taking the hero or heroine's journey to spiritual fulfillment. Riding as a passenger in a car may mention that you are allowing others to control the direction of your life. Riding in the back of a pickup truck may point to being taken for a ride or taken away from your own will.

Ring (M) Rings bring attention to the hands. Rings on the right hand may comment on your work. Rings on the left hand are associated with receiving a commitment. A wedding ring suggests commitment and a bond in marriage. Proudly wearing a canary diamond ring may mention that a woman possesses extremely rare and valuable talents.

Ritz crackers (M) Eating out of a box of Ritz crackers may represent your desire for wealth and "the good life." Crackers may also constructively point out that you are obsessed, as in going "crackers" over thoughts of wealth.

River (L) A river can represent the movement of the life force within your body. It can signify allowing yourself to be carried by life's energy or to surrender to the unknown.

Road (M) Roads may point to the path you are on in life and may present the obstacles and challenges you face on your way to a particular goal or destination. A narrow road thus can suggest a narrow path on which you have limited choices. A wide road may represent a broad view of life's opportunities. A winding road suggests backward and forward movement, which requires a lot of steering and concentration. Thus the road may be challenging.

Roadblock (M) A roadblock represents a barrier set up by some inner or outer authority who may want to control your progress. It may cause you to have to turn away from your desires and may present frustration.

Road cones (M) Bright orange cones marking lanes in a dream may point to roadwork on the way to your destination. They may suggest that you slow down for a while before proceeding with your plans. They may also represent waiting for someone else to complete his or her job before you proceed with yours.

Julia Roberts (L, M) As a radiant jewel, she is the archetypal princess who demonstrates that friendship and sex appeal win the man of her dreams. As a best friend to men, she may appear in the dream of a man to express the desire for female friendship and companionship. For a woman, she may arrive to teach you that having a satisfying relationship means being a man's best friend first.

Robots (M) Robots are mechanical men who imitate what it is to be human. The appearance of a robot in your dreams may point to someone who is cold and without feelings. It may mention that your behavior in a situation has become mindless and robotic. You may have lost your inspiration and freedom.

Rock climbing (M) Rock climbing signifies a difficult climb over a big obstacle in life, such as a difficult boss or a test of endurance.

Rock slide (L) A rock slide may represent the appearance of many obstacles to overcome as life lessons, which makes for a difficult crossing.

Rocket (M) Since a rocket explodes in space, it is often a response to sexual ecstasy. It may also mention that it is time to launch your ideas or a business. Your project will take off.

Rocky trail (L) In that rocks present obstacles in dreams, a rocky road may suggest that you have to travel a distance over some profound obstacles in order to fulfill your desires, whether financial, social, or a love relationship.

Roll (M) Eating a roll may point to the enjoyment of a roll or wad of money that is to come. It may also indicate concern that you are getting too fat.

Rolling hills (L) Representing the ups and downs of life's journey, driving past rolling hills can teach you to roll with the punches. It may mention that someone is moody.

Roof (M) The roof, being on top of the house, usually refers to the crown chakra or spiritual center. It crowns your glory. It may reflect your thoughts about self-protection, as it protects the house from weather and the elements. A leaking roof may signify emotions interfering with your thinking and ability to reason away difficulties. A burned roof may signify damaged thinking. A tile roof may mention hardheadedness.

Roofer (M) Dreaming about a roofer may signal the need to repair crown chakra, the connection to the spiritual dimensions. He may represent someone who is helping you to change your mind or improve your thinking.

Rooms (M) The rooms of a house each relate to the details and boundaries of different aspects of the soul or personality. For example, the bedroom often relates to your ideas about sexuality, and the kitchen reflects concerns about nurturing the family.

Roots (L) Examining the roots of a tree or of plants may mention to look at your roots or family genealogy in order to understand the reason why you think and behave the way you do. Roots may also suggest examining the root cause of an emotional outburst or other concern, or indicate a need to find roots or to get grounded.

Rope (M) A rope may represent the need to rescue or to be rescued. It signifies giving help. Rope may also mention that you are walking a tightrope and could take a fall easily. Used for hanging, it may represent feelings of persecution or punishment.

Rose (L) Roses, the expression of love and beauty, are a gift given to honor a woman's worth. A bud opening to fullness represents blossoming into love's expression. The red rose is associated with romantic love, the yellow with joyous beauty, the white with purity.

Rose-colored glasses (M) Wearing rose-colored glasses in a dream may point to your tendency or desire to see only the bright side of things.

Rose quartz (L) Opening to love is the message delivered from this pink quartz crystal. Rose quartz might also be offered as a tool for healing the wounded heart or for opening the closed heart. (See *Crystal.*)

Rubber band (M) Used to hold things together, a rubber band may represent the need to "hold it together" emotionally. As a rubber band expands it may offer the message to expand your way of thinking or to stretch the imagination.

Ruby (L) The gift of a ruby in a dream may signify your passionate side. The gem's deep red radiance can be sent to stimulate and improve sexual vitality and lend energy to the manifestation of your desires.

Ruby slippers (L, M) Clicking her heels together three times, a woman wearing ruby slippers in a dream may appear to ground magical power. As the amulets of power for Dorothy in *The Wizard of Oz,* ruby slippers signify the call to take a mythical heroine's journey to find the way home or the way to spiritual enlightenment.

Running (M) The act of running may comment on your avoidance or fear. Running a race may represent concerns about making a personal deadline or concerns about competing in business.

Meg Ryan (M) As the woman whose childlike innocence may result in repeated disappointment, this movie star may appear in a dream to comment on your overly positive attitude or tendency to see the world through rose-colored glasses. She can also represent the innocent and humorous woman.

Saddle (M) Dreaming about carrying a saddle may indicate that you are saddled with too much responsibility. It may point to the importance of mounting the horse and riding free to your purpose and destiny.

Safeway supermarket (M) "Don't step out of the mold" might be the message if you find yourself in a Safeway supermarket moving up and down the aisles for ideas to produce. It may express concerns about safely fitting into what is expected of you. It may also point to concerns about public safety.

Sagittarius (U) The Archer or Centaur, the astrological sign Sagittarius may support you in embarking on a quest for higher truth or to engage in more purposeful action. It combines strength and intellect in confronting a moral mission.

Sailboat (M) Propelled by the wind, a sailboat may mention to surrender to the elements or to a higher power. Thus, it may relate to your faith and trust in a higher power to move you safely to your destination in life. The sail may represent the mind and the hull the body. When the two are perpendicular, it represents the balance of mind and body.

Sailing (M) On the ocean blue, sailing is an activity that signifies letting go and allowing the forces of the winds and currents of spirit to propel you forward in life.

Salad dressing (M) Salad dressing brings flavor to salads and therefore may indicate that you need to add more flavor to a creative venture or product.

Salad dressing, Wishbone (M) The brand name Wishbone may metaphorically point to fulfillment, as it refers to the breastbone or the cavity where the heart is. It may call back a memory of a deep wish or desire that has been forgotten.

Sand (L) Sand represents hundreds of years of evolution at your feet. Made up of particles of eroded material, it may comment on the process of disintegration and regeneration of life. Sand may point to your personal evolution as it is connected to the evolution of the collective. As with "the sands of time," shifting through sand may mention that you are looking at the continuum of your life's passage in order to sift through the growth experiences of your life to measure how far you have come.

San Francisco (M) As the City by the Bay, San Francisco may be the setting for the individual who is concerned with developing a multicultural view. It may suggest that you are joining an elite group of Americans who value the arts. The ground of gay activism, San Francisco may represent frustration around the free expression of your sexual preference.

Carlos Santana (M) The Latin music sensation whose fame remained constant over three decades, Carlos's onstage performance in your dreams may signify the spiritual qualities and values of music. He may arrive as a teacher to the unmastered musician. He may bring a message of harmony.

Sapphire (L) Enhancing qualities of expression such as clarity, higher thought, truth, and wisdom, a sapphire may assist you in bringing forward a new expression of yourself. (See *Gems*.)

Satellite dish (M) A house with a satellite dish will receive signals from across the globe. It may mention that you are able to receive telepathic information through the dream state.

Saturn (U) A planet that represents hard work and lessons of limitations, Saturn's appearance in a dream may come as a sign of difficult times. However, it always brings strength and stability through self-discipline and mastery over life's challenges. It may appear to represent a time of fatherhood and appreciation of patriarchal structure.

Savanna (L) Associated with the wild game of Africa, a savanna is a wilderness with intrigue at every turn and interesting wildlife to explore. It suggests the multitude or varying experiences of life in one place. It teaches you to cherish and appreciate the variety in your environment and your life.

Saw (M) Used to cut wood, a saw may mention that it is time to divide your duties or the workload in your life with someone else.

Sawdust (M) Wading through sawdust may point to the debris that needs to be cleaned up from some project recently under construction. Sawdust may point to having witnessed something dirty.

Saxophone (M) A wind instrument used to play mostly jazz and ballads, a saxophone delivers its sound from deep within the soul. A character playing a saxophone in your dreams may announce a deep soul connection with someone who has entered your life.

Scale (M) Standing on a scale in your dreams may express concerns about your weight. It may mention the need to lose or gain weight. A broken scale may point to your reluctance to be weighed or measured against norms or external standards. It may reflect an unfair situation.

Scanner (M) Using a scanner may signify needing to transfer information from paper into a computer in order to process it. In this way, it may represent reading or taking in information through your perception and moving it to awareness so that it can be processed. It may also simply state "Take a look at her."

Scarab (L) Associated with Egyptian mysticism, the scarab represents reincarnation of the soul, death, resurrection, and immortality.

Scarf (M) A scarf worn around a character's neck in a dream may bring attention to the throat area, perhaps suggesting that he is covering up or not expressing who he is. As an expression of style, a scarf may represent a suave and sophisticated demeanor.

Scars (L) A scarred face may point to an old emotional wound that you need to face. It may also point to self-consciousness or embarrassment.

Scepter (L) Held in the hand of the king or queen, the scepter represents the assignment of position or rule passed from generation to generation. It may represent authority that is unquestioned.

School bus (M) The arrival of a school bus may suggest that you be taken on a journey to receive some important lessons for your personal growth. Sitting in the back of the bus may represent discrimination. Driving a school bus may suggest that you are in charge of others and interested in their welfare.

Schools (M) Schools in our dreams represent places of learning where we receive the lessons we need to grow intellectually and psychologically. Entering an elementary school represents learning something basic such as balancing your checkbook or getting enough to eat. A high school may represent that which prepares you for work in the world or lessons about your spiritual nature. Enrolling in a university or college might represent being ready to learn what it takes to graduate in life. It may represent concerns about your professional career or ways of achieving recognition and status in society.

Arnold Schwarzenegger (L, M) A hero with superstrength and a godlike body, Arnold may appear as a symbol of Hercules in a dream to perform superhuman feats. He, like Hercules, may appear to signify someone who must prove his worth through acts of strength yet who still appears inept or clumsy. This combination of greatness and self-doubt may comment on your poor self-concept or feelings that you are a misfit in society.

Scissors (M) A pair of scissors may appear as an instrument for cutting psychological or emotional ties. Perhaps you may need to cut the threads of an old relationship in order to let go of unfulfilled desires. Cutting hair may represent cutting off your personal power. Cutting fabric may comment on preparation for a new form, such as a new identity or career.

Scorpio (U) The sign associated with deep soul work, Scorpio may point to a solitary path for a while on which self-discipline can be established. Scorpio is a passionate and emotional sign that may deliver a sting in romantic relationships. A Scorpio may arrive in your life to assist you in healing sexual wounds and issues of betrayal.

Screaming (M) Screaming in a dream may represent the act of giving expression to your fears or anger. It may compensate for holding back your emotions in waking life. It may also be a response to a night terror or bad dream.

Screws (M) Turning a screw in a dream may mention that you need to tighten up or firm up some arrangements. It may point to someone who is literally screwing things up or screwing you out of what you deserve. Unwinding a screw may comment on a major screwup or mistake you have made.

Seal (L) The vocalization of pride is the attribute of Seal in the dreamscape. Seal may also come as a clown to spark the spirit of play and to coax out happiness at a depressing time.

Seat belts (M) Fumbling with seat belts in a car may reflect concerns about your safety while moving forward in life. It may compensate for feeling unsafe in a real-life situation. It may mention to hold yourself together, as in controlling your emotions.

Seaweed (L) Seaweed may comment on psychological and emotional growth. It may represent that which grows beneath the surface, or the growth of your creativity.

Seeds (L) Symbols of regeneration that sprout new offerings when cultivated, seeds are elements or ideas planted that present new growth. An acorn seed represents stamina and strength, a flower seed the regeneration of beauty, a pine cone is the symbol of masculine unfolding, a pumpkin seed is the planting of ideas for later harvest of wealth, and sunflower seeds represent masculine radiance.

Semi truck (M) A vehicle that carries a big load, a semi truck passing you on the road in your dreams may demonstrate how much of a workload or emotional load you are carrying. Perhaps you need to unload on a good friend.

Seven (L) The number seven represents the highest manifestation of spirit into matter and points to a spiritual life. It also represents higher knowledge, luck, and success.

7-Eleven (convenience store) (M) Stopping at a 7-Eleven in a dream may be a metaphor for enlightenment. It may be a sign reminding you that life is abundant. Anything your heart desires can be available to you twenty-four hours a day if you adopt the law of abundance.

7UP (M) Enjoying a 7UP may be a commentary on some experience or situation you find refreshing, such as joyful conversation with a friend. It may represent enthusiasm. In numerology, the number seven represents a dimension in which spirit is manifest. Thus dreaming of 7UP may point to a desire for a more spiritual life and a more enlightened view of your present circumstances. (See *Soda.*)

Sex (M) Dreaming about having sex may compensate for sexual inactivity. It may fulfill a desire for intimacy and sexual expression. Being caught having sex may mention that you feel exposed sexually or embarrassed about sexual feelings.

Shack (M) Living in a shack may represent that you feel that you are living with limited resources or that you don't desire the comforts of life. It may point to embarrassment about your circumstances.

Shaking hands (M) Shaking hands may predict a successful contract in business. It may also welcome an important individual who may soon appear in your life. It is a sign of commitment.

Shampoo (M) Washing hair with shampoo may suggest that you clean out dead psychic energy in order to free personal power. Shampooing may also mention that it is time to get someone "out of your hair."

Shark (L) Shark offers the medicine or power to confront your greatest fears. It can come as a response to a fearful situation. Once the fear is conquered, the courage and strength of Shark can deliver you to the bottom of the ocean of fear and beyond the limits of what you perceive as safe waters in order to conquer negative emotions. Being attacked by a shark in a dream might signify a confrontation with someone who could take advantage of your naïveté.

Sheets (M) Like linens, sheets bring comfort and luxury to the skin. Making a bed with fine linens may point to concerns about material comfort. Putting on fresh white sheets may signify bringing the essence of purity into your sex life.

Shells (L) Shells represent the treasures of the sea and point to your creativity. With their spiral structure, they often reflect the process of moving inward, as in self-exploration. They represent the window into the feminine and into creativity itself.

Shirt (M) For a man buttoning up a shirt may point to projecting an image of integrity without exposing your heart. It may comment on putting on a fresh new attitude for business. If the shirt is casual it may represent trying on a more relaxed or casual attitude.

Shoes (M) Shoes in their various styles protect your feet. They bring attention to how grounded you are on the earth and in the world. Losing shoes in a dream may represent ungroundedness or convey that you are losing touch with reality. Cowboy boots may point to a man who loves 'em and leaves 'em. High heels may mention a woman's need to dress up and look tall.

Shoestrings (M) Shoestrings may comment on living on a shoe-string or living on a limited budget. Untied shoes may remark on the lack of preparedness to move forward, or even laziness.

Shopping (M) Shopping for clothing may comment on deciding about and trying on new attitudes. It may express concerns about finding the right attitude to wear in a situation. Shopping for food may mention concerns about nutrition and feeding others, such as your family members.

Shopping cart (M) A shopping cart represents retrieving nourishment or the rewards from the world. A shopping cart with a loose wheel may point to instability. An empty shopping cart may point to coming up empty in a particular enterprise. It may also reflect concerns about the stock market.

Shorts (M) Wearing shorts in a dream may mention that you are selling yourself short. As shorts are associated with little boys, they may comment on childish behavior or wanting to have a youthful image in the world. In that they expose the legs, for a woman, wearing shorts may suggest her readiness to expose herself and her outer beauty.

Shoulders (L) Attention to the shoulders may mention your strength to carry a load. A man or woman with exaggerated broad shoulders may represent superior strength and the ability to take on responsibility. Shouldering too much responsibility may metaphorically be expressed as carrying a cement block or another heavy object on the shoulders.

Shower (M) The shower stall may represent a place for emotional and spiritual cleansing. It may suggest that you come clean and confess.

Shutters (M) Shutters on the window may represent the eyelids. Therefore, dreaming about shutters may mention that someone's eyes are shut to the truth.

Silk (M) Silk is a smooth and sensual fabric that denotes richness and wealth. Dreaming about silk may suggest that you have adopted an elegant style and have developed poise.

Silo (M) A place for storage of grain, a silo may represent a large bank account or mention the need to save money.

Silver (L) A precious metal associated with the attributes of the feminine aspect, silver brings the qualities of intuition, receptivity, passive sensitivity, and wisdom. Delivered or worn as a piece of jewelry, it signifies wearing feminine values. Often given as a wedding gift in the form of silverware, it represents the fine and elegant tools of feminine service. For instance, a silver platter represents receiving the wealth and abundance of the goddess presented through her grace.

Silver car (M) Driving a silver vehicle delivers feminine expression.

O. J. Simpson (L, M) O.J.'s appearance in a dream may comment on the shadow in the subconscious of a man or a woman.

He may come as a villain who seeks to kill your innocence or goodness. He may bring illumination to your own hatred, anger, and abusive nature. In that he may have been guilty of murder and judged innocent, he may represent transgressions you have gotten away with.

Singapore (M) With its crowds of people, the setting of Singapore may present concerns about being overcrowded or being just a face in a crowd. In this way, it may comment on lack of recognition or feeling insignificant. As a play on words, it may translate into "singing even if one is poor."

Singing (M) Singing is joyful expression, and dreaming about singing may comment on reaching fulfillment by changing your mood. It may signify harmony in some relationship.

Single bed (M) Discovering a room with a single bed in your dreams may refer to your independence and reluctance to commit to a relationship.

Sink (M) Dreaming about a kitchen sink may comment on having to stomach a great deal of family pressure. It may actually be a metaphor for the stomach, with the belly button as the drain and the garbage disposal as the intestines. A dirty sink might signal a need for a nutritional cleansing soon.

Six (L) Six is the number of decay of old forms into harmony, beauty, and balance of power. It may also symbolize uniformity, consciousness, the unification of the heart, and the creative center as manifesting love.

Skateboard (M) An adolescent riding a skateboard in a dream may mention an aspect of your personality that is fun-loving and free and finessing the way around the block with unique style. As an adolescent approach to moving through life, skateboarding suggests having fun by making something difficult look easy.

Skating (M) Roller-skating may represent skating through life without a care, worry, or concern. On concrete surfaces, it may show the exhilaration that comes with conquering a concrete project. Ice-skating may point to gliding through your fears and transforming them into a dance. It may mention the necessity to keep balance and poise in a fearful situation.

Skeleton (L) As the structure of the human body, a skeleton in your dreams may point to revealing the underlying beliefs that support and sustain your life. It may mention the skeletons in the closet or an old forgotten transgression about which you may feel guilty. Hauntingly, a skeleton may come as a messenger of death of the personality or ego.

Skiing (M) Downhill skiing may mention that you are successfully exercising control over your fears. Skiing down the north face of a mountain represents moving through your greatest fears with ease.

Skipping (M) Skipping relates to a lighthearted way of moving to your destination. It may also mention that you are skipping a necessary step.

Skirt (M) A full, long skirt worn by a character may suggest that a wise woman has entered the scene who expresses the qualities of a mature female.

Skull and crossbones (L) A symbol of poison, a skull and crossbones may come to reflect the poisoned ideals or negative influences that present a clear danger in your life. It may also indicate that you have been poisoned by the influence of another.

Skydiving (M) Skydiving may signify taking a leap of faith where you have to free-fall for a while and trust that you will have a gentle landing. Falling out of a plane without a parachute may mention that you are about to have a crash landing because of your lofty ideas or too-high ideals. Dreaming of skydiving may also tell you to get back on the ground quickly and be more realistic.

Sleeping (M) Being asleep in a dream may comment that you are unconscious of the facts in a situation. It may mention that you are out of touch.

Sleeping Beauty (L, M) The story of Aurora, the princess who was put under the spell or curse of a long sleep, may appear to present a lesson to a woman who is cursed by evil jealousy and kept from recognizing her own beauty. She may point to a woman who lives in a dreamworld and needs to wake up out of the spell of self-loathing.

Smoking (M) Smoking in a dream, especially if you are not a smoker, may point to worrying or the presence of unexpressed anger.

Smoky quartz (L) Grounding light and activating the root and sexual chakra, this crystal may be uncovered to help you reconnect with the earth. It may stimulate your sexuality and assist in the healing of sexual issues. (See *Crystal.*)

Snake (L) In general, the snake can be one of the most powerful forces emerging from a dream. The power of Snake brings active libidinous or sexual energy out of the subconscious for creative use. Snake power is healing power that when cultivated and used can heal your physical and emotional wounds. The undulating movement of Snake moves the energy known as kundalini up the spine of its initiate to activate a spiritual awakening. It may announce the call to the profession of a healer or shaman. Snake may signify wisdom in its association with the tree of knowledge. Snakes may sometimes represent deep-seated fears that disrupt your life, or sexual fears where there has been trauma or violation.

Snapdragon (L) A snapdragon may point to the bite of passion. It may point to someone you may fall deeply in love with and who will eventually betray you. It represents forgiveness.

Snickers (M) Eating a Snickers bar may be a response to a situation from which you derived a great deal of enjoyment. It points to a humorous conversation or interaction. It could be associated with someone with a good sense of humor.

Snoopy (L, M) Snoopy of Peanuts fame is an imaginative character who sleeps on top of his doghouse rather than inside. He can represent a friend who can't easily be controlled or led around on a leash. He may come with the message to stop daydreaming about being the Red Baron or to let go of other fruitless fantasies and join the real world. Or he might encourage you to use your imagination and to hold on to your dreams.

Snorkeling (M) Snorkeling may suggest that you are swimming on the surface of your emotions. It may represent seeing through the surface into the depths of a situation or searching for wealth.

Snow (L) As frozen or crystallized rain, snow may signify the release from fear resulting in a beautiful blanket of inner peace. It can point to the season of winter or the later years of life.

Snowboarding (M) Maneuvering skillfully down a slope on one board, snowboarding in a dream metaphorically translates into surfing or demonstrating finesse in conquering your fears.

Snow White (L, M) Snow White may convey deep patterns of jealousy and envy that threaten a woman's innocence, beauty, and spiritual purity. She may elicit you to embrace your innocence in a situation where you felt ridiculed or judged.

Soap (M) Used for cleaning the skin, a bar of soap may urge you to cleanse your body and soul of emotional garbage. It may come as a recommendation to do a physical or nutritional cleanse. Or dreaming about soap may state "Get clean" or confess.

Soccer (M) Since it's a game played with the feet, playing soccer in a dream may comment on stepping onto the playing field of life grounded and ready to make a goal. A soccer ball alternates five-sided and six-sided geometric patterns in black and white, and the pentagon is the construct of creativity and the hexagon the construct of productivity. Therefore, it may metaphorically combine these structures to suggest playing creatively with a team in order to be productive. Soccer may also appear as a play on words, suggesting "Sock her," remarking on abuse on a woman's pride.

Social security card (M) As a form of identification, dreaming about your social security card or number may point to an over-identification with the authoritarian structures of society. As a play on words, it may also mention feelings of insecurity in social situations.

Socks (M) Socks bring warmth and comfort to the feet. Throwing away a pair of socks may signify a readiness to let go or to go beyond your comfort zone. Having mixed socks in a dream may comment that you are wearing two identities in the world. Or it may represent an embarrassment.

Soda (M) Drinking a soda can be a sweet, refreshing experience.

In a dream, soda may refer to an event where you experienced a great deal of pleasure. Soda may also represent the need to quench your desire for uplifting fulfillment, or it may represent a refreshing idea. (See *7UP, Coca-Cola, Pepsi, Sprite*.)

Sofa (M) Representing concerns about comfort with social relationships, a couch whose fabric is stained might suggest that you are concerned about your reputation being stained by the carelessness of others.

Software (M) Dreaming about programs installed in your PC may signify patterns of belief that have been programmed into your mind that "run" or drive your personality. New software—new beliefs—may also be installed in your bio-computer for personal growth.

Soldier (M) A soldier may appear to suggest that it is time to commit to service or to a purpose. He may bring the message that perhaps you have become too patriotic in allegiance to your country. He may also represent a militaristic attitude.

Sore throat (M) Having a sore throat in a dream may mention your inability to speak your mind. It may also suggest that you are tired of trying to get your point across or that there is some unexpressed anger that may need to be soothed.

Sorting (M) Sorting objects may comment on needing to sort out a problem at hand. Sorting through things in the closet might mention that you are involved in sorting out the past and the attitudes and beliefs that have influenced you.

Soup (M) With its many ingredients, preparing soup may suggest a project containing a variety of ideas being cooked up and simmered, to be served as a product of your creativity. (See *Campbell's soup*.)

South (L) The direction of transformation and manifestation, the south brings your vision, needs, and desires into manifestation. Associated with liberation and purification through fire, it liberates the soul from the past. Traveling toward the south is to travel to personal freedom. (See *Compass, Four directions.*)

South America (M) Landing in South America in a dream may represent entering a passionate phase of your life where life is colorful and celebratory.

Spaghetti (M) Long, sticky, and stringy, spaghetti may point to being involved in a long and endless conversation that is uncomfortable and messy. It may also comment on a long and enjoyable conversation. Dreaming about spaghetti may also suggest feeling entangled within a relationship.

Sparrow (L) Sparrow comes to deliver the message "look to the ordinary events of life as meaningful and special." It can signify the practice of contemplation. Sparrow's message is that what is most common can be good, or that the road most traveled is the one to take. (See *Birds.*)

Speakers (M) Coming upon a speaker in an incongruent place may bring attention to the need to express feminine values, as in "speak her." The appearance of a speaker may, more simply, amplify your desire to speak up and be heard.

Speedboat (M) Symbolizing skimming over the currents of life, riding on a speedboat may signify getting through some emotional issue quickly. It could point to overconfidence.

Sphinx (L) A symbol of ancient Egypt, the Sphinx signifies the mystery and power of Ra, the sun god. With its human head, body of a bull, feet of a lion, and wings of an eagle, it symbolizes a combination of physical, intellectual, and spiritual power.

Spider (L) Spiders weaving webs in dreams mention the creativity at hand or what is being created in your life. Spider spins and weaves dreams into realities through time and patience. The web is the fabric of the tapestry of your life that you create with your thoughts. The appearance of a spider may point to a need to take on a creative project or to cultivate through some art form.

Spinach (L) A leafy vegetable containing a great deal of iron for the blood, spinach may appear in a dream as a symbol of super-strength.

Spiral (L) A symbol of movement inward, the spiral is a circular journey toward the core self or spiritual center. It is a symbol that points to the penetration of the deepest aspects of the soul and its wisdom.

Spiral staircase (U) As a path spiraling upward to spiritual attainment, a spiral staircase may appear to bridge the mind with a higher intelligence. It may signify the upward path to heaven to receive the blessing of God.

Spock (L, M) As the half-human, half-Vulcan adviser of the Starship *Enterprise,* Mr. Spock may appear in a dream to give sound and objective advice. He may bring the power of reason separated from the emotional function and comment on not letting your emotions rule in important decisions. He may appear as a levelheaded guide helping you to navigate safely toward a personal mission.

Sponge (L) Porous and soft, a sponge may symbolically represent spongy exterior boundaries. It may comment that you too easily absorb the energy of others. As in "sponging off someone," it may mention that you could be using people or are too dependent.

Spoon (M) A tool used for eating soup may suggest the act of nurturing yourself or others. It may represent the giving of compassion and love. A bent spoon may point to being fed slanted or distorted beliefs about another.

Sports (M) Playing sports represents being active and aggressive in pursuing your goals in life through fairness and good sportsmanship. Dreaming about sports may comment on a competitive endeavor. Observing sports events may point to witnessing your progress in achieving your goals. It may suggest that you are being competitive.

Sports arena (M) As a spectator in a sports arena, you may capture the greater view or the whole picture as to your position in life's game. You may gain an overall sense of your performance.

Sportswear (M) Sports and athletic wear point to team identification and may comment "Join them and win." A man appearing in a woman's dream wearing an athletic jersey may indicate that the man is a real player: "Watch out."

Sprite (M) Sprite, a soft drink bottled by Coca-Cola, as an outstanding symbol may appear to bring attention to its name or relate to a refreshing experience. It may announce a mystical fairy buzzing around your head in the night, perhaps to bring the message of a small blessing. It may also comment on living vivaciously.

Square (L) Anything square appearing in a dream may comment on the importance of structure. It may represent fixed or concrete ideas. It may also represent the four corners or directions as bringing form to your ideas. A square denotes rigidity.

Squid (L) Sometimes a monster emerging out of the depths of the subconscious, Squid may appear as a frightening reminder of something that could be clinging to you. But in actuality it may appear to ask you to see what monstrous beliefs, patterns, or feelings lie twenty thousand leagues below that may be tormenting you. A creature that holds his own ink like a fountain pen, Squid may come to deliver the message to write a book.

Staff (L) A symbol of power for the sage, a staff represents the forces of higher knowledge and spiritual power. The staff brought to life as a snake, as with the staff of Moses, represents the creative power of God brought into manifestation. It may also represent a crutch.

Stage (M) Being onstage may mention that you are performing in life and may not be expressing your authentic nature. It may also represent the stage on which we play out our life dramas and comedies. It may point to the need for self-reflection.

Staircase (M, U) A staircase may represent the passage or connection between the mind and the body. Or it may suggest the movement from the structures of your own thoughts to a higher consciousness. A spiral staircase may reflect the steps to higher spiritual levels, each step mastering important spiritual principles. It may represent achievement.

Staples (M) Staples fasten pages together and thus signify the need to keep things or your life in order. They may indicate a need to remedy feeling scattered or disorganized.

Star (U) As radiant energy, a star may appear in a dream to represent your own radiant qualities and as a sign of self-fulfillment. It may make a wish come true, as in "Wish upon a star." Or it may lead you to destiny, fame, and recognition. Starlight in dreams offers the light in the darkness, which is like a beacon to follow. It may arrive as a sign of the birth of a new idea. It may also reflect your connection to the cosmos.

- **Four-pointed star** (L) The star of Bethlehem is the four-pointed star that appeared in the sky as a sign of the birth of Christ. This star is associated with Sirius, the Dog Star, which for the ancient Egyptians represented heavenly power. In your dream, it may be a sign of a great spiritual awakening or the birth of Christ-like qualities.

- **Five-pointed star** (L) The pentagram with its five radiating points is the insignia of the goddess and a symbol of her fertility and creativity. The same five radiating points are found in the flora within nature, from the morning glory to the violet blossom. This star symbolizes the creative power within nature. The Wicca tradition uses this star as a symbol of protection and power. As a more modern symbol, it appears on the American flag to represent the states and, therefore, uniqueness and individuality. If the five-pointed star appears on a pair of Converse sneakers in your dream, it may recommend that you step into your personal power.

- **Six-pointed star** (L) The Star of David, a symbol of the Judaic tradition, consists of two interlocking triangles merged together. This symbol joins the power of the heart with the power of creativity to manifest love. It may also signify the union of heaven and earth. As a sign, it points to the return of the Messiah or true king.

- **Twelve-pointed star** (L) The twelve points symbolize twelve principles of spiritual attainment through service. They are love, charity, hope, compassion, truth, light, creativity, faith, honor, enlightenment, joy, and peace.

Star Wars (L, M) Any of the characters from *Star Wars,* whether Luke Skywalker or Obi-Wan Kenobi, may point to a personal quest for the light against the forces of evil.

Statue (M) A statue is a likeness carved or sculptured out of earthen material. It may represent an idol of worship. In that it holds no life, a statue appearing in dreams may represent your projections. It may point to a stationary existence, or to someone who is lifeless.

Statue of Liberty (M) The Statue of Liberty was a gift from France to the United States. It represents cultural freedom. Thus, it may appear as a symbol of liberty and freedom for all. As the gateway to New York, it may represent free enterprise. In your dreams it may stand as a symbol of your own freedom.

Steamroller (M) A steamroller may point out that you have allowed someone to flatten your spirit. It may be the response to a conversation in which you felt run over by the persuasive ideas of another. Or you may have felt that you have been pushed away from your own intention. It may be a response to emotional trauma.

Steel (L) Structures or containers created from steel signify strength, stability, and impenetrability. They may also point toward an individual's resilience or untarnished reputation. As a personality trait, steel is associated with a powerful will and bravery, as in "nerves of steel."

Steering wheel (M) The steering wheel of a vehicle is used to change directions. Difficulty steering a vehicle down a road may reflect difficulty in changing the direction of your life or staying on the road with your short- and long-term goals.

Steps (M) The front steps to a house may demonstrate the difficulty you have in getting close to someone. It may represent the steps of achievement toward ownership. Each step in a staircase may represent a step of growth.

Stereo (M) A stereo in a room may comment on two people talking at the same time. Or it may point to a partnership that demonstrates equality.

Sting (L, M) The British rock star Sting appears as the musical alchemist who turns poetry into music and then into gold records. As the alchemist, he demonstrates that music transforms the culture.

Stolen car (M) Discovering that your car has been stolen may signify having your identity taken from you, perhaps by an event such as losing your job.

Stork (L) Carrying its own mail sack, Stork is the deliverer of a message you may or may not expect. It can offer the happy news of pregnancy, or any other good news. (See *Birds*.)

Stove (M) As an appliance used to cook food, a stove may reflect concerns about nurturing others as well as yourself. The oven may represent the womb of a female and may announce pregnancy.

Strawberries (L) Picking strawberries may signify the discovery of your sensual side, which is ripe, red, and luscious. If strawberries are offered to you in your dreams, they may represent an invitation to be passionate with a romantic partner.

Stream (L) A stream may signify following a stream of thought or being in the flow of things. It delivers you with ease to life's purpose. It may also represent a soothing and relaxing situation.

Street (M) Whether residential or commercial, a street may suggest different avenues of expression and concerns. If you are driving through a residential area in your dreams, you may be looking at family values or concerns. A commercial area with shops and stores suggests exploring new options or shopping for ideas.

Street sign (M) A street sign is a landmark that identifies a location. The name of a street in a dream may provide important information as to the area of psychological work or personal enterprise you are proceeding toward. For instance, Park Avenue may represent movement toward financial success and status, or Oak Street may reflect a direction toward a solid or stable enterprise.

String (M) Unwinding string from a ball in a dream may mean that you have felt strung along by someone. Being given string may represent someone's suggestions that you may decide to follow.

Stripes (M) Stripes may mean that someone is making a bold statement. Horizontal stripes may denote straightforwardness. Vertical stripes may signify nonconformity or well-roundedness. Vertical black-and-white stripes may point out that you are a prisoner of your own limited thinking.

Study (M) Walking into a study in a dream may indicate the need for quiet in order to concentrate and focus on your studies or work. It may also point to something you have to learn.

Stuffed animal (M) Discovering a stuffed animal in the attic may point to childhood issues and feelings that have been repressed. A stuffed animal is an object of emotional comfort and attachment.

Subway (M) A form of rapid transit that travels through underground tunnels, the subway may symbolize exploring the underworld and moving through psychological milestones to your destination of wholeness. A subway may also indicate a preoccupation with getting to work and may reflect concerns in making a deadline.

Suitcase (M) A packed suitcase may signify that you are about to travel or may predict a future trip. As baggage, it may also illustrate the tendency to carry the legacy of patterns from your family of origin around with you.

Sun (U) The sun symbolizes the source of light in our solar system. As all the planets rotate around it, the sun demonstrates the source of light within you. Considered to have masculine qualities, it may come to represent reason, logic, and the strength of the will put into action. As the sun god Ra, the sun brings with it the mystical knowledge of ancient Egypt whose temples prepared the initiate for eternal life. A rising sun may represent a new beginning or a new lease on life. A setting sun represents the end of an important chapter in your life. In a dream, the sun's arrival may predict a powerful new man in a woman's life or the rising of her own masculine qualities.

Sun and moon (L, U) These two symbols combined represent the solar, or masculine aspect, in union with the lunar, or feminine aspect, of the soul. Bringing together the qualities of vision, inspiration, and intuition with the radiant powers of reason and logic put into action, the sun and moon represent balance.

Sunflower (L) The sunflower is a sturdy and tall flower that represents radiance and masculinity.

Sunglasses (M) Used to block out the rays of the sun, sunglasses may offer protection. They may also mention that you are hiding your identity. The wearer may be secretive or deceptive. Sunglasses may humorously represent acting cool.

Supermarket (M) Shopping in a supermarket may express concerns about life's staples, food, clothing, and shelter. It may also signify that there are many choices in life that can help fulfill your desires. Food itself may represent that which nurtures and sustains. A supermarket may also indicate shopping for a relationship or discovering your position in society, or it may represent the delivery of the fruits of your labor.

Surfboard (M) A surfboard may represent the tool or platform of creative thought.

Surfing (M) Surfing may be the next best thing to walking on water, and surfing a giant wave may comment on riding the curl of a great creative wave, which may result in a great deal of productivity. Surfing may comment on how competent you feel or point to some forward-moving energy that could carry your idea a long way. Each wave you surf represents a new manifestation of your creativity or a new opportunity.

Swastika (L) A symbol associated with the Third Reich of Hitler's Germany, the swastika (with blades moving counterclockwise) represents forces of destruction. Inverted to its clockwise rotation, it signifies creativity and regeneration.

Sweater (M) Putting on a sweater in a dream may be a remedy of comfort after having come in contact with someone who was emotionally cold toward you. A sweater offers comfort and warmth around the upper body, including the heart, and thus may mention the need to improve your mood. A pink sweater may express love, and a blue sweater may communicate peace.

Sweeping (M) Using a broom and sweeping up dirt in a dream may be a comment on the process of cleaning up a mess in your family, or at work, or it may represent an emotional cleansing. It may point to a clean sweep or an experience you benefited from.

Swimming (M) Swimming in a pool may offer a refreshing experience and a release from tensions. It may represent a spiritual experience with others. Swimming in the ocean may indicate your readiness to explore the subconscious as well as your feelings.

Sword (L, M) A symbol of valor, the sword cuts to the essence of truth that dispels the darkness. The sword brings significant spiritual power to the individual who holds it. Associated with the Archangel Michael, this symbol represents higher truth and the cutting away of evil through celestial power brought to earth.

Synthesizer (M) Playing a synthesizer may suggest that you need to synthesize or integrate some new information into understanding. This electronic keyboard may also comment that harmony is the key to resolving a situation of conflict.

Syrup (M) Having syrup poured on pancakes in a dream may indicate that someone is being sickeningly sweet. Syrup may also express the desire for a smooth and sweet encounter.

Tape measure (M) A tape measure may point to feelings that you don't measure up or that you are not good enough, or it may offer a comparison. Measuring something in a dream may reveal the size of a conflict or issue in your life that needs further analysis.

Tasmanian Devil (L, M) As the whirlwind of destructive intention, this cartoon character represents a mischievous, angry, devilish aspect of the personality that may need to be embraced or tamed. This devil also brings comedy to our angry moments and may summon you to look at the destructive aspects of your personality.

Tattoo (L) Tattoos portray archetypes with which you may identify. They may act as metaphors for what is deeply imprinted within the soul, whether devil or angel. Tattoos may make a strong statement about another's identity. Some people, such as the Hawaiians, wear tattoos that connect them with an ancestral lineage and with their spirit guides, called Amakua.

Taurus (U) Stability, beauty, and pleasure are the message of Taurus, the sign of the bull. Taurus may also signify your stubborn side and your resistance to change.

Taxi (M) A taxi may indicate your tendency to "drive" others or to act as a chauffeur. It may also represent a way to get to your destination through someone else's efforts.

Tea (M) A cup of tea may represent something soothing being offered, as well as leisurely conversation with a friend. Tea may suggest refinement and point to the execution of good manners with an important client.

Teaching (M) Being in front of a classroom in a dream may indicate your desire to teach others or to share what you know. Teaching in a dream may compensate for feelings that you are unable to influence others in the way you would like. Standing in front of an empty classroom may signify feelings of frustration that no one seeks your knowledge or advice.

Teapot (M) Pouring tea from a teapot may represent feminine service and hospitality.

Teeth (L) Teeth represent the power of assertive communication. Decaying teeth and teeth falling out represent losing the ability to communicate your feelings or thoughts effectively. Tooth decay may also refer to a situation where you failed to get your point across, especially with an authority figure.

Telephone (M) Waking up to the ring of a telephone in a dream may mean that someone is trying to communicate something telepathically to you through the dream state. If you are in the middle of having a conversation with someone and the phone suddenly goes dead, this may indicate frustration about being cut off by someone. Dialing a wrong number may represent that your perceptions of someone are wrong or that you are approaching the wrong person for what you need.

Television (M) Watching television in a dream may point to a need to view something that is important for the conscious mind to comprehend. It may also represent leisure time and concerns over what's new and what's news. A television may indicate that it is time to "tell a vision" for the future that you have been carrying around in your mind.

Temple (U) The appearance of a temple may reflect concerns about worshiping God. A temple is a sacred spiritual space where you may receive spiritual insights and revelations and solidify your spiritual connection. It may refer to the need to pray or the desire to be close to God.

Ten (L) Ten is the number of the creative paradigm, the totality, the microcosm within the macrocosm, and the beginning of a new cycle. Ten denotes strength and success.

Tennis (M) Tennis is a sport in which a racquet is used by each player to volley a ball over a net that separates the players. The game of tennis may metaphorically refer to the process of networking for prospects for your business, or it may comment on a "racket" or scheme underlying a business deal.

Tent (M) Moving into a tent may point to the desire to free up your life. A tent may also signify setting up a temporary residence or comment on a desire to enjoy nature by camping in the outdoors. Having difficulty in putting up a tent may comment on frustration with your living situation and the impermanence in your life.

Thermometer (M) Because a thermometer measures your temperature, its appearance in a dream may comment on your tendency to be hotheaded or point out that you are heated up about an event or situation in your life. It may also signify the need to diagnose an illness.

Thermostat (M) A thermostat regulates heat and may signify an uncomfortable situation that leaves you cold. To turn up the heat in the home in a dream would suggest that you want to warm up to guests or provide a cozy atmosphere. A broken thermostat may reflect difficulties in regulating or controlling your environment or your mood.

Thighs (L) Thighs relate to childhood issues. Fat thighs may indicate having had to protect yourself during childhood from the pain of abuse.

Thirty-three (L) Thirty-three is the number of the Christ light and the embodiment of love. It represents the giving of unconditional love through spiritual service.

Thoroughfare (M) Traveling on a thoroughfare may suggest that you can count on power and prestige at the end of the road for adopting a thorough and fair approach to business.

Three (L) The number three represents spiritual power. As the spiritual trinity, it signifies the Father, the Son, and the Holy Spirit. Three may also be interpreted as the integration of body, mind, and spirit. It may point to a triangulation as a dysfunctional pattern in relationships.

Thumb (L) The thumb is used to grasp, hold, and press down.

The presence of a thumb may remark that you are under someone's thumb or are being manipulated. A broken or damaged thumb may suggest difficulty in grasping information or holding on to something for very long.

Thumbtack (M) Stepping on a thumbtack may signify a painful message, perhaps about your work. Pressing down on a thumbtack may signify a pressing issue that is on your mind.

Thunder (U) A clap of thunder may signify a big wake-up call from the spiritual dimensions. Thunder may announce an approaching lightning storm or a spiritual storm that is meant to enlighten you, or it may represent shocking news.

Thunderbird (L) A bird with supernatural powers, the thunderbird may arrive to summon you to use your personal power wisely or to make a loud and important statement to the world. A thunderbird may come as a sign that powerful circumstances or a turn in events are sure to happen soon.

Ticket (M) Purchasing an airplane ticket may be a sign of preparation for a trip or vacation in the near future. A ticket may also represent your passport to personal freedom.

Tidal wave (L) A tidal wave can point to a huge emotional shock, the result of a trauma of childhood, which emerges out of the sea of the unconscious as a warning. A tidal wave may also predict a serious illness or a huge emotional upset.

Tide laundry detergent (M) Tide is the most well-known brand name in laundry detergent. Tide may comment on the need to deter the tides from washing away your prospects. Tide may signify that the tide has risen and it is a great time to launder your emotional attitudes.

Tides (L) The ebb and flow of the tides, which are influenced by the lunar cycles, expresses the arrival of your wishes over time. The tides may comment on your readiness to experience the emotional qualities of life.

Tie (M) Wearing a tie may mean that you are ready to do business. A tie separates the head from the heart and thus might be telling you about someone who values his thinking more than the love inside him.

Tiger (L) The cultivation of personal authority and power may be the message of a tiger in a dream. The tiger signifies the power to exert your will in the world and the possession of leadership qualities. It holds a regal authority that is seldom challenged. A tiger may come to mention that you take the lead in orchestrating much-needed reforms in some community service.

Tigger (L, M) Bouncy, bouncy Tigger in the Winnie-the-Pooh adventures comes to demonstrate an enthusiastic individual who holds a positive outlook on life. He displays that you can bounce back from difficult times by keeping a positive attitude.

Tile (M) Tile may represent the pieces or concepts of yourself that make up your personality. In that tiles are usually square, they may reflect rigid attitudes that could be easily cracked or broken.

Tin (L) A thin, soft metal that is easily dented, tin may suggest some pliability regarding your personality. It may also indicate that your self-esteem can be easily damaged. If given as a gift, tin can represent a cheap offering of little monetary value. The tin cup is the beggar's tool, and the Tin Man is hollow and doesn't have a heart.

Tires (M) Tires on your vehicle represent the emotional qualities you ride on. A flat tire may arrive as a response to a big emotional issue that deflated you and stopped your progress temporarily. A flat tire on the right-hand side might reflect trouble related to the masculine side of the personality, which is associated with reason or logic. One on the left side symbolizes that an emotional issue may have wounded your feminine side or intuitive and receptive nature. Back tires relate to emotional issues of the past, and front tires signify more recent issues. Therefore, a flat left rear tire would metaphorically represent a big emotional issue from the past that affects your intuition.

Toaster (M) Turning bread into toast may metaphorically represent making money. It may also have associations with a surprise gift of money.

Toes (L) Toes help you to walk forward in a balanced manner. Therefore, a stubbed or injured toe may appear as a response to an emotional injury that caught you off balance.

Toilet (M) Sitting on the toilet in a dream may signify the need to release emotions, worries, or thoughts.

Toilet paper (M) Toilet paper may be associated with processing and releasing old beliefs or feelings.

Tokyo (M) As the embodiment of American capitalistic values, arriving in Tokyo may mean that you are seeking the rewards of materialism. A trip to Tokyo might also be associated with concerns about your productivity and reflects a competitive attitude.

Tomato (L) As a ripe fruit served in a salad, a tomato may represent a potential mate. In a man's dream, a tomato may signify a voluptuous woman.

Tombstone (M) A tombstone may indicate the need to revisit the gravesite of a dead relative symbolically in order to unravel limiting attitudes and patterns learned from this person. The headstone may also point to the need to grieve a loss, whether a real death or a personal failure.

Tony the Tiger (M) "Frosted Flakes are grrrrreat!" is the message of Tony the Tiger. His appearance in a dream may warn of a hard-pitching salesperson or an authority who may be trying to sell you on something sweet rather than something of substance.

Toolbox (M) A toolbox may contain your tools or skills for work. An empty toolbox may mean that you feel ill-equipped or unprepared for work.

Toothbrush (M) Brushing your teeth in your dreams may signify preparation for an important conversation in which you must be assertive and clear, or it may be a simple reminder to practice better oral hygiene.

Toothpaste (M) Toothpaste freshens the mouth and cleans the teeth. Receiving a tube of toothpaste in a dream may suggest the need to watch your words; you may be putting a bad flavor in the air. Toothpaste may also bring a literal message, commenting that you had better brush your teeth more regularly because you have bad breath.

Toothpick (M) A toothpick in a dream may indicate that you are being picky. Toothpicks may also indicate the need to remove deeply embedded beliefs about a topic of communication before saying anything more. On the other hand, a toothpick may also comment on the need for assertive communication.

Topaz (L) With its golden brown ray, topaz offers clarity of mind and balance to your creative intelligence. Topaz can also signify the need to possess an open mind and trust your intuition.

Tornado (L) Tornadoes may point to huge destructive changes, destroying old structures in your life and personality. This may signal a need to rebuild your life. As with Dorothy in *The Wizard of Oz,* the house swept up by the tornado signifies a transformation of the soul that allows acceptance of a new transcendent worldview or revised spiritual destiny.

Toto (L, M) Dorothy's loyal and frisky friend in *The Wizard of Oz* may appear to represent the mischief of a friend that might be about to create some real trouble. Toto may also appear as a guardian of the heroine, who protects you through loyal companionship on the quest home.

Toucan (L) An exotic bird with a huge beak, the toucan's message is that "two can" accomplish much, whether in a partnership, a business venture, or a creative project. The toucan may also speak of the good fortune that comes through relationship or marriage. (See *Birds.*)

Towels (M) Towels of soft fabric bring comfort and absorb water from the skin. A towel may signify receiving comfort from a friend after an emotional release. It may also be a sign that you need to dry some tears.

Tower (M) A high tower may represent that you feel exiled or placed in a position that separates you from others. A tower may comment on feeling isolated or lonely, or it may indicate that your expectations are too high.

Toyota 4Runner (M) As four is the number of grounding on the material plane, a 4Runner may suggest the need to ground your ideas quickly. The vehicle may also suggest that your forward-looking ideas keep you ahead of others. It may also signify someone on the run who needs to escape.

Train (M) A train transports a large group of people or products on a track laid by others. Dreaming of a train may indicate that you have adopted the values of a large group of people and therefore are on track.

Transmission (M) Transmission problems in a car or truck may be a response to an inability to shift gears and to proceed with increased power. Problems with transmission may also reflect your denial or inability to receive a message.

Tree (L) Trees represent life and wisdom. With roots in the Lower World, trees pump up the power of the earth and demonstrate our deep connection to the core of the earth through our own bodies. Their branches can represent branches of knowledge that reach toward the sky, or the Upper World, to obtain higher knowledge. Trees demonstrate the creative power of nature and point to your own potential to regenerate your life. The wood itself is an element used to build with. Trees symbolically have been associated with the Garden of Eden and returning to innocence. Trees also symbolize the fulfillment and enlightenment that can come through a direct relationship with nature.

• **Bare tree** (L) A barren tree can represent your need to embrace your own beauty, naked and unadorned. A bare tree is a winter tree and may indicate an understanding of the cycles of life, maturation, and the embracing of old age and its wisdom. The barren tree may also signify a time of loss or a fruitless venture.

• **Birch tree** (L) The birch tree signifies wisdom and naked beauty.

• **Blossoming tree** (L, M) As a sign of spring, a tree in bloom is associated with potential or new beginnings.

- **Fruit-bearing tree** (L) A tree with ripe fruit is associated with accepting the bounty of life. On the other hand, unripened fruit on a tree might represent having to wait for a project's fruition before enjoying the rewards.

- **Oak tree** (L) An oak tree symbolizes strength and stability.

- **Olive tree** (L) The olive tree brings the gift of peace. Its branches are an offering of peace for humanity.

- **Palm tree** (L) The palm represents victory and resurrection.

- **Willow tree** (L) The willow tree signifies flexibility and mourning. Red willow, for Native Americans, represents manifestation.

Trident (L) As a harpoon associated with Triton, the ruler of the undersea, the trident represents seizing the power of creative currents. As a lightning bolt from the heavens, it may be an indication of God's power as the supreme authority.

Trimming (M) Trimming a tree may suggest cutting away old branches or knowledge that are no longer useful. A trimming also may represent a feeling of being criticized or "cut apart" for your beliefs.

Tripod (M, L) Used to hold a camera steady, a tripod may be a support for your own vision for the future. As an ancient symbol, it may represent a spiritual triad—past, present, and future—in the moment.

Trowel (M) Used to smooth out plaster, a trowel may represent a necessary tool for smoothing over a problem, perhaps with a relationship.

Truck (M) Trucks, in general, carry a large load. Thus, a truck may represent the capacity to carry responsibility. A pickup truck usually represents masculine power. A semi may indicate that you are carrying a huge responsibility in your life, or that you are about to confront the legacy of patterns you are carrying from the past.

- **Dodge Ram** (M) This symbol of masculine power combines the symbology of Aries, the Ram, with a truck that symbolizes male-driven ideas and power. It might suggest that you possess the initiative and power to take on the challenges facing you. It may also announce someone you could have to go to war with to battle for your rights.

- **Ford Ranger** (M) A Ford Ranger beside you on the road of life may comment on your angry side. The word "ranger" breaks down to read "r-anger" or "our anger." It may appear to remind you to cool off.

True Value hardware (M) Visiting a True Value hardware store may suggest a search for intrinsic value. It may also indicate a search for tools or skills that are valuable for your work.

Tugboat (M) Being pulled by a tugboat in a dream may signify being rescued from an emotional issue or a confrontation, or it may represent slow movement.

Tulip (L) A pot of tulips may mean the first kiss of new beginnings. The first sign of spring, a field of tulips may represent an experience that begins a new cycle of life.

Tunnel (L) A dark tunnel may represent a dark passage in life where you may have to confront your fears. A tunnel may be related to a birth memory or to some passage of rebirth. Also, a tunnel may signify a symbolic death in which you usually find the proverbial light at the end.

Turkey (L) For Native Americans, the turkey comes to honor the act of giving and receiving. If a turkey comes gobbling into your dream, you may expect to receive a gift. Associated with Thanksgiving, the turkey may mean you are entering a time of appreciation for life's fulfillment.

Tina Turner (L, M) Tina may arrive in a dream as a bold voice from the past who still may have a strong impact on a woman's psyche in the present. She also may arrive to say "Age really makes no difference." In addition, she may come to represent a woman who, despite early abuse, can reclaim her power and keep going strong.

Turnip (L) As a root vegetable, the turnip may point to the need to "turn up" what has been buried underground in the subconscious.

Turquoise (L) A sacred stone used in Native American jewelry, turquoise, with its range in color from deep blue-green to green, signifies spiritual mastery. Turquoise offers the opportunity to open up expression to communicate your spiritual beliefs and higher truth.

Twelve (L) Twelve represents liberation from karma, spiritual freedom, cosmic order, and innocence. As a dozen, it may represent a bargain.

Twenty-two (L) Twenty-two is the number of a spiritual master. It signifies mastery of all planes—intuition and mental power combined into action.

Twins (L) The appearance of twins in a dream may point to the union of opposites or two opposing personalities within your psyche that have equal power.

Twix (M) Since there are two bars contained in every wrapper, Twix may represent the sharing of love and sensuality between two people or lovers.

Two (L) The number two represents partnerships, marriages, and the balance of the masculine and feminine aspects of the psyche. A dream including the number two may express concern about finding a mate or concerns about problems in a relationship or marriage. The number two also signifies duality, separation, or the union of opposites.

Typewriter (M) Clanking on a typewriter whose keys get stuck may mean that you are holding on to an old method of doing business or communication tactics that no longer work.

Typing (M) Typing on a computer may symbolize programming your mind to complete a necessary project. Typing may also refer to your desire to write or indicate a need to complete a task you've left undone.

Mike Tyson (M) Mike may appear as the overinflated ego who demonstrates strength without understanding, morality, or valor. He may announce that someone who is overpowering has come into your life.

Underwear (M) Hanging out underwear may be a sign that you are exposing your underlying beliefs, attitudes, and feelings to the world. Looking down and seeing yourself in underwear may be a response to an embarrassing situation in waking life in which you felt exposed.

Unicorn (L) This mythical and mystical animal can represent the power of your visionary abilities applied to the future. In that its horn projects from the middle of its forehead, the unicorn points to the power of the third eye to direct your decisions and movement forward. The unicorn also represents uniqueness and mystical knowledge.

Uphill (M) Climbing an uphill path may represent having to exert effort to attain your immediate or long-term goals. It may also mean that you are steadily climbing in status in your profession through consistent achievement.

Uranus (U) As the harbinger of great change, the presence of Uranus in a dream may signify that forces of change are at hand. Much like a tornado hitting your house, Uranus may initiate a crisis that causes you to reevaluate what is important in life. Being fired from your job or breaking up with a girlfriend or boyfriend may bring about a needed change to realign the personality with more serious endeavors. Uranus may also be part of a prophetic dream indicating earth changes or political turbulence arising out of the collective unconscious.

Vacuum cleaner (M) As a modern appliance that cleans the carpets, a vacuum may mention the need to clean your thoughts of dust and dirt. Rugs and carpets relate to the second or sexual chakra and, thus, their cleaning may represent the restoration of your creative power and flourishing sexuality freed from shame.

Darth Vader (L, M) "The dark force is with you" may be the message of Darth Vader's guest appearance in a dream as a shadow character. He may also come to comment on the mythological pattern of feeling betrayed by one's father.

Saint Valentine (U) This Holy Roman priest of the thirteenth century, whose feast is celebrated on February 14, Saint Valentine may appear to mention the sacredness of relationships and to honor romance as a sacred path of the heart.

Valley (L) A valley can represent the gifts of feminine wisdom acquired by descending into the womb or the bosom. Traveling from the peaks to the valley represents moving from inspiration to wisdom and fruition.

Vampire (L) A vampire may represent a shadow character who sucks the blood of others. He therefore may mention that you have been sucked dry by someone else's psychic power.

Van (M) Driving a van may represent moving forward with concerns about family. Because a van can carry many passengers, when it arrives at your front door in a dream it may indicate the arrival of a whole community of new friends. A commercial van may arrive with an important delivery that is necessary for a business enterprise, such as the tools or the help needed to solve a problem.

Vanity (M) A vanity with beauty tools and makeup may bring the message that you are too vain. It may also point to a desire to look pretty or to get some aid in developing your own beauty.

Vase (M) A vase may represent the female body or the receptacle for holding feminine values. If full of flowers, a vase may symbolize that you have arranged something beautiful to be presented as a reflection of your creative nature. As a container whose shape may be expressed as curved or as straight lines, a vase may signify the female body and its contours.

VCR (M) Putting in a tape into a VCR in your dreams may point to needing to view a drama from the past. In this way, patterns that play out in your life may be reviewed and their lessons learned.

Vehicle (M) A vehicle is one of the symbols most commonly found in our dreams, since it literally takes us to new realms and dimensions.

- **Dented vehicle** (M) Going out and finding that your vehicle has been dented may come as a response to an event that "dented" your self-esteem. It could come after a personal insult that caused you to feel degraded. A huge dent may have even damaged your reputation.

- **Recreational vehicle** (M) On the open road, this vehicle may represent an early retirement from work. It may signify a desire to travel and see the countryside. It points to a leisurely lifestyle and thus may mention "Take your time and enjoy a little scenery."

Veil (M) A veil on a hat may signify a mysterious woman who may bring enchantment into a man's life. It may also indicate that your vision is veiled from the truth. A wedding veil may represent the qualities of the bride, which traditionally were kept concealed until the ceremony was complete. In this way, a veil may be an indication of a woman's sexuality.

Venus (U) As the planet of feminine beauty and love, Venus may emerge as the naked romantic lover to a man or as the qualities of a woman's own beauty. As a planet, it might suggest a place where you are embraced by love's arms. Venus may also announce a new relationship on the horizon.

Video camera (M) A character holding a video camera may appear to reflect back the dramas and comedies of your life with commentary relating to your behavior.

Village (M) Entering a village may represent a short getaway to an enchanting place or dealing with more primitive or ancient styles of approaching life. A village is where the commoners live, so a village could represent the desire to live a more simple and straightforward lifestyle.

Violet (L) Violets, in their variety of purple hues, illuminate the darkness and point to spiritual vision or psychic abilities. (See *Flowers*.)

Violin (M) Violin music in a dream may point to a romantic event that fulfilled a desire for romantic love. A violin played badly may suggest that you need to stop whining.

Virgo (U) With its sensual and inquisitive nature, Virgo as a sign of the zodiac implies the need to taste, touch, and inspect every detail in life before digesting anything. She may call you to embrace the feminine aspect and her discerning nature.

Vitamins (M) Being offered a bottle of vitamins in a dream may be a direct message that you are missing necessary nutrients in your diet and need a supplement, or it may point to a need to strengthen your will.

Vulture (L) The scavenger of the bird tribe, the vulture teaches us to honor death as part of a natural cycle of life. The vulture picks the meat down to the bone to reveal the power in having examined something down to its internal structure or the bare bones. A vulture may come to liberate you from the fear of death and, in shamanistic terms, to reduce the personality to its original structure. The vulture also signifies respect for all the dead who have passed on to other levels of evolution. The appearance of a vulture in a dream may be a response to someone who is taking advantage of what another has accomplished. (See *Birds*.)

VW Bug (M) This vehicle is associated with someone who strives for simplicity or is a bit of a "hippie."

Wading (M) Wading in shallow water may be a sign of your hesitation to go deeply into your feelings.

Walking (M) Walking down the street in a dream expresses exploring life on foot as a slow-moving method that allows you to have more direct contact with your experiences.

Wallpaper (M) Putting up wallpaper in a room may represent putting up a new decorative surface on the interior of your personality that covers up the cracks or damage from the past. The action may also comment on a new or more functional pattern of behavior that you are ready to display.

Walls (M) Walls are the divisions between rooms and reflect separation from others or the boundaries and barriers we erect to protect us from intimacy. Demolishing a wall in a dream may, therefore, indicate your readiness for a more intimate relationship or more openness.

Wal-Mart (M) An experience of shopping at Wal-Mart may reflect the variety of values that are readily available in America. It may be a sign that you live in a material world concerned only with being a consumer. On the other hand, you may find yourself shopping for items, such as tools or skills, that will help you survive in the real world.

Warehouse (M) Entering a warehouse may point to the exploration of the ideas, feelings, and attitudes that were stored away in the past. If the warehouse is empty, it could represent that you have a vast empty space in your head or heart to fill.

Washing machine (M) A washing machine may point to the need to clean up your attitude in order to perfect your image in the world.

Watch (M) A watch in a dream expresses concerns about time and deadlines. Losing your watch may point to the loss of your sense of time or to your resistance to being on time. It may also represent anxiety about being late or forgetting an appointment. A broken watch may indicate that time has run out.

Water (L) An element that is associated with the emotions and the subconscious, water reflects our responses to emotional issues. It represents the fluid movement of creative energy as waves or ripples coming onto the shore of the conscious mind. In a dream, water represents hidden emotions that need to become fluid and made conscious before being released.

Waterfall (L) As a natural shower, a waterfall may signify a need for emotional cleansing or the need to cry.

Water pistol (M) Shooting a water pistol at someone in a dream may indicate a need to let off steam without injuring the other person. It may represent playful aggression.

Waterskiing (M) Pulled by a boat on the surface of the water, the dreamer who is waterskiing may be experiencing the force of someone else's decisions pulling him or her. Falling while water-skiing could easily indicate an emotional fall.

Weather (L) The qualities of weather appearing in dreams express the alchemy of emotions and thoughts that generate your many moods. Whether it's stormy or clear blue skies that lie ahead, the weather can offer a prediction of what is ahead for you. Much of a person's mood depends on life's events, which may trigger emotional responses translated into weather conditions in night dreams. Mother Nature's consequences, such as hurricanes and tornadoes, may come to represent life's big and little shocks, both of which affect your mood and can alter life's direction.

Sigourney Weaver (L, M) With her roles as a man's equal, Sigourney will cut off her breasts like the Amazon queen in order to fight for her equality under natural laws. Like the goddess of the hunt, Artemis, she may appear to mirror the attributes of assertive strength, a woman with a mission, and the protector of a woman's honor. She needs no man to validate her worth. She may appear to mention that a woman's strength can even be superior to a man's.

Weeder (M) A tool used to pull weeds, a weeder may indicate the need to pull out the negative influences that strangle either new psychological growth or your creative expression.

West (L) The west is where the sun sets, and it represents the emotional qualities of life. The west may indicate the essential or authentic self and the child within. It is the direction taken toward depth and the understanding of emotions. If you are moving toward the west, you are ready for the introspection it takes to face and cope with your emotions. (See *Compass, Four directions.*)

Whale (L) The elephant of the sea, the whale, navigates long distances. Traveling in groups called pods, whales can come to assist your navigation through the vast unseen potential of the subconscious. The sound of the whale is a song that demonstrates the power of music in bringing about harmony and healing. The appearance of whales in a dream may indicate a need to migrate to a new environment.

Wheat (L) A staff of wheat, often associated with the goddess Demeter, represents fertility and sustenance brought through the manifesting power of the mother or feminine principle. Wheat may also appear in a dream as a symbol of fertility and prosperity.

White (L) White denotes purity, clarity, and innocence. Wearing all white in a dream may indicate a character's pure intentions. It may also represent virginity.

Robin Williams (L, M) The comic relief of Robin Williams as the sensitive-fool archetype leads the dreamer into the divine comedy of life. As the fool, he demonstrates the power of improvisation. He may come to state that the easiest way through a difficult situation is to ad-lib.

Bruce Willis (M) A sensitive type with boyish appeal, Bruce may arrive to give definition to what the "will is" in the consciousness of a male. He may announce someone appearing in your life with equal charisma.

Wind (L) As the movement of air, wind brings about a change in life's circumstances and direction, and reflects a change in thinking. Wind from the east signifies a change in spiritual view. Wind from the south expresses soul transformation. A westward wind reflects a change of emotions, and a northern wind denotes a change in understanding.

Windex glass cleaner (M) Polishing your window with Windex may point to putting a clear shine on the third eye or the all-seeing eye. It may also signify a time to look out toward the future with clear vision or to improve your visual acuity.

Winding road (M) Seen as a metaphor for life, a winding road represents the twists and turns life may present on the journey to your destination and to fulfillment.

Window (M) The windows of a house represent the eyes into the future or the way you look into the soul of another. Windows also allow air in and out and may express the avenue for sending out a thought or wish for future manifestation.

Window box (M) A window box full of flowers may welcome you to look into the eyes of another, or it may represent the beauty of someone's eyes.

Windowpanes (M) A window with many panes may appear in a dream to point out the "pain" in looking out at something negative that is happening in the neighborhood or the world, or it may represent the fear of the future.

Window seat (M) A window seat may represent a place to contemplate your fate or future. It may signify the need to wait for a messenger or for someone to arrive in order to fulfill a promise. It may also be an indication of loneliness.

Winery (M) Exploring a winery in a dream may express concerns about spiritual matters and fulfillment. Wine is a substance of spiritual and physical intoxication. A winery may indicate "tasting" a variety of enjoyable experiences.

Oprah Winfrey (L, M) As an archetype of feminine wisdom, Oprah appears each day to guide the TV viewing public on a journey through the labyrinth to expose the truth about often-painful issues. As Ariadne, the goddess of the labyrinth, she slays the minotaur of ignorance. Oprah's guest appearance in a dream may signify some compassionate wisdom coming your way that may challenge you to look more deeply into painful issues.

Winnie-the-Pooh (L, M) The golden teddy bear belonging to Christopher Robin was brought to life by his father, A. A. Milne, in these delightful tales. Pooh offers the attributes of unconditional love and patience. His appearance in a dream indicates a loving friendship.

Wire cutters (M) Wire cutters may appear in a dream when you need to break a difficult tie with someone or to cut off a difficult communication.

Wiring (M) Exposed wiring may be a message intended to bring attention to problems with the nervous system, or it may reveal crossed or disconnected wires of communication. Crossed wires may symbolize thoughts being disrupted by another's intentions. Disconnected wires might signify disconnected thinking or even a diagnosis of a brain dysfunction.

Wolf (M) Wandering the edge of the forest, the wolf protects its domain. The appearance of a wolf in a dream may be to offer its keen senses to protect one's individual boundaries. A wolf may offer some self-defense to the dreamer whose psychic boundaries are too fuzzy. The wolf may also speak to your untamed nature. On the other hand, it may point to someone who is like the wolf in "Little Red Riding Hood," ready to deceive and devour a woman who trusts too much.

Wombat (L) Native to Australia, this large marsupial burrows a home in the dirt. Waddling forward on short legs, it looks pretty silly but it displays an enormous ability to hold on for dear life. Wombats come to bring the message of the power of the element of earth as a home, which can protect you as long as you are grounded. Wombats may be saying to you, "Make your home here on earth. It's a safe shelter." In other words, get grounded on the planet.

Working (M) Dreaming about working relates to concerns about upward movement in your career. It may point to events at work that have created some conflict for you. It may also mean that you are working too hard—or not hard enough.

Wounds (M) In general, wounds on the body in dreams are the result of painful experiences that affected you deeply. Bruises may make a poignant statement that you feel bruised by an argument, a betrayal, or an abusive situation. Open wounds in a dream may suggest that the emotional pain is on the surface and may need attention and a remedy to heal.

Wrench (M) Used to fix plumbing, a wrench may represent a personal healing tool to fix your own flow of energy. It may also represent a turn of events.

Writing (M) Writing in a dream may indicate your desire to express yourself through words. It may also indicate a wish to be creative or to write a book.

X (L) As the symbol of partnership, an "X" may point to an important contract. It may also refer to a kiss. An "X" is also the symbol of Christ, the resurrected Son of God.

Xena (L, M) Xena is the medieval princess warrior who, like an Amazon, demonstrates superstrength for a woman. She may come to announce a woman who will not be easy to seduce into giving away her power. In a woman's dream, she may point to suppressed personal power and the desire to be respected.

X ray (M) Viewing an X ray may represent a need to receive a clear picture of something within the subconscious. It may reveal a disease in the physical body that you may not yet be conscious of, but more often it points to an emotional issue.

Yellow (L) Yellow is the color of the intellect. It represents a positive attitude or outlook. It may also be a sign of cowardliness.

Yellow Brick Road (L, M) For Dorothy, the Yellow Brick Road delivered her to Oz and finally back to her home. The Yellow

Brick Road may appear as a modern mythical path to enlightenment. (See *Brick road*.)

Yin and yang (L) This common symbol represents the balancing of the masculine and feminine energies into a whole expression. The concept of yin and yang symbolizes the balance between intuition and reason.

Yoda (L, M) Yoda, the Master Jedi in *Star Wars,* may bring special powers to the dreamer. He represents a spiritual guide or teacher in your mythological quest as a hero. His message may be to use "the Force" to fight against evil in your life. He may remind you that anyone can be a hero.

Zebra (L) As the dancing horse of Africa, the zebra brings the alchemy of movement and the integration of the dark and light into a prancing power. Its appearance may be a call to use dance as an art for enjoyment or as a tool to foster transforming energy. Its pattern of stripes integrates the feminine or dark aspect of the psychic with the masculine (light) aspect into a sacred union through movement. The zebra's appearance in a dream, therefore, can signify the healing and transforming power of dancing through life.

Zest deodorant soap Being handed a bar of Zest may suggest that you need to refresh your attitude and cleanse yourself of any negative energy you may have taken on. It may also be a comment on the need to put some "zest" into your life.

Zodiac See listings for specific signs of the Zodiac.

Zoo (M) Strolling through a zoo in a dream may indicate pent-up emotions or primal power. It may also humorously symbolize that you are living in a "zoo"—an overwhelming place where a variety of influences are demanding your attention.

Zorro (L, M) The masked Spanish bandit carried a sharp sword and may ride into your dream to undo a wrong in a fight for fairness. He may represent a secret desire to rescue humanity from its woes or to steal back power. He may indicate a suppressed desire to help. Leaving his mark, a giant "Z," Zorro may be there to indicate your need to gain some attention while maintaining your anonymity.

Index